Crime in the Making

ROBERT J. SAMPSON
AND JOHN H. LAUB

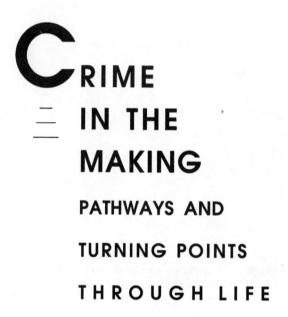

CRIME
IN THE
MAKING

PATHWAYS AND

TURNING POINTS

THROUGH LIFE

HARVARD UNIVERSITY PRESS

CAMBRIDGE, MASSACHUSETTS

LONDON, ENGLAND

First Harvard University Press paperback edition, 1995

Library of Congress Cataloging-in-Publication Data

Sampson, Robert J.
    Crime in the making : pathways and turning points through life /
Robert J. Sampson and John H. Laub.
        p.   cm.
    Includes bibliographical references and index.
    ISBN 0-674-17604-9 (alk. paper) (cloth)
    ISBN 0-674-17605-7 (pbk.)
    1. Juvenile delinquency—Longitudinal studies.   2. Juvenile
delinquents—Longitudinal studies.   3. Criminals—Longitudinal
studies.   4. Glueck, Sheldon, 1896–1980. Unraveling juvenile
delinquency.   I. Laub, John H.   II. Title.
HV9069.S246   1993
364.3'6—dc20   92-35723
                                                              CIP

CONTENTS

ACKNOWLEDGMENTS

Many individuals and institutions have played key roles in facilitating the research program that underlies this book. First and foremost, our debt to Sheldon and Eleanor Glueck is most obvious. Were it not for their pioneering vision and spirited commitment to the collection of data, this book would never have materialized in its current form. Indeed, the Gluecks and their research team collected an extraordinary body of data that will be examined again and again well into the next century. We dedicate this book to Sheldon and Eleanor Glueck as a testament to their lifelong persistence and determination in the collection of multifaceted data on human development over time.

Resurrecting the Gluecks' data presented us with numerous and serious obstacles. Fortunately, many have helped us over the hurdles. Throughout the project we received assistance from the staff of the Manuscript Division of the Harvard Law School Library. In particular, we thank Erika Chadbourn, David de Lorenzo, Judy Mellins, and David Warrington for their enthusiasm and support of our endeavors. We also thank Richard LaBrie, Louis Maglio, Sheila Murphrey, Mary Moran, and Charles Eliot Sands for taking the time to talk with us about the Gluecks and their research.

The Henry A. Murray Research Center at Radcliffe College proved to be the perfect home for the Gluecks' data. Without the backing of Anne Colby, Director, and the technical expertise and patience of Erin Phelps, the Gluecks' data would not have been in any shape for a study such as ours. Copeland Young and the rest of the staff at the Center also deserve special thanks.

Of course, a project of this magnitude needs hard cash as well as other forms of support. We gratefully acknowledge financial support from the National Institute of Justice, the Henry A. Murray Research Center of Radcliffe College, Northeastern University Research and

Scholarship Development Fund, the College of Criminal Justice at Northeastern University, and the departments of sociology at the University of Illinois at Urbana-Champaign and the University of Chicago. Without these sources of support, our long-term collaborative project would have been difficult if not impossible to sustain.

Throughout the project we were fortunate to have an excellent team of data coders and research assistants. Lou Ann Enos, Kenna Davis (Kiger), Sandra Gauvreau, and Janet Lauritsen deserve special recognition for their hard work.

Although we sometimes disagreed with them, we were also lucky to have colleagues who offered criticism, encouragement, and helpful suggestions throughout the process of writing this book. There are simply too many individuals to list here, but we especially wish to acknowledge Al Blumstein, Dave Bordua, Avshalom Caspi, Jacqueline Cohen, Tony Earls, Glen Elder, David Farrington, Mike Gottfredson, John Hagan, Travis Hirschi, Temi Moffitt, Dan Nagin, Al Reiss, Mac Runyan, and George Vaillant.

We began working with the Gluecks' data more than six years ago. Our families know only too well how this project consumed many of our waking hours during this period. Trips to Illinois or Boston became integral parts of our family calendars, like birthdays and other family events. Our families managed to cope with each project-related crisis, no matter how large or small. We would like to express our thanks by dedicating this book as well to our families—Nancy, John, and Laura (RS) and Joanne and Calies (JL)—for the time we can never replace.

We are also grateful to those we worked with at Harvard University Press. Our editor, Michael Aronson, was enthusiastic and excited about the book from his first reading and never wavered from this view. His suggestions and insights helped to sharpen our focus and widen our lens. Our manuscript editor, Mary Ellen Geer, helped us to write better.

Although we present new empirical and theoretical analyses in this book, some of the material is an outgrowth from our earlier publications. We are grateful to the following journals and publishers for allowing us to use, in part, materials published elsewhere: John H. Laub and Robert J. Sampson, "Unraveling Families and Delinquency: A Reanalysis of the Gluecks' Data," *Criminology* (1988), 26:355–380; John H. Laub, Robert J. Sampson, and Kenna Kiger, "Assessing the Potential of Secondary Data Analysis: A New Look at the Gluecks' *Unraveling Juvenile Delinquency* Data," in *Measurement Issues in Criminology*, ed.

Kimberly Kempf (New York: Springer-Verlag, 1990), 241–257; Robert J. Sampson and John H. Laub, "Crime and Deviance over the Life Course: The Salience of Adult Social Bonds," *American Sociological Review* (1990), 55:609–627; John H. Laub and Robert J. Sampson, "The Sutherland-Glueck Debate: On the Sociology of Criminological Knowledge," *American Journal of Sociology* (1991), 96:1402–1440; Robert J. Sampson and John H. Laub, "Crime and Deviance in the Life Course," *Annual Review of Sociology* (1992), 18:63–84.

INTRODUCTION

The origins of this book can be traced to two puzzles. Eight years ago we stumbled across the first puzzle in the form of dusty cartons of data in the basement of the Harvard Law School Library. Originally assembled by Sheldon and Eleanor Glueck of Harvard University, these cartons contained the original case files from their classic study, *Unraveling Juvenile Delinquency* (1950). These data, along with the Gluecks' eighteen-year follow-up of the 1,000 subjects from *Unraveling*, were given to the Harvard Law School Library in 1972. The Gluecks also gave the library their personal papers, correspondence, books, photographs, and the like. The papers and other items were sorted and fully cataloged as part of the Glueck archive. The cartons of data were simply stored in the sub-basement of the library.

We sensed that these data were of immense importance. Yet the obstacles to analyzing them were formidable. For example, the data for the 500 delinquent subjects alone were contained in more than fifty 12-by-15 cartons and seemed nearly impenetrable. How could we possibly recode and computerize these data? Moreover, as we began to sort through the case files, we soon discovered that these were not conventional data. And, as we went on, we found out that the Gluecks themselves were not conventional researchers (Laub and Sampson, 1991). Nevertheless, after several years of a true group and institutional effort, we reconstructed a good portion of the Gluecks' data. These data are the major source of information analyzed in this book.

While we were trying to piece together the Gluecks' data, we were confronted with a rancorous debate that has embroiled recent criminology over age and crime, longitudinal and cross-sectional research, and the usefulness of the concept of "criminal careers" (see especially Gottfredson and Hirschi, 1986, 1990; Blumstein et al., 1986, 1988a). On the one hand, Gottfredson and Hirschi (1990) argue for the importance of effective child rearing in producing self-control during the early formative years of a youth's development. Since self-control is posited as a stable phenomenon that is sufficient for understanding patterns of crime throughout the life course, they view the longitudinal study of lives as unnecessary. We were attracted to this theoretical conception because of its emphasis on the importance of families in explaining the origins of juvenile delinquency.

On the other hand, we were troubled by key aspects of their stability argument. Is efficacy in child rearing all we need to know to explain patterns of adult crime? What about individual change and salient life events in adulthood? Are longitudinal data really unnecessary for understanding crime? In probing these issues we came to believe that the critics of Hirschi and Gottfredson (for example, Farrington, 1986a; Blumstein et al., 1988a, 1988b) had some important things to say regarding the study of crime. By using longitudinal data properly (that is, longitudinally) and in a theoretically informed fashion, we believed new insights could be gained into the causes of crime. In our view, the theoretical puzzle provided by the two sides in the debate in essence can be reduced to the following challenge: can we develop and test a theoretical model that accounts for the unfolding of childhood antisocial behavior, adolescent delinquency, and adult crime in longitudinal perspective? In other words, can we unravel crime and deviance over the full life course?

In the end, our solutions to both puzzles, and hence our attempt to forge some integration and reconciliation in the criminology debate, remain to be judged by the reader. Rather than trying to be all things to all theories, we take what we believe to be empirically and theoretically correct from each side of the debate, and weave together what we hope is a coherent argument that is greater than the sum of its individual parts.

These debates, of course, are not merely academic. We believe that our analyses of the Gluecks' data can contribute to public discourse on crime and crime policy. In particular, the Gluecks' data provide an unusual opportunity to advance a comparative understanding of crime in contemporary society as well as in the past. The overemphasis on "current data" stems from a mistaken belief that the time dimension is irrelevant in social research. As Thernstrom argued in his seminal study of social mobility among Boston residents: "Historical analysis of social phenomena is thus not a luxury for those interested in the past for its own sake. A study of the present that neglects the processes of change by which the present was created is necessarily superficial" (1973: 3). In this sense, we believe that our book has a bearing on general discussions of the crime problem in contemporary society.

For example, today we often hear discussions of crime that assume criminal behavior is inevitably linked to race and drugs (see Kotlowitz, 1991). Yet crime in the historical context we are analyzing was not committed primarily by blacks, but rather by members of white ethnic groups in structurally disadvantaged positions. And even though drugs were not pervasive, crime and alcohol abuse were quite rampant. The men in the Gluecks' delinquent sample were persistent, serious offenders, and many of them can be labeled "career criminals" using contemporary language. Therefore, the fact that sample members were drawn from settings of social and economic disadvantage yet were all white provides an important comparative base for assessing current concerns of race, crime, and the underclass (see Jencks, 1992). Furthermore, because the use and sale of drugs like cocaine and heroin were not prevalent in this study, a unique opportunity is presented to learn about the relationship between alcohol and criminal behavior. In our view, the crime policy agenda is too often determined without data, theory, or a historical/longitudinal perspective; our book embraces all three dimensions.

Along similar lines, we strongly disagree with the narrow focus on incarceration as the solution to the crime problem. We believe that crime policy must be broader in scope and look to nongovernmental institutions like families, schools, work settings, and neighborhoods as the centerpiece of a crime reduction policy. The government can and should take the lead in strengthening these basic institutions of our society. We do not mean to imply that individuals who commit serious crimes should never be incarcerated. Rather, our reservations about current crime policies that rely heavily on long terms of incarceration—especially for juvenile offenders—reflect our fears that such policies do not reduce crime and may in fact be counterproductive.

We believe that crime is a pressing social problem that demands attention. Both of us have written in the past about the devastating effects of crime and the fear it produces in communities, especially with respect to quality of life and social cohesion (Sampson, 1987, 1988; Garofalo and Laub, 1978; Laub, 1983a). Reflecting this concern, we offer in this book a theoretical and empirical framework with which to think in new ways about policies on crime. Public discourse about crime is dominated by television shows and radio call-in programs, forums we believe are inappropriate for discussing the causes of crime and the solutions to the crime problem. In our view, it is foolhardy to think that the study of crime can be reduced to a 10-second sound bite, as we have in fact been asked to do in the past. Media accounts notwithstanding, we believe that most citizens realize and appreciate the complexity of the crime problem, a complexity that is realized in our analyses that follow. Although at times these analyses may seem daunting, they are necessary as a foundation from which to extract the "big picture." Building on this knowledge, we aim to reach those who are concerned about crime and who, like us, remain optimistic that social science research can inform dialogue on crime policy. We maintain that a well-reasoned and informed crime policy is possible, and we hope that our work can contribute to the development of that policy.

Our piecing together of the empirical and theoretical puzzles and our larger concerns with current policy debates take the following form. The first three chapters present the major theoretical strategy of the book. More specifically, Chapter 1 outlines the life-course framework and the main tenets of our theoretical model of age-graded informal social control and crime. Chapter 2 describes in detail the Gluecks' *Unraveling Juvenile Delinquency* study together with the follow-up longitudinal data. In this chapter, we also situate the "Glueck perspective" on criminology in its historical and institutional context and respond to both the methodological and ideological critics of the Gluecks' research. Chapter 3 delineates how the Gluecks' data were recast for modern use, including our efforts at empirical validation. We also place the subjects of the Gluecks' study in history and discuss the role of cohort and period effects in understanding individual lives through time.

The two following chapters examine the causes of antisocial and delinquent behavior in adolescence. Chapter 4 presents and assesses our theory of informal family social control, and Chapter 5 focuses on school factors, siblings, and peer groups. Within these chapters we analyze the cross-sectional data originally generated in the *Unraveling* study.

The next three chapters explore stability and change in crime and deviance in the adult life course. This analysis centers on an examination of persistence in and desistance from crime among the 1,000 men in the *Unraveling* study. We begin in Chapter 6 with an examination of continuity between childhood delinquent behavior and adult out-comes. Chapter 7 explores the effects of adult social bonds on changes in criminal behavior for the original 500 delinquent subjects. Chapter 8 examines the late onset of crime and deviance for the original group of 500 nondelinquent subjects. In these sets of analyses we use the Gluecks' follow-up data collected from official records and interviews with the men at age 25 and again at age 32. New data are also presented regarding criminal activity for the men between the ages of 32 and 45.

Chapter 9 merges the quantitative and qualitative data collected by the Gluecks' research team. Drawing on the rich narrative information, we explore the life histories of antisocial behavior and social control of 70 men who represent key contrasts in our theory. Finally, in Chapter 10, we provide a synthesis of findings and discuss the implications of our results for criminological theory and research. We conclude with the implications of our study for current policy debates on crime.

TOWARD AN
AGE-GRADED
THEORY
OF INFORMAL
SOCIAL CONTROL

1

Accepted wisdom holds that crime is committed disproportionately by adolescents. According to data from the United States and other industrialized countries, rates of property crime and violent crime rise rapidly in the teenage years to a peak at about ages 16 and 18, respectively (Hirschi and Gottfredson, 1983; Farrington, 1986a; Flanagan and Maguire, 1990). The overrepresentation of youth in crime has been demonstrated using multiple sources of measurement—official arrest reports (Federal Bureau of Investigation, 1990), self-reports of offending (Rowe and Tittle, 1977), and victims' reports of the ages of their offenders (Hindelang, 1981). It is thus generally accepted that, in the aggregate, age-specific crime rates peak in the late teenage years and then decline sharply across the adult life span.

The age-crime curve has had a profound impact on the organization and content of sociological studies of crime by channeling research to a focus on adolescents. As a result, sociological criminology has traditionally neglected the theoretical significance of childhood characteristics and the link between early childhood behaviors and later adult outcomes (Robins, 1966; McCord, 1979; Caspi et al., 1989; Farrington, 1989; Gottfredson and Hirschi, 1990; Loeber and LeBlanc, 1990; Sampson and Laub, 1990). Although criminal behavior does peak in the teenage years, evidence reviewed in this chapter indicates an early onset of delinquency as well as continuity of criminal behavior over the life course. By concentrating on the teenage years, sociological perspectives on crime have thus failed to address the life-span implications of childhood behavior.

At the same time, criminologists have not devoted much attention to the other end of the spectrum—desistance from crime and the transitions from criminal to noncriminal behavior in adulthood (Cusson and Pinsonneault, 1986; Shover, 1985; Gartner and Piliavin, 1988). As

Rutter (1988: 3) argues, we know little about "escape from the risk process" and whether predictors of desistance are unique or simply the opposite of criminogenic factors. Thus, researchers have neglected not only the early life course, but also the relevance of social transitions in young adulthood and the factors explaining desistance from crime as people age.

Finally, in all phases of the life course, criminologists have largely ignored the link between social structural context and the mediating processes of informal social control. Most researchers have examined either macro-level/structural variables (for example, social class, ethnicity, mobility) or micro-level processes (for example, parent-child interactions, discipline) in the study of crime. We believe both sets of variables are necessary to explain crime, but from the existing research we do not know precisely how structural variables and the processes of informal social control are related.

In this book we confront these issues by bringing both childhood and adulthood back into the criminological picture of age and crime. To accomplish this goal, we synthesize and integrate the research literatures on crime and the life course and develop a theory of age-graded informal social control and criminal behavior. The basic thesis we develop is threefold in nature: (1) structural context mediated by informal family and school social controls explains delinquency in childhood and adolescence; (2) in turn, there is continuity in antisocial behavior from childhood through adulthood in a variety of life domains; and (3) informal social bonds in adulthood to family and employment explain changes in criminality over the life span despite early childhood propensities. Our theoretical model thus acknowledges the importance of early childhood behaviors and individual differences in self-control (Gottfredson and Hirschi, 1990) but rejects the implication that later adult factors have little relevance (Wilson and Herrnstein, 1985; Gottfredson and Hirschi, 1990). In other words, we contend that social interaction with both juvenile *and* adult institutions of informal social control has important effects on crime and deviance. Thus, ours is a "sociogenic" model of crime and deviance that seeks to incorporate both stability and change over the life course.

We test our theoretical model through a detailed analysis of unique longitudinal data consisting of two samples of delinquent and nondelinquent boys followed from childhood and adolescence into their forties. Before describing our research strategy, we present a brief overview of the life-course perspective.

THE LIFE-COURSE PERSPECTIVE

The life course has been defined as "pathways through the age differentiated life span," where age differentiation "is manifested in expectations and options that impinge on decision processes and the course of events that give shape to life stages, transitions, and turning points" (Elder, 1985: 17). Similarly, Caspi, Elder, and Herbener (1990: 15) conceive of the life course as a "sequence of culturally defined age-graded roles and social transitions that are enacted over time." Age-graded transitions are embedded in social institutions and are subject to historical change (Elder, 1975, 1992).

Two central concepts underlie the analysis of life-course dynamics. A *trajectory* is a pathway or line of development over the life span, such as work life, marriage, parenthood, self-esteem, or criminal behavior. Trajectories refer to long-term patterns of behavior and are marked by a sequence of transitions. *Transitions* are marked by life events (such as first job or first marriage) that are embedded in trajectories and evolve over shorter time spans—"changes in state that are more or less abrupt" (Elder, 1985: 31–32). Some transitions are age-graded and some are not; hence, what is often assumed to be important are the normative timing and sequencing of role transitions. For example, Hogan (1980) emphasizes the duration of time (spells) between a change in state and the ordering of events such as first job or first marriage on occupational status and earnings in adulthood. Caspi, Elder, and Herbener (1990: 25) argue that delays in social transitions (for example, being "off-time") produce conflicting obligations that enhance later difficulties (see also Rindfuss et al., 1987). As a result, life-course analyses are often characterized by a focus on the duration, timing, and ordering of major life events and their consequences for later social development.

The interlocking nature of trajectories and transitions may generate *turning points* or a change in the life course (Elder, 1985: 32). Adaptation to life events is crucial because the same event or transition followed by different adaptations can lead to different trajectories (Elder, 1985: 35). The long-term view embodied by the life-course focus on trajectories implies a strong connection between childhood events and experiences in adulthood. However, the simultaneous shorter-term view also implies that transitions or turning points can modify life trajectories—they can "redirect paths." Social institutions and triggering life events that may modify trajectories include school, work, the military, marriage, and parenthood (see Elder, 1986; Rutter et al., 1990; Sampson and Laub, 1990).

In addition to the study of patterns of change and the continuity between childhood behavior and later adulthood outcomes, the life-course framework encompasses at least three other themes: a concern with the social meanings of age throughout the life course, intergenerational transmission of social patterns, and the effects of macro-level events (such as the Great Depression or World War II) on individual life histories (Elder, 1974, 1985). As Elder (1992) notes, a major objective of the life-course perspective is to link social history and social structure to the unfolding of human lives. To address these themes individual lives are studied through time, with particular attention devoted to aging, cohort effects, historical context, and the social influence of age-graded transitions. Naturally, prospective longitudinal research designs form the heart of life-course research.

Of all the themes emphasized in life-course research, the extent of stability and change in behavior and personality attributes over time is probably the most complex. Stability versus change in behavior is also one of the most hotly debated and controversial issues in the social sciences (Brim and Kagan, 1980; Dannefer, 1984; Baltes and Nesselroade, 1984; Featherman and Lerner, 1985; Caspi and Bem, 1990). Given the pivotal role of this issue, we turn to an assessment of the research literature as it bears on stability and change in crime. As we shall see, this literature contains evidence for both continuity *and* change over the life course.

STABILITY OF CRIME AND DEVIANCE

Unlike sociological criminology, the field of developmental psychology has long been concerned with the continuity of maladaptive behaviors (Brim and Kagan, 1980; Caspi and Bem, 1990). As a result, a large portion of the longitudinal evidence on stability comes from psychologists and others who study "antisocial behavior" generally, where the legal concept of crime may or may not be a component.[1] An example is the study of aggression in psychology (Olweus, 1979). In exploring this research tradition our purpose is to highlight the extent to which deviant childhood behaviors have important ramifications in later adult life, whether criminal or noncriminal in form.

Our point of departure is the widely reported claim that individual differences in antisocial behavior are stable across the life course (Olweus, 1979; Caspi et al., 1987; Loeber, 1982; Robins, 1966; Huesmann et al., 1984; Gottfredson and Hirschi, 1990; Jessor et al., 1977, 1991). The stability of crime and antisocial behavior over time is often defined as *homotypic continuity*, which refers to the continuity of similar behaviors or phenotypic attributes over time (Caspi and Bem, 1990: 553). For example, in a widely cited study of the aggressiveness of 600 subjects, their parents, and their children over a 22-year period, Huesmann and colleagues (1984) found that early aggressiveness predicted later aggression and criminal violence. They concluded that "aggression can be viewed as a persistent trait that . . . possesses substantial cross-situational constancy" (1984: 1120). An earlier study by Robins (1966) also found a high level of stability in crime and aggression over time.

More generally, Olweus's (1979) comprehensive review of more than 16 studies on aggressive behavior revealed "substantial" stability: the correlation between early aggressive behavior and later criminality averaged .68 for the studies reviewed (1979: 854–855). Loeber (1982) completed a similar review of the extant literature in many disciplines and concluded that a "consensus" had been reached in favor of the stability hypothesis: "Children who initially display high rates of antisocial behavior are more likely to persist in this behavior than children who initially show lower rates of antisocial behavior" (1982: 1433). Recent empirical studies documenting stability in criminal and deviant behavior across time include West and Farrington (1977), Wolfgang et al. (1987), Shannon (1988), Elliott et al. (1985), and Jessor et al. (1991).

Although perhaps more comprehensive, these findings are not new. Over 50 years ago the Gluecks found that virtually all of the 510 reformatory inmates in their study of criminal careers "had experience in serious antisocial conduct" (Glueck and Glueck, 1930: 142). Their data also confirmed "the early genesis of antisocial careers" (1930: 143). In addition, the Gluecks' follow-up of 1,000 males originally studied in *Unraveling Juvenile Delinquency* (1950) revealed remarkable continuities. As they argued in *Delinquents and Non-Delinquents in Perspective:* "While the majority of boys originally included in the nondelinquent control group continued, down the years, to remain essentially law-abiding, the greatest majority of those originally included in the delinquent group continued to commit all sorts of crimes in the 17–25 age-span" (1968: 170). Findings regarding behavioral or homotypic continuity are thus supported by a rich body of empirical research that spans several decades (for more extensive discussion see Robins, 1966, 1978; West and Farrington, 1977; Gottfredson and Hirschi, 1990). In fact, much as the Gluecks had reported earlier, Robins (1978) summarized results from her studies of four male cohorts by stating that "adult antisocial behavior virtually *requires* childhood antisocial behavior" (1978: 611).

In short, there is considerable evidence that antisocial behavior is relatively stable across stages of the life course. As Caspi and Moffitt (1992) conclude, robust continuities in antisocial behavior have been revealed over the past 50 years in different nations (for example, Canada, England, Finland, New Zealand, Sweden, and the United States) and with multiple methods of assessment (including official records, teacher ratings, parent reports, and peer nominations of aggressive behavior). These replications across time and space yield an impressive generalization that is rare in the social sciences.

Sociological approaches to crime have largely ignored this generalization and consequently remain vulnerable to attack for not coming to grips with the implications of behavioral stability. Not surprisingly, developmental psychologists have long seized on stability to argue for the primacy of early childhood and the irrelevance of the adult life course. But even recent social theories of crime take much the same tack, denying that adult life-course transitions can have any real effect on adult criminal behavior. In particular, Gottfredson and Hirschi (1990: 238) argue that ordinary life events (for example, jobs, getting married, becoming a parent) have little effect on criminal behavior because crime rates decline with age "whether or not these events occur." They go on to argue that the life-course assumption that such events are important neglects its own evidence on the stability of personal characteristics (1990: 237; see also Gottfredson and Hirschi, 1987). And, since crime emerges early in the life course, traditional sociological variables (such as peers, the labor market, or marriage) are again allegedly impotent (Wilson and Herrnstein, 1985). The reasoning is that since crime emerges before sociological variables appear, the latter cannot be important in modifying life trajectories.

From initial appearances it thus appears that the evidence on stability leaves little room for the relevance of sociological theories of age-graded transitions in the life course. As it turns out, however, whether one views the glass of stability as half empty or half full stems at least as much from theoretical predilections as from empirical reality. Moreover, not only are there important discontinuities in crime that need to be explained, but a reconsideration of the evidence suggests that stability itself is quite compatible with a sociological perspective on the life course.

CHANGE AND THE ADULT LIFE COURSE

In an important paper Dannefer (1984) sharply critiques existing models of adult development, drawn primarily from the fields of biology and psychology, for their exclusive "ontogenetic" focus and their failure to recognize the "profoundly interactive nature of self-society relations" and the "variability of social environments" (1984: 100). He further argues that "the contributions of sociological research and theory provide the basis for understanding human development as socially organized and socially produced, not only by what happens in early life, but also by the effects of social structure, social interaction, and their effects on life chances throughout the life course" (1984:106). Is there evidence in the criminological literature to support Dannefer's general observations regarding change over the life course and the importance of social structure and interaction?

We begin to answer this question with a seeming paradox: although the studies reviewed earlier do show that antisocial behavior in children is one of the best predictors of antisocial behavior in adults, "most antisocial children do not become antisocial as adults" (Gove, 1985: 123). Robins (1978) found identical results in her review of four longitudinal studies, stating that most antisocial children do not become antisocial adults (1978: 611). A follow-up of the Cambridge-Somerville Youth study found that "a majority of adult criminals had no history as juvenile delinquents" (McCord, 1980: 158). Cline (1980: 665) states that although there is "more constancy than change . . . there is sufficient change in all the data to preclude simple conclusions concerning criminal career progressions." He concludes that there is far more heterogeneity in criminal behavior than previous work has suggested, and that many juvenile offenders do not become career offenders (Cline, 1980: 669–670). Loeber and LeBlanc make a similar point: "Against the backdrop of continuity, studies also show large within-individual changes in offending, a point understressed by Gottfredson and Hirschi" (1990: 390).

Caspi and Moffitt's (1992) review reaches a similar conclusion when they discover large variations in the stability of antisocial behavior over time. Antisocial behavior appears to be highly stable and consistent only in a relatively small number of males whose behavior problems are quite extreme. Loeber's (1982) review also found that extremes in antisocial conduct were positively linked to the magnitude of stability. Moffitt (1991) builds on this information to argue that stability is a trait among those she terms "life-course persistent" delinquents. In other words, whereas change is the norm for the majority of adolescents, stability characterizes those at the extremes of the antisocial-conduct distribution. This conceptualization points out the dangers of relying on measures of central tendency that mask divergent subgroups.

Moffitt's (1991) review further suggests that social factors may work to modify childhood trajectories for the majority of youth who are not "life-course persistent." In support of this idea, recent criminological research suggests that salient life events influence behavior and modify trajectories—a key thesis of the life-course model. A follow-up of 200 delinquent boys found that marriage led to "increasing social stability" (Gibbens, 1984: 61). Knight, Osborn, and West (1977) discovered that while marriage did not reduce criminality, it reduced antisocial behavior such as drinking and drug use (see also Osborn and West, 1979; West, 1982; Rand, 1987). Osborn (1980) examined the effect of leaving London on delinquency and found that subjects who moved had a lower risk of re-offending when compared with a similar group who stayed in London (see also West, 1982). Rand (1987) found mixed results for the effect of going into the armed forces on later offending, but for some subgroups criminal behavior declined after serving in the military. And there is some evidence that episodes of unemployment lead to higher crime rates (Farrington et al., 1986).

In the context of personality characteristics, Caspi (1987) found that although the tendency toward explosive, under-controlled behavior in childhood was evident in adulthood, "invariant action patterns did not emerge across the age-graded life course" (1987: 1211). Similarly, using a prospective longitudinal design to study poverty, Long and Vaillant (1984) found both discontinuity and continuity across three generations of subjects. Their finding that the transmission of "underclass" or dependent life styles was not inevitable or even very likely refutes the hypothesis that the chances of escape from poverty are minimal. As they observe: "The transmission of disorganization and alienation that seems inevitable when a disadvantaged cohort is studied retrospectively appears to be the exception rather than the norm in a prospective study that locates the successes as well as the failures" (Long and Vaillant, 1984: 344; see also Vaillant, 1977).

This is an important methodological point that applies to the stability of crime. Looking *back* over the careers of adult criminals exaggerates the prevalence of stability. Looking *forward* from youth reveals the successes and failures, including adolescent delinquents who go on to be normal functioning adults. This is the paradox noted earlier: adult criminality seems to be always preceded by childhood misconduct, but most conduct-disordered children do not become antisocial or criminal adults (Robins, 1978).

A recent study of adult crime supports a dual concern with stability and change using prospective longitudinal data. Rutter, Quinton, and Hill (1990) analyzed follow-up data from two groups of youth. One was a sample of youth institutionalized in group homes because of family dysfunctions (for example, parental criminality, abuse, desertion). The other was a quasi-random sample of the population of noninstitutionalized individuals of the same age living in inner-city London. Both groups were thus similar in composition but varied on childhood adversity. Consistent with the stability literature, Rutter and colleagues found that the high-risk institutionalized youth went on to experience a diversity of troublesome outcomes in adulthood, including but not limited to crime. By comparison, those in the control group were relatively well adjusted in later life.

Yet Rutter and colleagues also found that in both groups there was considerable heterogeneity in outcomes that was associated with later adult experiences. In particular, marital support in early adult life provided a protective mechanism that inhibited later deviance. Positive school experience among females was another factor that promoted desistance from crime, especially indirectly through its effect on planning and stable marriage choices. These results maintained despite controls for numerous measures of childhood deviance (1990: 152), leading Rutter and colleagues to rule out individual self-selection bias as an explanation (cf. Nagin and Paternoster, 1991). As they concluded: "The data showed substantial heterogeneity in outcomes, indicating the need to account for major discontinuities, as well as continuities in development. In that connection marital support from a nondeviant spouse stood out as a factor associated with a powerful protective effect" (1990: 152). Adult transitions in the life course can thus "modify the effect of adversities experienced in childhood" (Rutter et al., 1990: 152). They also pointed out a key reason why change is possible: because the chain of stability "relied on multiple links, each one dependent on the presence of some particular set of features, there were many opportunities for the chain of adversity to be broken" (Rutter et al., 1990: 137).

RETHINKING CHANGE AND STABILITY

Taken as a whole, the foregoing review suggests that conclusions about the inevitability of antisocial continuities have been either overstated or misinterpreted. In regard to the former, long-term stability coefficients are far from perfect and leave considerable room for the emergence of discontinuities. In retrospect, criminologists should have been forewarned not to make sweeping generalizations about stability in light of the lengthy history of prediction research showing that childhood variables are quite modest prognostic devices. In a situation known as the false positive problem, prediction scales often result in the substantial overprediction of future criminality (Loeber, 1987; Farrington and Tarling, 1985). Likewise, prediction attempts often fail to identify accurately those who will become criminal even though past behavior suggests otherwise (false negatives).

In probably the best recent study on this topic, White and colleagues (1990: 521) document that, consistent with past research, "early antisocial behavior is the best predictor of later antisocial behavior." Nevertheless, their data clearly show the limitations of relying only on childhood information to understand behavior over time. As White and colleagues (1990: 521) argue, a high false positive rate precludes the use of early antisocial behavior alone as a predictor of later crime. They go on to note the general inaccuracy of specific predictions and the fact that the heterogeneous nature of delinquency in later adolescence (and, by implication, in adulthood) thwarts accurate prediction.

The prediction literature thus reinforces the need to look at both stability and change, and hence the futility of either/or conceptions of human development. That is, although there is longitudinal consistency, research has established large variations in later adolescent and adult criminal behavior that are not directly accounted for by childhood propensities. Furthermore, there is some evidence that these changes in adult criminality are structured by social transitions and adult life events in the life course (Rutter et al., 1990), underscoring the utility of a life-course perspective.

Equally important, however, is the fact that the conception of stability traditionally used in criminology is very specific and has been frequently misinterpreted. Rank-order correlations and other measures of stability refer to the consistency of between-individual differences over time and consequently rely on an aggregate picture of relative standing. As Huesmann and colleagues (1984) note, what remains stable over time is the aggressiveness of an individual relative to the population (1984: 1131). Stability coefficients do not measure the consistency or heterogeneity of individual behaviors over time (that is, individual change). Consider Gottfredson and Hirschi's (1990) argument that "if there is continuity over the life course in criminal activity . . . it is unnecessary to follow people over time" (1990: 230). The continuity to which they refer is relative stability, which does not mean that individuals remain constant in their behavior over time. Thus, individual change is possible, if not likely, despite the stability of relative rank orderings.

Even if propensity for crime is stable over time, the commission of a criminal act depends on a host of social factors that vary with key life-course transitions. For example, in Gottfredson and Hirschi's (1990) theory, heterogeneity among individuals in low self-control is established early in life and remains stable over time (see also Nagin and Paternoster, 1991). From their viewpoint the diversity of adult crimes and antisocial behaviors in childhood are all expressions of the same underlying trait. Yet the idea of self-control cannot be divorced from the life course because its changing manifestations over time are structured by social opportunities to commit crime, differential reactions by the criminal justice system, and constraints imposed by aging (see also Shover, 1985; Gartner and Piliavin, 1985). As Gottfredson and Hirschi argue: "Crimes are short-term, circumscribed events that presuppose a peculiar set of necessary conditions (e.g., activity, opportunity, adversaries, victims, goods). Self-control, in contrast, refers to relatively stable differences across individuals in the propensity to commit criminal (or equivalent) acts. Accordingly, self-control is only one element in the causal configuration leading to a criminal act" (1990: 137). This argument clearly implies that the causes of crime may be very different from the causes of propensity (low self-control). Combined with the recognition that stability is an aggregate between-individual concept that does not preclude within-individual change, Gottfredson and

Hirschi's distinction between crime and lack of self-control (criminality) aids in resolving the seemingly contradictory data on stability, change, and prediction of criminal events over time.

Based on this conceptualization of past research, our theoretical model is premised on the fact that both stability and change are present over the life course, and that we need to explain both. As Gottfredson and Hirschi (1990) note, the tendency of individuals to remain relatively stable over time on the dimension of deviance points to the early life course—especially family socialization and child rearing—as a key causal explanation of early delinquency and a stable self-control. While we agree with this conception, we are also concerned with adult behavior and how it is influenced not only by early life experiences and self-control, but also by modifying events and socialization in adulthood. Because we hypothesize that the adult life course accounts for variation in adult crime that cannot be predicted from childhood, change is a central part of our explanatory framework. Our theoretical model is laid out in detail in Chapters 4–9, but it will be useful at this point to provide a brief overview of our key strategy and ideas.

INFORMAL SOCIAL CONTROL AND SOCIAL CAPITAL

Our theory emphasizes the importance of informal social ties and bonds to society at all ages across the life course. Hence the effects of informal social control in childhood, adolescence, and adulthood are central to our theoretical model. Virtually all previous studies of social control in criminology have focused either on adolescents or on official (that is, formal) social control mechanisms such as arrest and imprisonment (for reviews see Gottfredson and Hirschi, 1990; Horwitz, 1990). As a result, most criminological studies have failed to examine the processes of informal social control from childhood through adulthood.

Following Elder (1975, 1985), we differentiate the life course of individuals on the basis of age and argue that the important institutions of informal and formal social control vary across the life span. For example, the dominant institutions of social control in childhood and adolescence are the family, school, peer groups, and the juvenile justice system. In the phase of young adulthood, the institutions of higher education or vocational training, work, and marriage become salient. The juvenile justice system is also replaced by the adult criminal justice system. Finally, in middle adulthood, the dominant institutions of social control are work, marriage, parenthood, investment in the community, and the criminal justice system.

Within this framework, our organizing principle derives from the central idea of social control theory (Durkheim, [1897] 1951; Reiss, 1951a; Hirschi, 1969; Janowitz, 1975; Kornhauser, 1978): crime and deviance result when an individual's bond to society is weak or broken.[2] As Janowitz (1975) has cogently argued, many sociologists mistakenly think of social control solely in terms of social repression and State sanctions (for example, surveillance, enforced conformity, incarceration). By contrast, we adopt a more general conceptualization of social control as the capacity of a social group to regulate itself according to desired principles and values, and hence to make norms and rules effective (Janowitz, 1975: 82; Reiss, 1951a; Kornhauser, 1978). We further emphasize the role of *informal* social controls that emerge from the role reciprocities and structure of interpersonal bonds linking members of society to one another and to wider social institutions such as work, family, and school (see also Kornhauser, 1978: 24).

In applying these concepts to the longitudinal study of crime, we examine the extent to which social bonds inhibit crime and deviance early in the life course, and the consequences this has for later development. Moreover, we examine social ties to both institutions and other individuals in the adult life course, and identify the transitions within individual trajectories that relate to changes in informal social control. In this context we contend that pathways to crime *and* conformity are mediated by social bonds to key institutions of social control. Our theoretical model focuses on the transition to adulthood and, in turn, the new role demands from higher education, full-time employment, military service, and marriage. Hence, we explore the interrelationships among crime and informal social control at all ages, with particular attention devoted to the assessment of within-individual change.

We also examine social relations between individuals (for example, parent-child, teacher-student, and employer-employee) at each stage of the life course as a form of social investment or social capital (Coleman, 1988, 1990). Specifically, we posit that the social capital derived from strong social relations (or strong social bonds), whether as a child in a family, as an adolescent in school, or as an adult in a job, dictates the salience of these relations at the individual level. If these relations are characterized by interdependence (Braithwaite, 1989), they represent social and psychological resources that individuals can draw on as they move through life transitions that traverse larger trajectories. Thus, we see both social capital and informal social control as linked to social structure, and we distinguish both concepts as important in understanding changes in behavior over time.

Recognizing the importance of both stability and change in the life course, we develop three sets of thematic ideas regarding age-graded social control. The first concerns the structural and intervening sources of juvenile delinquency; the second centers on the consequences of delinquency and antisocial behavior for adult life chances; and the third focuses on the explanation of adult crime and deviance in relation to adult informal social control and social capital. Although this model was developed in the ongoing context of our analysis of the Gluecks' data and represents the best fit between our conceptual framework and available measures, we believe that our theoretical notions have wider appeal and are not solely bound by these data.

Structure and Process in Adolescent Delinquency

In explaining the origins of delinquency, criminologists have embraced either structural factors (such as poverty, broken homes) or process variables (such as attachment to parents or teachers). We believe such a separation is a mistake. In Chapters 4 and 5, we join structural and process variables together into a single theoretical model. In brief, we argue that informal social controls derived from the family (for example, consistent use of discipline, monitoring, and attachment) and school (for instance, attachment to school) mediate the effects of both individual and structural background variables. For instance, previous research on families and delinquency often fails to account for social structural disadvantage and how it influences family life. As Rutter and Giller (1983: 185) have argued, socioeconomic disadvantage has potentially adverse effects on parents, such that parental difficulties are more likely to develop and good parenting is impeded. If this is true, we would then expect poverty and disadvantage to have their effects on delinquency transmitted through parenting.

The effects of family process are hypothesized to mediate structural context in other domains as well. As described in Chapter 4, our model and data enable us to ascertain the direct and indirect effects of other key factors such as family disruption, parental criminality, household crowding, large family size, residential mobility, and mother's employment. All of these structural background factors have traditionally been associated with delinquency (for a review, see Rutter and Giller, 1983). It is our major contention, however, that these structural factors will strongly affect family and school social control mechanisms, thereby playing a largely indirect (but not unimportant) role in the explanation of early delinquency. As detailed in Chapters 4 and 5, the intervening processes of primary interest are family socialization (discipline, supervision, and attachment), school attachment, and the influence of delinquent siblings and friends. Overall, these two chapters provide our accounting of the causes of early delinquency and what Gottfredson and Hirschi (1990) refer to as low self-control.

The Importance of Continuity between Childhood and Adulthood

Our second theme concerns childhood antisocial behavior (such as juvenile delinquency, conduct disorder, or violent temper tantrums) and its link to troublesome adult behaviors. As noted earlier, the theoretical importance of homotypic continuity has been largely ignored among sociological criminologists. Criminologists still focus primarily on the teenage years in their studies of offending, apparently disregarding the connections between childhood delinquency and adult crime. Reversing this tide, our main contention (as discussed in Chapter 6) is that antisocial and delinquent behavior in childhood—measured by both official and unofficial sources—is linked to later adult deviance and criminality in a variety of settings (for example, family violence, military offenses, "street crime," and alcohol abuse). Moreover, we argue that these outcomes occur independent of traditional sociological and psychological variables such as class background, ethnicity, and IQ.

Although some criminologists have explored the connections among conduct disorder, juvenile delinquency, and adult crime, we argue that the negative consequences of childhood misbehavior extend to a much broader spectrum of adult life, including economic dependence, educational failure, employment instability, and marital discord. In Chapter 6 we thus explore the adult worlds of work, educational attainment, and marriage as well as involvement in deviant behavior generally. As Hagan and Palloni (1988) argue (see also Hagan, 1989: 260), delinquent and criminal events "are linked into life trajectories of broader significance, whether those trajectories are criminal or noncriminal in form" (1988: 90). Because most research by criminologists has focused either on the teenage years or on adult behavior limited to crime, this basic idea has not been well integrated into the criminological literature.

The Significance of Change in the Life Course

Our third focus, drawing on a developmental perspective and stepping-stone approach (Loeber and LeBlanc, 1990: 433–439), is concerned with changes in deviance and offending as individuals age. As discussed in Chapter 7, our thesis concerns adult behavior and how it is influenced not just by early life experiences, but also by social ties to the adult institutions of informal social control (such as family, school, and work). We argue that trajectories of both crime and conformity are significantly influenced over the life course by these adult social bonds, regardless of prior individual differences in self-control or criminal propensity.

The third major theme of our research, then, is that changes that strengthen social bonds to society in adulthood will lead to less crime and deviance. Conversely, changes in adulthood that weaken social bonds will lead to more crime and deviance. This premise allows us to explain desistance from crime as well as late onset. In addition, unlike most researchers, we emphasize the quality, strength, and interdependence of social ties more than the occurrence or timing of discrete life events (cf. Hogan, 1978; Loeber and LeBlanc, 1990: 430–432). In our view, interdependent social bonds increase social capital and investment in social relations and institutions. As discussed more fully in Chapters 7 and 8, our theoretical model rests on social ties to jobs and family as the key inhibitors to adult crime and deviance.

DATA ON CRIME IN THE LIFE COURSE

Our concerns in this chapter have been primarily theoretical and conceptual. Nevertheless, it is important to recognize that scientific knowledge regarding crime and delinquency has also been hampered by the sheer lack of good data, especially data of a longitudinal nature. Recently the National Academy of Sciences Panel on Criminal Careers (Blumstein et al., 1986; see also Farrington, Ohlin, and Wilson, 1986) made several recommendations regarding criminological research. The NAS panel called for prospective longitudinal studies to examine (1) the developmental experiences engendering compliant behavior, (2) behavioral precursors of subsequent criminality, (3) the influence on subsequent behavior of interactions with the juvenile and adult criminal justice systems, and (4) factors associated with career termination (Blumstein et al., 1986: 200).

What sort of data base would suffice to carry out such a mandate? The panel's answer included data on "crime and arrest sequences; on each individual's early childhood experiences; on his parents, siblings, and peers; on school experiences and work experiences; on deviant behavior of various sorts; and on interactions with the justice system" (1986: 200). This description sounds discouraging because, according to the panel, "No single data source yet collected contains so rich a set of information on an appropriately broad sample" (Blumstein et al., 1986: 209). Furthermore, collection of new longitudinal data is costly and time-consuming (Gottfredson and Hirschi, 1987).

Counteracting these concerns, we executed a research strategy that involved recoding, computerizing, and analyzing a major prospective data base that has been virtually inaccessible to the research community—the three-wave, matched-sample longitudinal study of juvenile delinquency and adult crime pioneered by Sheldon and Eleanor Glueck of Harvard Law School. This data base contains virtually all the necessary characteristics delineated by the NAS panel for a rigorous study of crime and delinquency in the life course. Moreover, several important theorists and methodologists have noted the value of both the matched-sample research design employed in the *Unraveling Juvenile Delinquency (UJD)* study, and the quality and scope of longitudinal information collected by the Gluecks' research team (Reiss, 1951b; Hirschi and Selvin, 1967; Wilson and Herrnstein, 1985: 175–179; Farrington, 1986a: 209). Quite simply, the Gluecks' data are some of the best that the field of criminology has to offer.

Among the numerous advantages provided by the Gluecks' data, at least three stand out. First, the data cover a long period of time—information is available from birth to age 32 and, in some instances, to age 45. To date, most criminological research has been cross-sectional in design, or, to a lesser extent, has consisted of short-term panel studies. By contrast, there are few long-term longitudinal data sets (see Farrington, 1979, and Farrington, Ohlin, and Wilson, 1986), and even fewer prospective longitudinal studies (for example, Elliott et al., 1985; Robins, 1966; McCord and McCord, 1959; West and Farrington, 1973, 1977; Thornberry et al., 1991; Loeber et al., 1991; Huizinga et al., 1991). Thus, it is perhaps unsurprising that information gleaned from prior longitudinal studies often simply reaffirms the results of cross-sectional data (Gottfredson and Hirschi, 1987). When the same variables are measured over a short period for the same cohort of individuals, one is precluded from studying developmental change and how constructs manifest themselves across varying stages of the life course.

Second, the sampling design of the *UJD* study allows a full-scale assessment of serious and persistent offending. As reviewed by the NAS panel (Blumstein et al., 1986: 198–209; see also Cernkovich et al., 1985), prior data bases often do not include sufficient samples of serious or persistent criminal offending. In fact, many studies of juvenile delinquency are characterized by an analysis of truancy, running away, and other relatively minor offenses, and by samples where State sanctions are infrequent. Although specialization is not a trademark of delinquency (Gottfredson and Hirschi, 1990; Blumstein et al., 1986), the juvenile justice system does react more harshly to violent and persistent offending. Focusing on minor deviance therefore precludes the study of how the mechanisms of official delinquency control may alter later adult development (cf. Moffitt, 1991). We elaborate on this point in Chapters 6 and 7, where we examine the long-term negative consequences of incarceration for adult outcomes.

Third, and probably most important, the Gluecks' data are rich in the number and quality of measures across a variety of dimensions of juvenile and adult development. Many longitudinal studies fail to measure the developmental course of informal social control and major life events. For example, although the birth cohort study by Wolfgang et al. (1972; see also Tracy et al., 1990) has provided key information on criminal offending and has served as a stimulus for research, explanatory characteristics were limited largely to structural and demographic variables (such as poverty and race). Many other longitudinal studies have also been limited to demographics and a restricted age range. As many researchers have argued (Farrington, Ohlin, and Wilson, 1986; Tonry et al., 1991; Blumstein et al., 1986), to distinguish effectively the causal influences on crime one must account for important background factors and the changing nature of life events—especially during the transition from late adolescence to young adulthood. Informal social controls in adulthood seem especially salient to us, and the Gluecks' data permit refined analyses of this dimension.

INTEGRATING CRIMINOLOGY AND THE LIFE COURSE

Building on earlier work (Laub and Sampson, 1988; Sampson and Laub, 1990), our theoretical framework represents a challenge to several assumptions and ideas found in contemporary criminological thought. We believe that the field of criminology has been dominated by narrow sociological and psychological perspectives, coupled with a strong tradition of research using cross-sectional data on adolescents. As a result, scientific knowledge in the field has been hindered by a focus on a limited age range, a limited range of variation in crime and State sanctions, an examination of either structural *or* process variables, and by serious limitations found in previous research designs and analytic strategies. The overall consequence is that major gaps appear in the existing body of criminological literature.

In this book we confront several of these knowledge gaps and, we hope, expand and enrich the focus of criminological theory and research. We do so by merging a life-course perspective on age and informal social control with the existing criminological literature on crime and delinquency. With this strategy we believe that key issues of current debate in the field, such as the age-crime relationship and longitudinal versus cross-sectional data needs, can be resolved (see Gottfredson and Hirschi, 1986, 1988; Blumstein et al., 1988a, 1988b). Rather than pitting one view against the other in an either/or fashion, our theory of social bonding integrates what is conceptually sound and empirically correct from each perspective.

Take, for example, the issue of stability versus change. We posit that life-event transitions and adult social bonds can modify quite different childhood trajectories. Thus our conception of change is that adult factors explain systematic variations in adult behavior independent of childhood background. This does not deny the significance of childhood—in fact, Chapters 4 and 5 are devoted to the explanation of delinquency by focusing primarily on early child-rearing practices. Our theory thus incorporates the juvenile period with the adult life course to provide a more unified picture of human development. The unique advantage of a sociological perspective on the life course is that it brings the formative period of childhood back into the picture yet recognizes that individual behavior is mediated over time through interaction with age-graded social institutions.

By choosing the route of data restoration, we avoid legitimate criticisms regarding expenditures of large funds on long-term projects (Gottfredson and Hirschi, 1987). We also take advantage of the unique substantive properties of the Gluecks' data, which will likely never be repeated given current research restrictions. Our strategy thus permits the linking of theoretical concerns with the rich nature of the Gluecks' longitudinal data. We now turn to a description of these data and our efforts to restore them.

UNRAVELING JUVENILE DELINQUENCY AND FOLLOW-UP STUDIES

2

For more than forty years, Sheldon Glueck (1896–1980) and Eleanor (Touroff) Glueck (1898–1972) carried out fundamental research on crime and delinquency at Harvard University. Their primary interests were discovering the causes of juvenile delinquency and adult crime and assessing the overall effectiveness of correctional treatment in controlling criminal careers. For their time, the Gluecks' research projects were unusually large investigations that included extensive follow-up periods. Their major studies included the Massachusetts Reformatory study (1930, 1937, 1943), the Women's Reformatory study (1934a), the Judge Baker Foundation study (1934b, 1940), and the *Unraveling Juvenile Delinquency (UJD)* study (1950) plus later follow-ups (1956, 1962, 1968, and 1970). The result was that the Gluecks generated four relatively large data sets and more than 280 articles and 13 books during the course of their professional careers (for an overview see Glueck and Glueck, 1964 and 1974).

This chapter has three main objectives in presenting the empirical and intellectual context of the Gluecks' research. The first is to describe in detail the research design of the *UJD* study and subsequent data collection efforts during the period from 1940 to 1965. Second, we seek to provide an intellectual history of the Gluecks and their research program in order to establish what we call the "Glueck perspective" on crime and criminological research. Third, we address the methodological and ideological critics of the *UJD* study specifically and the Gluecks' research program in general. It is our contention that the Gluecks' research contributed crucial knowledge on the causes of crime and, more important, that their research agenda set the stage for current battles in criminology regarding the proper focus of the discipline and the role of the scientific method (Laub and Sampson, 1991). Despite their seminal contributions to the field, the substance of the Gluecks' works has either been ignored or criticized—especially by sociologists. As a result, contemporary researchers rarely, if ever, read their original studies. When perfunctory cites do appear, they are usually to allege fatal flaws in the Gluecks' position. Therefore, we offer here a revisionist assessment of the Gluecks' research along with an overview of one of the most comprehensive longitudinal data bases in the history of criminological research.

THE *UNRAVELING JUVENILE DELINQUENCY* STUDY

Undoubtedly, the work for which the Gluecks are known best is *Unraveling Juvenile Delinquency* (1950).[1] The *UJD* project, a study of the formation and development of delinquent behavior, began in the fall of 1939. Originally, the Gluecks had planned for a delinquent sample to be drawn from the juvenile court (letter to Dr. Elizabeth Hincks, 2/14/38); however, a major obstacle was finding a court that would grant access to subjects without interference. Five hundred officially delinquent boys were eventually selected from the Massachusetts correctional system. More precisely, the sample of "persistent delinquents" contained white males, ages 10 to 17, recently committed to one of two correctional schools—the Lyman School for Boys in Westboro, Massachusetts, and the Industrial School for Boys in Shirley, Massachusetts (see Glueck and Glueck, 1950: 27).

The 500 nondelinquents, also white males of ages 10 to 17, were chosen from the Boston public schools. Nondelinquent status was determined on the basis of official record checks and interviews with parents, teachers, local police, social workers, and recreational leaders as well as the boys themselves. The Gluecks' sampling procedure was designed to maximize differences in delinquency—an objective that by all accounts succeeded (see Glueck and Glueck, 1950: 27–29).[2] Still, as Long and Vaillant note, even though the nondelinquent boys were certainly different from the Boston youth remanded to reform school, compared with national averages the nondelinquents "did *not* represent a particularly law-abiding group" (1984:345). So the nondelinquents were not atypical "saints" but rather "normal" youth who were not involved in official or serious, persistent delinquency as reported by parents, teachers, and others at the time of the study. Although clearly not a random selection, the samples thus appear representative of the populations of persistent official delinquents and generally nondelinquent youth in Boston at the time.[3]

Matching Design

A unique aspect of the *UJD* study was the matching design. Specifically, the 500 officially defined delinquents and 500 nondelinquents were matched *case by case* on age, race/ethnicity (birthplace of both parents), neighborhood (for example, "boys who are living in clearly defined delinquent areas"), and measured intelligence (Social Case Histories—Policy Memo, November 1939).

The matching on neighborhood ensured that both delinquents and nondelinquents had grown up in lower-class neighborhoods of central Boston. The neighborhoods included Roxbury, East Boston, Charlestown, South Boston, Dorchester, the West End, and the South End. Using census tract data, property inventory data for the city of Boston, and personal observation of the areas themselves, the Gluecks targeted "underprivileged neighborhoods"—slums and tenement areas—for selection in the study. These areas were regions of poverty, economic dependence, and physical deterioration, and were usually adjacent to areas of industry and commerce—what Shaw and McKay (1942) would have termed socially disorganized neighborhoods (Glueck and Glueck, 1950:29). One such neighborhood is described vividly in interviewer notes found in a subject's case file:

> The neighborhood is a congested area; main streets all around are heavy with traffic; factories, businesses, and second class tenements all around; no play places. [In relation to the subject's home, there is] street life (1 block); barrooms (1 block); alleyways (all around); gangs (men and boys 1 block); dumps and empty lots (1 block); railroad yards and tracks (6 blocks); vice (1 block, all around); cheap commercialized recreation (5 minute walk); supervised indoor recreational facilities (none); and supervised outdoor play places (none).

The physical characteristics of the subjects' homes also revealed the underprivileged aspect of the neighborhoods. In general, the homes of the subjects were crowded, and often lacking in basic necessities like sanitary facilities, tubs/showers, and central heating. Interviewer notes found in the case materials for one of the subjects describe more graphically the physical conditions of the household:

> The family lived in the cellar of a two story building. The house was very old and in poor condition. It was a rickety wooden house in an alley. Living conditions in the house were crowded—2 bedrooms for 6 people. There was an oil burner in the parlor and in the kitchen. No gas. There was an ill smelling toilet in the hall.

Given the similarity in neighborhood conditions, the areas were in essence matched on delinquency rate along with poverty: 59 percent of the delinquents and 55 percent of the nondelinquents lived in neighborhoods in which the delinquency rate was 10–24.9 per thousand; 20 percent of the former and 23 percent of the latter came from areas with a delinquency rate of 25–49.9 per thousand; and 15 percent of the delinquents and 17 percent of the control group resided in areas of high delinquency (50–100 per thousand; Glueck and Glueck, 1950:36).

In addition to growing up in similar high-risk environments of poverty and exposure to antisocial conduct, the delinquent and control groups were further matched on an individual basis by age, IQ, and ethnicity. The delinquents averaged 14 years, 8 months and the nondelinquents 14 years, 6 months when the study began. As for ethnicity, 25 percent of both groups were of English background, another fourth were Italian, a fifth Irish, less than a tenth old American, Slavic, or French, and the remaining 20 percent were Near Eastern, Spanish, Scandinavian, German, or Jewish. And as measured by the Wechsler-Bellevue Test, the delinquents had an average IQ of 92 and the nondelinquents 94.

In brief, the 1,000 male subjects in the *UJD* study were matched on key criminological variables thought to influence both delinquent behavior and official reactions by the police and courts (Sampson, 1986). That 500 of the boys were persistent delinquents and 500 avoided delinquency in childhood thus cannot be attributed to residence in urban slum areas, age differences, ethnicity, or IQ.

Data Sources and Follow-Up

A wealth of information on social, psychological, and biological characteristics, family life, school performance, work experiences, and other life events was collected on the delinquents and controls in the period 1939–1948. For example, some key items regarding families include parental criminality and alcohol use, economic status, family structure (for example, divorce/separation), family relations, and patterns of supervision and discipline by parents. Items on grades, school-related behavior, and educational/occupational ambitions are included as well. There are also numerous indicators of recreational and leisure time activities, peer relationships, church attendance, and complete psychiatric profiles gleaned from psychiatric interviews.

These data were collected through detailed investigations by the

Gluecks' research team that included interviews with the subjects themselves and their families, employers, school teachers, neighbors, and criminal justice/social welfare officials. These interview data were supplemented by extensive record checks across a variety of social agencies. The Gluecks were especially concerned with independent sources of measurement and hence provided a means to validate many of the key concepts. For example, most of the social variables (family income, parental discipline, and so forth) were collected from a variety of sources, such as home interviews conducted by the Gluecks' research team along with independent visits by social welfare agencies. This level of detail and the range of information sources found in the Glueck study will likely never be repeated, given contemporary research standards on the protection of human subjects.

Also important was the Gluecks' collection of *self-reported, parent-reported,* and *teacher-reported* measures of delinquent behavior. As Weis (1986: 42) has recently argued: "Direct observations and informant reports (e.g., teachers, parents, peers) are useful approaches in gaining some sense of troublesome behavior among children that might have substantial predictive validity." Foreshadowing these contemporary concerns with predictive validation of official records, the Gluecks' research team asked a variety of questions on antisocial and delinquent conduct that can be used with the extensive information on the nature and history of criminal records (see Glueck and Glueck, 1950:60–61). The combination of self, parent, and teacher reports along with official records provides an excellent opportunity to develop reliable and valid measures of delinquent and antisocial conduct.

The original sample in the *UJD* study was followed up at two different points in time—at the age of 25 and again at the age of 32. This data collection effort took place during the 1949–1963 period (see Glueck and Glueck, 1968 for more details). As a result, extensive data are available for analysis relating to criminal career histories, criminal justice interventions, family life, school and employment history, and recreational activities for the matched subjects in childhood, adolescence, and young adulthood. Moreover, data are available for 438 of the original 500 delinquents (88 percent) and 442 of the original 500 nondelinquents (88 percent) at all three age periods. We calculate that when adjusted for mortality, the follow-up success rate is approximately 92 percent—very high by current standards (see, for example, Wolfgang et al., 1987). The low attrition is testimony to the Gluecks' rigorous research strategy, but also to lower residential mobility and interstate migration rates in the 1940s and 1950s as compared to today. It should be noted, though, that the follow-up of criminal histories and official records covered 37 states—the most common being California, New York, New Hampshire, Florida, and Illinois (Glueck and Glueck, 1968: xix). Thus, criminal history data from first offense to age 32 were gathered through extensive record checks of police, court, and correctional files.

In addition, follow-up information from interviews and record checks was collected on key life events over the time of the follow-up period. Of particular interest are items such as the nature and change of a subject's living arrangements as an adult—including marriage/divorce, frequency of moves, number of children, and military experiences; employment history and work habits (number and type of jobs, weekly income, unemployment, public assistance); and schooling history (age at final academic achievement, reason for stopping schooling, adult education). There are also a host of items concerning factors such as participation in civic affairs, aspirations, types of companions, and nature of leisure-time activities.

As if anticipating future concerns, the Glueck data also overcome a key problem noted by Blumstein and colleagues (1986) in existing criminological research. Many previous studies lack a sufficient number of persistent and serious offenders; moreover, few studies have been able to trace the factors associated with adult initiation of a criminal career. By contrast, during the period between ages 17–32, approximately 90 of the Gluecks' delinquents were arrested for robbery, 225 for burglary, and over 250 for larceny. As for the frequency of offenses, we estimate that overall the delinquent group generated about 6,300 arrest charges from birth to age 32. Moreover, 55 percent had an arrest in Massachusetts from age 32 to age 45 (these data are described later). Clearly, the Gluecks' delinquent group consisted of persistent and serious offenders.

What is perhaps even more interesting, approximately 100 members of the original nondelinquent group (20 percent) initiated criminal behavior as adults. The factors that led to the initiation of crime in adulthood among the nondelinquent group are of considerable interest to criminological theory, as are the factors associated with desistance among those in the delinquent group.

Our efforts in locating, reconstructing, and validating the Gluecks' original case records from the *UJD* study and follow-ups are described more fully in Chapter 3. Before turning to our empirical strategy, however, we now present in some detail the historical and institutional setting in which the Gluecks established their program of research. This social context is crucial for understanding not only the nature of the Gluecks' data, but also the reception that their ideas received by the criminological community.

HISTORICAL AND INSTITUTIONAL CONTEXT

The historical context and institutional affiliations of the Gluecks had an important effect on their research program, especially their methodological stance toward the study of crime and its causes. First, the Gluecks' educational background was eclectic and interdisciplinary in nature. Sheldon Glueck in particular was something of an academic maverick. He first attended Georgetown University (1914–1915) and then transferred to George Washington University, where he received his A.B. degree in the humanities in 1920. He went on to receive LL.B. and LL.M. degrees from National University Law School in 1920.[4] After being denied admission to Harvard Law School, he entered the Department of Social Ethics at Harvard University, an interdisciplinary precursor to the sociology department (see Potts, 1965 for a description of that department). There he received an A.M. in 1922 and a Ph.D. in 1924. Reflecting this diverse educational setting, Sheldon Glueck's Ph.D. thesis (1925) integrated the interests of sociology, law, and psychiatry in its focus on criminal responsibility, mental disorder, and criminal law.

Eleanor Glueck's academic terrain was similarly eclectic. After attending Barnard College (A.B. in English, 1920), the New York School of Social Work (1921), and working in a settlement house in Dorchester, Massachusetts, she enrolled in the School of Education at Harvard. She received an Ed.M. degree in 1923 and a doctorate (Ed.D.) in 1925. Eleanor Glueck's early research focused on the sociology of education, especially the relationship between schools and the community and evaluation research methods in social work (1927, 1936; see also Gilboy, 1936).[5]

Overall, then, the Gluecks were not beholden to any one discipline in an a priori sense, and as a result, they published extensively in the leading journals of criminology, social work, psychology, sociology, education, law, and psychiatry. The price they paid for such an interdisciplinary outlook was steep (see Laub and Sampson, 1991). Indeed, as Geis recognized over 20 years ago: "The Gluecks belong to no single academic discipline, and they are suffering the déclassé fate of aliens and intruders" (1966: 188).

Second, the Gluecks' social positions within the academic community were unique at the time, and would be even today. After teaching for a few years in the Department of Social Ethics at Harvard, Sheldon Glueck was appointed to the Harvard Law School as assistant professor of criminology in 1929. He became a full professor in 1932 and was appointed the first Roscoe Pound Professor of Law in 1950 (*Current Biography Yearbook*, 1957). Sheldon Glueck's position as a professor of criminology in a law school was an unusual institutional arrangement that led him to a somewhat isolated and "outcast" perspective. Specifically, although law professors and students do not often conduct (or reward) social science research, that was his specialty and main interest. Moreover, research on the causes of crime was a particular anomaly in a law school setting, even though during the 1930s the Harvard Law School had a tradition of research on the administration of justice (for example, the Cleveland Crime Survey and the Harvard Crime Survey). Sheldon Glueck's institutional arrangement was also a structural constraint in another crucial respect: there was no opportunity to train Ph.D. students who might carry on the Gluecks' research agenda.

Perhaps more salient was the institutional treatment accorded Eleanor Glueck. Although armed with a doctorate in education[6] and a prolific publishing record, Eleanor Glueck was unable to secure a tenured faculty position or any teaching position at Harvard. In fact, she was employed from 1930 to 1953 as a research assistant in criminology at the Harvard Law School.[7] Some twenty years after her appointment as a research assistant she was "promoted" to research associate in criminology in 1953, a position she retained until 1964. At the same time, from 1929 to 1964, she was co-director of the project on the causes and prevention of juvenile delinquency.[8] In short, Eleanor Glueck's entire career at Harvard University consisted of a social position akin to what many Ph.D. candidates face today before graduation. As such, she was an outcast from mainstream academia at Harvard and in the academic field at large.

A third fact central to understanding the Gluecks' approach was that their intellectual mentors were a diverse group drawn from a variety of disciplines and all unusual thinkers in their own right. The group included such figures as Roscoe Pound, Felix Frankfurter, Richard Cabot, Bernard Glueck, William Healy, Augusta Bronner, and Edwin B. Wilson. This diversity of intellectual influence is evident throughout the Gluecks' research careers. Early on the Gluecks were influenced personally as well as professionally by Sheldon Glueck's older brother, Bernard Glueck. The latter was a forensic psychiatrist at Sing Sing prison and had a long-standing interest in crime (see B. Glueck, 1916, 1918). Equally important, it was Bernard Glueck who arranged the first meeting between one of his graduate students, Eleanor Touroff, and Sheldon Glueck.

At Harvard the Gluecks were influenced by Richard C. Cabot, a professor in the Department of Social Ethics. It was in a seminar with Cabot that the idea for a study of 500 offenders from the Massachusetts Reformatory first originated. Cabot's own research utilized the follow-up method in assessing the accuracy of diagnoses of cardiac illnesses (Cabot, 1926). Sheldon Glueck noted that in the field of penology no studies had been done assessing the post-treatment histories of ex-prisoners. Excited by the prospects of such research, Cabot arranged financing for the Gluecks' research, which culminated in *500 Criminal Careers* (1930).

Felix Frankfurter served as director of the Harvard Crime Survey in 1926 and was also quite influential in the Gluecks' early studies. In fact, the Harvard Crime Survey, of which the Gluecks' *One Thousand Juvenile Delinquents* (1934b) was the first volume, can be seen as an early model of scientific inquiry in the social sciences. According to Frankfurter, the Survey was "not an agency for reform" but a contribution of scientific knowledge to society in the areas of criminal behavior and social policy that "heretofore had been left largely to improvisation, crude empiricism, and propaganda" (1934: xii). Moreover, Frankfurter (1934) believed that the formulation of the problem and use of the scientific process to address the problem would eventually lead to prudent social policies. This general viewpoint can be found in all the Gluecks' research.

William Healy and Augusta Bronner were probably the most influential thinkers in the Gluecks' intellectual history. The Gluecks had met Healy and Bronner, directors of the Judge Baker Foundation, when they first arrived in Boston, a meeting facilitated in part by Bernard Glueck. The Gluecks had read Healy's *The Individual Delinquent* (1915) and were favorably disposed to his research. Healy was also interested in issues relating to Sheldon Glueck's doctoral thesis and was one of the reviewers who encouraged its publication by Little, Brown (S. Glueck, 1964:319). Most important to the Gluecks was the "scientific attitude" of Healy and Bronner; in a memorial address for Healy, Sheldon Glueck stated that Healy was "a major catalyst of our work" (1964: 319). Like the Gluecks, Healy focused on the individual as the most important unit of analysis, embraced a multiple factor approach in the study of crime causation, and utilized knowledge across a variety of disciplines (see Healy, 1915 and Healy and Bronner, 1926). In fact, Snodgrass (1972: 326) has referred to *Unraveling Juvenile Delinquency* as "essentially a modernized *Individual Delinquent.*"

Three factors thus worked together to develop a fiercely independent and even iconoclastic outlook on the part of the Gluecks. Namely, interdisciplinary educational training combined with Sheldon Glueck's unusual position in the law school and apparent gender discrimination against Eleanor Glueck served to create an almost bunker mentality, especially regarding the discipline of sociology.[9] The Gluecks were also constrained by their lack of involvement in the training of graduate students. Added to this was the intellectual diversity of a set of mentors who fostered empirical research beyond the confines of any one discipline. It is only within this context that we can understand the Gluecks' distinctive theoretical and methodological perspective.

THE GLUECK PERSPECTIVE

During their 40-year career at the Harvard Law School, the Gluecks produced four major data bases relating to crime and delinquency. The first was the study of 510 male offenders from the Massachusetts Reformatory during the period 1911–1922. These offenders were studied over a 15-year span, which resulted in three books (Glueck and Glueck, 1930, 1937, 1943). A second although similar study of women incarcerated at the Women's Reformatory resulted in the publication of *Five Hundred Delinquent Women* (1934a). The Gluecks' third major research effort focused on a sample of juveniles who had been referred by the Boston Juvenile Court to the Judge Baker Foundation (the existing court clinic at the time). These results were published in *One Thousand Juvenile Delinquents* (1934b), and a follow-up analysis ten years later produced *Juvenile Delinquents Grown Up* (1940). The results of these studies are summarized in a volume entitled *After-Conduct of Discharged Offenders* (1945). Finally, the works that the Gluecks are best known for are *Unraveling Juvenile Delinquency* (1950) and the follow-up of the *Unraveling* sample, *Delinquents and Non-Delinquents in Perspective* (1968), both described earlier.

The Gluecks' methodological approach to the study of crime can be characterized by three distinct features. The first is an emphasis on longitudinal and follow-up prediction studies, including, when possible, control groups for comparative purposes. Second, the Gluecks' work emphasized a criminal career focus, especially the study of serious, persistent offenders (1950: 13). The Gluecks thought that the study of the formation, development, and termination of criminal careers was a research priority, and that the causes of the initiation of crime were distinct from the causes of continuing crime and processes of desistance (1930: 257; 1934b: 282; 1945: 75, n.1). Third, the Gluecks stressed the importance of collecting multiple sources of information (for example, parent, teacher, self-reports) in addition to official records of crime and delinquency.

As for substantive findings, the Gluecks, like Goring ([1913] 1972), uncovered the important relationship between age and crime. The Gluecks argued that age of onset was a key factor for etiology and policy, and that career criminals started offending very early in life. The Gluecks also stressed that crime declined strongly with age. Specifically, in all of their research the Gluecks found that as the population of offenders aged, their crime rate declined. Furthermore, even among those who continued offending the seriousness of the offenses declined (Glueck and Glueck, 1940, 1943, 1945, 1968). The Gluecks sought to understand the age-crime curve in terms of "delayed maturation" (Glueck and Glueck, 1974: 169–176). The nature of the relationship between age and crime was one of the major sources of battle between the Gluecks and Edwin Sutherland, and their dispute foreshadowed a contemporary debate along similar lines (Laub and Sampson, 1991).

Research by the Gluecks also revealed the stability of delinquent patterns over the life cycle. They argued that the data showed "beyond a reasonable doubt that, in all of life's activities considered in this inquiry, the men who as boys comprised our sample of juvenile delinquents have continued on a path markedly divergent from those who as juveniles had been included in the control group of nondelinquents" (Glueck and Glueck, 1968: 169–170). The Gluecks' hypothesis regarding the stability of deviance would also turn out to be a major sticking point with those, like Sutherland, who advocated an exclusively sociological perspective on crime.

According to the Gluecks, the most important factor that distinguished delinquents from nondelinquents in early life was the family. In particular, the Gluecks developed a prediction scale of delinquency in their major work, *Unraveling Juvenile Delinquency*, that centered on family variables—disciplinary practices, supervision by parents, and child-parent attachment. Those families with lax discipline combined with erratic and threatening punishment, poor supervision, and weak emotional ties between parent and child generated the highest probability of delinquency. Although a focus on the family was to become extremely unpopular in sociology during the 1950s and 1960s (see Wilkinson, 1974), it was one of the Gluecks' major interests.

Perhaps most important, the Gluecks promoted a multi-disciplinary perspective and had little patience for those criminologists who were wedded to any one particular discipline. As a result the Gluecks rejected unilateral causation, whether sociological, biological, or psychological in focus, and embraced instead a multiple causal approach emphasizing differentiation between offenders and nonoffenders. This approach is seen most clearly in *Unraveling*, where they focused not only on the family but on personality development, temperament, and constitutional factors such as body structure (for example, mesomorphy) that may have distinguished offenders from nonoffenders. As the Gluecks stated, "The separate findings, independently gathered, integrate into a dynamic pattern which is neither exclusively biologic nor exclusively socio-cultural, but which derives from an interplay of somatic, temperamental, intellectual, and socio-cultural forces" (1950: 281). The Gluecks, along with Healy (1915; see also Healy and Bronner, 1926) thus established the multiple factor approach to the study of crime.

In short, the Gluecks were stubbornly driven by what their data revealed, and refused to pigeonhole their interpretations into any one disciplinary box, tempted though they were. This emphasis on fact gathering prevented them from ever developing a systematic theoretical framework. As they argued: "Neither hunches nor theoretical speculation, can conjure away the facts, even though those facts may not fit neatly into various preconceptions about human nature and crime causation" (1951: 762). Their mode of analysis was to cross-tabulate all possible factors with delinquency (cf. Lazarsfeld, 1955). As a result,

Unraveling is very difficult to read and seems to present nothing but table after table. As Geis has said regarding their work: ". . . the paradox of studies by the Gluecks: they do such good work so badly" (1970: 118).

METHODOLOGICAL AND IDEOLOGICAL CRITICS OF THE GLUECKS

Despite their collection of a wealth of data on crime and delinquency, the substantive contributions of the Gluecks have not been well integrated into modern criminological theory and research. One of the main reasons for this can be traced to the methodological critiques of their work (for example, Reiss, 1951b; Hirschi and Selvin, 1967; Wilkins, 1969). A well-known and damaging criticism relating to the cross-sectional *UJD* study concerns the Gluecks' attempt to predict delinquency among school-age children. They constructed a prediction table based on five factors: the discipline of the boy by the father, the supervision of the boy by the mother, the affection of the father for the boy, the affection of the mother for the boy, and the cohesiveness of the family (Glueck and Glueck, 1950: 261). The Gluecks claimed great success with their prediction scheme, but, as Reiss (1951b) correctly pointed out, given a sampling design that has 50 percent delinquents and 50 percent nondelinquents, these proportions must be representative of the general population in Boston or else "the tables will yield very poor prediction" (1951: 118). Using an estimate of 10 percent delinquents in the general population, Reiss found that the Glueck prediction table led to a disappointing 8.6 percent reduction in the expected errors in prediction (1951b: 118–119).[10]

Despite this admittedly dismal attempt at predicting delinquency, the cross-sectional *UJD* data can still be used to assess the correlates of delinquency and antisocial behavior. As Hirschi and Selvin argue (1967: 248–250), a sample of 50 percent delinquents and 50 percent nondelinquents is not a problem if the data are used to explicate a set of factors relating to the delinquent and nondelinquent populations as opposed to being used to predict delinquency from a set of factors. Hirschi and Selvin contend:

> The Gluecks' prediction tables thus illustrate an important methodological point: If an investigator wishes to make statements about the population

from which his sample was drawn, he must percentage within categories representative of that population. The Gluecks can (perhaps) make accurate statements about distributions of their independent variables within the delinquent and nondelinquent populations; they cannot make accurate statements about the distributions of delinquency within categories of their independent variables for some larger population. (1967: 250)

Thus, the Gluecks' data may not be ideal for prediction tables, but they are well suited to the explication of factors that distinguish serious and persistent delinquents from nondelinquents. Moreover, the Gluecks' longitudinal data can be used to assess both between-group and within-group variation in criminal and deviant behavior over the life course. These data can also be employed in an investigation of *intraindividual* change.

The Gluecks were further criticized for their matching design and poor analyses of both cross-sectional and longitudinal data (Reiss, 1951b; Hirschi and Selvin, 1967; Short, 1969; Wilkins, 1969). We argue, however, that these criticisms have been overblown and often confuse concerns relating to the quality of the data analysis used by the Gluecks and their interpretation of the findings with the overall quality of the data the Gluecks collected. In other words, the conclusion that the Gluecks' data analysis was ill-conceived ought not to lead to the conclusion that their data were of equally poor quality. More to the point, most of the criticisms can in fact be empirically addressed through a reanalysis of their basic data.

One such important issue concerns causal ordering. The analysis by the Gluecks did not examine in a systematic manner issues relating to causal order and spuriousness (see Robins and Hill, 1966; Hirschi and Selvin, 1967). Hirschi and Selvin write that "in their study of five hundred delinquents and five hundred nondelinquents, the Gluecks fail to distinguish consistently between factors that preceded delinquency and those that may well have resulted from either delinquent acts or institutionalization" (1967: 54). Robins and Hill (1966) make essentially the same point. Moreover, few of the many tables presented by the Gluecks in *UJD* and *Delinquents and Nondelinquents in Perspective* examined three or more variables simultaneously. Yet the issues of causal order and spuriousness can be addressed through a detailed reanalysis of the data. For instance, by examining the effects of early childhood behavioral difficulties on family and school processes, one can ascertain their role as antecedents of delinquent behavior. Similarly, by controlling for time spent in correctional institutions before the measurement of individual or family characteristics, the effect of institutionalization (if any) can be empirically assessed. As Hirschi and Selvin point out: "If institutionalization has an effect on certain personality or physiological characteristics of delinquents, the strength of this effect should vary with the length of time spent in the institution" (1967: 58).

The issue of spurious relationships can also be handled through data analysis. While it is true that the Gluecks did not examine relationships among key independent variables, a reanalysis of their data can assess the extent of redundancy to determine how this may affect various findings. It should also be recognized that the larger issue of causal order is a constant problem in social science research, especially in cross-sectional designs. Like measurement error, it is a problem that can never be totally resolved, and as Hirschi and Selvin assert, "it is . . . wrong to let some uncertainties about causal order preclude causal inferences" (1967: 69).

The Gluecks have also been criticized for the quality of their matching design, especially in relation to age (Reiss, 1951b; Kamin, 1986). In contrast, it is our contention that the overall accuracy and detail of the case-by-case matching are quite impressive. Differences between matched individuals are for the most part negligible (see Glueck and Glueck, 1950: Appendix B), and residual age differences can be assessed empirically by examining the findings after controlling for age. Other concerns of the matching design can be examined in a similar manner.

In his review of *UJD*, Reiss (1951b) further chastised the Gluecks for their poor data analysis. Their analytical strategy did in fact suffer in at least three respects. First, in *UJD* the Gluecks did not use any multivariate analysis in their work, in part because such statistical packages were simply unavailable at that time.[11] The Gluecks used what can be called a "hit and run" technique, which in effect gave equal weight to all findings (Hirschi and Selvin, 1967). Thus, there is a need to go beyond their somewhat simplistic analyses by using more sophisticated analytic techniques such as multiple and logistic regression analysis.

Second, the Gluecks did not use their data to test the relative strengths of competing theoretical approaches. For instance, it is possible to assess the relative strengths of sociological, psychological, and biological factors in the explanation of delinquency and adult crime using their data. Thus, a reanalysis could address some of the substantive criticisms raised about their work. For example, some have argued that the Gluecks underemphasized the role of social factors in the explanation of delinquency. The role of peers and socioeconomic status in particular can be reexamined to counteract this criticism. This strategy is important in light of current theoretical conceptions that attach salience to these variables in fostering delinquent behavior (for example, Elliott et al., 1985). The issue of age and crime—especially maturation—also demands more attention with respect to the Gluecks' longitudinal data.

Third, the Gluecks can be criticized for misusing basic statistical techniques and procedures. For example, they routinely presented tests of significance without mentioning that the meaning and appropriateness of these tests are unclear when applied to nonprobability, matched samples. Similarly, the Gluecks often percentaged their tables in the "wrong" direction (Hirschi and Selvin, 1967)[12] and used a percentage point difference to assess the strength of relationships. Although important descriptively, the latter procedure is limited because the measure of association used is sensitive to the distribution of the independent variable (Hirschi and Selvin, 1967).

Finally, the Gluecks have been criticized for the fact that their *UJD* research design used a simple dichotomy distinguishing delinquents from nondelinquents on the basis of official records. They also relied heavily on official records in the follow-up studies to *UJD* (for example, Glueck and Glueck, 1968). The debate over the use of official records is long and contentious, and has been reviewed at length elsewhere (see Blumstein et al., 1986). Although the uncritical use of official records is clearly problematic, it is worth emphasizing a crucial factor that works to the advantage of the Glueck data: the factors controlled by design are exactly those factors that have received the most attention as being "extralegal" or discriminatory in their potential to influence official police reaction. That is, race/ethnicity, age, neighborhood SES, and IQ have all been hypothesized by various theorists to influence the probability of arrest independent of actual delinquency (see, for example, Sampson, 1986). Since subjects are matched on these variables, differential arrest risk cannot be invoked to explain differences in the delinquent and nondelinquent group. Moreover, as a group the delinquents committed delinquency on a persistent and often serious basis, averaging 3.5 convictions per youth. Given this level of frequency and seriousness, it is unreasonable to argue that official delinquents were selected, convicted, and incarcerated solely on the basis of discriminatory practices. In addition, as shown in the following chapters, the results from the official delinquency criterion match quite well not only with *unofficial* measures of delinquency that the Gluecks collected (both in *UJD* and follow-ups) but also with the results of past research.

In sum, we believe that each of the criticisms raised above can be addressed through a reanalysis of the basic Glueck data. As Reiss wrote in a review of *Unraveling Juvenile Delinquency* more than 30 years ago, the Gluecks "present a body of data . . . which can be reworked and re-evaluated. Thus the scientific study of delinquency can be advanced by the further utilization of the basic data which the Gluecks have provided" (1951b: 120). To date, no researcher has accepted Reiss's challenge, and as a result one of the largest efforts to study the causes of delinquency and adult crime has not been fully taken advantage of by the criminological research community.

Other Sources of Criticism

Given the Gluecks' stubborn empiricism, it is ironic that the ideological and disciplinary-based critiques of their research have been equally if not more powerful than the methodological ones. Probably the most important critic of the Gluecks' research was the sociologist Edwin Sutherland. Sutherland was fundamentally opposed to the multiple factor approach to the study of crime and instead sought to establish criminology as a purely sociological discipline with an emphasis on general theory rather than "gathering empirical facts" (see Laub and Sampson, 1991). Sutherland thus attacked the Gluecks' interdisciplinary framework and subsequent research so that sociology could establish proprietary rights to criminology. These critiques coincided with the rise of sociology in the study of crime as well as the rise of Sutherland as the dominant criminologist of the twentieth century. The power of Sutherland's critique cannot be overestimated; to this day a substantive version of sociological positivism is dominant and the Gluecks are often seen as relics of a distant past (see Laub and Sampson, 1991 for more discussion of this point).

Another reason the Gluecks' contributions have been ignored is their interest in biology and crime. For example, Sutherland often placed the Gluecks in the same camp as William Sheldon and E. A. Hooton, two researchers at Harvard interested in the biological causes of human behavior (see, for example, Cohen et al., 1956: 270–326). The result is that the Gluecks were perceived as being interested in *only* the biological basis of crime. Indeed, virtually every citation to the Gluecks in major criminology texts refers to their assertion that mesomorphy is a major predictor of delinquency—a finding stemming from the cross-sectional analysis of *UJD* (see, for example, Vold and Bernard, 1986: 61–62; Siegel, 1989: 126). There exists a long-standing aversion among sociologists to biological explanations of human behavior. As Rowe and Osgood note: "In most sociological treatments of crime and delinquency, genetic explanations are either ignored or ridiculed" (1984: 526). With reference to the Gluecks' work, Bordua has argued that "Sociological criticism . . . of the Gluecks often is well taken but seems to have led to an agreement to ignore their findings. The results of *UJD* agree fairly well with those of comparable control group studies" (Bordua, 1962: 259).

A major exception to this posture is the work of Wilson and Herrnstein (1985). They provide a fair and we think accurate summary of the Gluecks' work. For example, they state: "Sheldon and Eleanor Glueck conducted what was, and has remained, one of the most detailed and comprehensive longitudinal and cross-sectional studies of male delinquency" (Wilson and Herrnstein, 1985: 175). Not surprisingly, the work of Wilson and Herrnstein, like that of the Gluecks, has been severely criticized for its focus on individual factors in crime causation and its examination of nonsociological variables such as genetic predisposition to crime. But, in an excellent review of the Wilson and Herrnstein book, Cohen contends that sociology is "the only branch of social science that has . . . failed to recognize openly the possible influence of nature on human behavior, and nowhere is this more evident than in our studies of crime" (Cohen, 1987: 204).

In brief, we contend that ideological critics of the Gluecks' research have used ideology to destroy empirical facts, without assessing the validity of the empirical findings. The more appropriate strategy, in our view, is to use empirical data to answer empirical questions, independent of allegiance to any particular discipline. Moreover, criticisms from Sutherland and others notwithstanding, the Gluecks' research on such key areas as age and crime, longitudinal research/criminal careers, stability of crime and antisocial behavior, and social control theory with a focus on family processes has been shown to be either (1) essentially correct, or (2) currently dominating the research agenda in criminology (see Laub and Sampson, 1991 for more details).

It is also important to underscore how the Gluecks' own professional interests further contributed to their weak standing in the field and amplified the hostile reaction by sociologists. We have identified six specific reasons why sociology, especially after Sutherland's death in 1950, was so negative about the Gluecks' work. First, the Gluecks had a tendency to infuse their works with moral statements that reflected a middle-class bias. For instance, about the management of income, the Gluecks wrote that families of delinquents were "living from day to day, borrowing without thought of their ability to make reimbursement and showing little comprehension of the value of limiting their expenditures to conform to a meager income" (1950: 108). On most accounts, the Gluecks simply viewed delinquents and their families as inferior. Moreover, although the Gluecks' data were derived from multiple reports describing actual behaviors, the Gluecks often injected moral judgments in their summary coding scheme, using categories such as good, fair, and poor to describe these behaviors (see *UJD* and *Delinquents and Nondelinquents in Perspective* for numerous examples).

Second, the Gluecks were not only atheoretical in their approach to the study of crime; they were *anti*-theory. Although they emphasized an empirical tradition and sought to identify any and all characteristics that might be related to crime and delinquency, they regarded abstract theory as idle speculation, something that was not useful from a scientific point of view. Thus, the Gluecks did not present a theory of crime or even any systematic theoretical ideas in their numerous works. In fact, their idea of a theoretical statement was to present a "tentative causal formula or law" that merely summarized their findings distinguishing offenders from nonoffenders (see Glueck and Glueck, 1950: 281–282).

Third, despite embracing a multiple factor approach, the Gluecks downplayed or ignored traditional sociological variables like stratification, peer group, culture, and community characteristics. As noted earlier and also by Snodgrass (1972: 9), the Gluecks' focus on the "bio-constitutional and psycho-social" downplayed social factors (for example, delinquent associates; employment opportunities) in favor of morphology, temperament, and early family influences (see Glueck and Glueck, 1943: 69; 1950; 1956; 1962; 1968: 170). Overall, the Gluecks' research reflected a restricted range of interest in key sociological variables presumed to be related to crime.

Fourth, it is significant that Sheldon Glueck was a law professor and Eleanor Glueck a soft-money research assistant. Because of their social position within the academic institution, the Gluecks were denied the opportunity to train graduate students and develop the sort of following that others like Sutherland had. Quite simply, no one had a stake in defending the Gluecks. We believe this context is crucial in understanding the lack of transmission of the Gluecks' legacy.

Fifth, our analysis of the Gluecks' papers (Laub and Sampson, 1991), especially their personal correspondence (notes and letters), leads to the conclusion that the Gluecks suffered from social awkwardness and a severe difficulty with public relations. Whereas Sutherland was well liked and perceived to be "humble" and "gentle" (see Laub's 1983b interviews with Cressey, Cohen, and Ohlin), the Gluecks were stubborn, pompous, and had great difficulty accepting any criticism of their work, justified or not, as something other than a personal attack on their integrity (see also S. Glueck, 1960). This no doubt impeded their attempts to establish a cadre of supporters.

Sixth, and probably most important, the Gluecks' research was driven by pragmatic concerns. More precisely, by using their prediction tables, they sought to influence social policy in two distinct ways. One was to improve the process of decision making by judges, probation officers, parole boards, and military officials.[13] The second was to identify potential delinquents at school age or perhaps even as early as age 2 or 3 (see E. Glueck, 1966) to provide therapeutic intervention. For example, the Gluecks argued that the identification of potential delinquents at an early age "would make possible the application of treatment measures that would be truly crime preventive" (1950: 257). Moreover, the Gluecks promoted this interest in the popular literature as well as in scholarly books and journals (see, for example, Glueck and Glueck, 1952; Morgan, 1960; Callwood, 1954; Dressler, 1955).

As discussed earlier, the Gluecks' research on prediction has been severely criticized on methodological grounds. However, this concern reflected their professional interests and intellectual history. Although at the time sociology was not explicitly linked to social policy, such practical applications were the norm for the disciplines reflected in the background of the Gluecks—law, psychiatry, education, and social work. In addition, this pragmatic orientation was consistent with the interests of the Gluecks' mentors, such as Bernard Glueck and William Healy. Thus, through their interest in prediction techniques, the Gluecks promoted an emphasis on individual-level analysis and advocated the application of psychiatric expertise to the formal systems of social control. The Gluecks even envisioned a criminal justice system based on "the rational exercise of discretion enlightened by the reports of psychiatric, psychological, and social workers who ought . . . to be indispensable adjuncts to criminal courts and to classifying agencies and correctional establishments" (S. Glueck, 1962: 139). Furthermore, the Gluecks encouraged the use and expansion of court clinics and child guidance centers. The result of this focus on social policy, along with the explicit promotion of the professional interests of the field of psychiatry, was to alienate the Gluecks further from mainstream sociology, especially as reflected in the works of Edwin Sutherland.

CONCLUDING REMARKS

Sheldon and Eleanor Glueck spent some 25 years compiling what is widely recognized as one of the most seminal data bases in criminological research history (Farrington, 1979, 1986a; Farrington, Ohlin, and Wilson, 1986; Wilson and Herrnstein, 1985). Unfortunately, the Gluecks were not sophisticated analytically, and the quality of their data analyses has been properly questioned (Reiss, 1951b; Hirschi and Selvin, 1967; Short, 1969). Moreover, recent advances in research methodology (for example, multiple linear and logistic regression, covariance structure analysis, event history models) were not available to them.

Perhaps most important, though, is the fact that the Gluecks did not bring a consistent theoretical or policy perspective to bear on their data. As a consequence, the analyses they conducted (Glueck and Glueck, 1950, 1968) were unsatisfactory on both methodological and substantive grounds. When this shortcoming is combined with the widely publicized criticisms of their interdisciplinary paradigm by Edwin Sutherland and their own unique professional interests and biases, it is not hard to understand why the Gluecks' substantive contributions on crime and delinquency have been largely invisible to the modern social science community.

Furthermore, after the publication of *Delinquents and Nondelinquents in Perspective* (1968), the original data lay relatively dormant as the Gluecks retired from their scholarly careers. This comprehensive longitudinal data base—three waves of interdisciplinary information gathered on an original sample of 500 delinquent and 500 nondelinquent urban males matched by race/ethnicity, age, IQ, and low-income residence—has remained inaccessible to the research community as a source of information on crime and deviance from a longitudinal perspective. To rectify this situation, we devoted considerable time and effort to reconstructing and validating these data. As a result, for the first time, data from one of the most important studies ever conducted on crime and delinquency over the life course will be reassessed in light of current theory and empirical techniques.

RESTORING, SUPPLEMENTING, AND VALIDATING THE DATA

3

In October 1986 the Henry A. Murray Research Center of Radcliffe College acquired on a long-term loan basis the *Unraveling Juvenile Delinquency* data plus all of the follow-up data on the original 1,000 cases. The data for the 500 cases in the delinquent group are currently held in the data archive at the Murray Center. The data for the 500 control-group cases are currently held at the Dartmouth Medical School in Hanover, New Hampshire, under the auspices of Dr. George Vaillant. In the course of our work, we devoted a considerable amount of time to coding, recoding, and computerizing the Gluecks' longitudinal data set. In addition, we paid special attention to the reconstruction and validation of measures found in the raw data.

The major purpose of this chapter is to describe our multiple strategies in resurrecting the Gluecks' data. At the end of the chapter, however, we also set the macro-level context in which these data were gathered (for example, Great Depression, World War II) and generally situate the lives of the 500 delinquents and 500 nondelinquents in history. Included in this effort is a discussion of how the timing of key life transitions varies by birth year of the subjects.

DATA RESTORATION AND VALIDATION

Early in the project we discovered several boxes of computer cards derived from the Gluecks' *UJD* plus subsequent follow-up studies. Considering the amount of coding we faced, we first constructed a data set using the Gluecks' computer cards. Although the cards were very old and contained multiple punches in a majority of columns (most modern card readers cannot read multiple-punched cards successfully), we embarked on a strategy to computerize the data. Eventually we read more than 15,000 cards, and hence one component of our strategy was to build a file using the Gluecks' coded data. This process allowed us to secure a wide range of data—over 2,500 variables—in a relatively short time frame (under one year).

We then developed a technical validation scheme. First, we checked (whenever possible) frequencies for the coded variables against frequencies in the published sources of data. Second, we compared the frequency distributions for each variable (column by column) on the cards to the original IBM sheets found in the Gluecks' papers in the Harvard Law School Library. These sheets contained the handwritten counts for each variable (column by column). Third, we generated a 10 percent random sample of cases and compared the value for each variable to the values found in the raw interview files. We completed this validation procedure for the delinquent group and found an extremely high level of agreement between the raw data and the coded data (98 percent or higher for the 2,600 variables we examined). The high level of agreement increased our confidence in the quality of preserved files.

In addition to the technical validation scheme, we examined the substantive validity of numerous measures of delinquency and other theoretical constructs. Unknown to most criminologists, the Gluecks collected data regarding delinquent acts and other forms of misbehavior from parents, teachers, and the subjects themselves. This serves as an example of the serendipity that can result when an investigator has access to raw records from the original study. Moreover, we believe that the combination of self, parental, and teacher reports plus official records provides an excellent opportunity to develop alternative measures of delinquent and antisocial conduct for our substantive analysis as well as assisting us in validating the Gluecks' data overall. As noted by Keicolt and Nathan (1985), when data can be assessed with multiple independent sources, confidence in the validity of the data is increased if these sources arrive at similar conclusions.

Self-reported Data

During wave 1 of the Gluecks' data collection, psychiatric interviews were conducted with each of the boys in the study. These interviews dealt with personality and behavioral characteristics and were intended to supplement information that had been derived from the extensive social investigation of the home environment as well as other investigations (for example, Rorschach tests). In addition to asking questions concerning the boys' various activities, such as club memberships, play places, academic/vocational ambitions, and church attendance, the psychiatrist also questioned the boys about their misbehavior.[1] As noted by the Gluecks, the initial hesitancy on the part of the boys in discussing their misbehavior (particularly those who had not yet come to the attention of the police) dissipated as the boys realized the confidential nature of the study (1950: 61).

The interviews of the boys regarding their own misbehavior began in 1939. Virtually all literature reviews of the early self-report studies cite Short and Nye (1957, 1958) as the first definitive self-report study and Porterfield (1947) and Wallerstein and Wyle (1947) as the earliest but crude versions of this method (see, for example, reviews in Hinde-lang et al., 1981; Weis, 1986). As with many of the Gluecks' contributions to criminology, their early use of a general self-report method to study delinquent and deviant behavior has been overshadowed by concern for their lack of a singularly sociological focus as well as by perceived methodological inadequacies in their research (Laub and Sampson, 1988, 1991).

Parent-reported Data

The Gluecks' research team conducted interviews with parents (usually mothers) in the homes of each boy in the study to obtain information about the home atmosphere, family finances, family background, and genealogy as well as the boy's developmental health history and his leisure-time habits. Within the context of this interview, there were also questions asked about the boy's misbehavior. These home interviews were also supplemented by information from the records of various social agencies (Glueck and Glueck, 1950: 160).

Teacher-reported Data

In addition to obtaining school records for each boy in the study that contained information on their grades, truancies, and other possible misbehavior, the Gluecks' investigators also interviewed the boy's most recent teacher. The focus of the interview was to "determine how the delinquents and non-delinquents behaved in school during their most recent full year" (1950: 149). Inquiries were made about the boy's adjustment to his schoolmates and participation in curricular and extra-curricular activities as well as his misbehavior in school (1950: 51). Teachers were provided with a list of behavioral characteristics regarding conduct at school and were asked to record which characteristics described the subject (1950: 149).

In sum, the Gluecks collected information from a variety of different sources on a wide range of delinquent and other antisocial behaviors. The Glueck data come very close to the suggestion of Farrington, Ohlin, and Wilson (1986: 18–19) that "data about crime should include arrest reports, self-reports, and (to the extent possible) the reports of peers, parents and teachers. Moreover, these reports should focus not only on crime and delinquency, but other measures of misconduct like truancy, drug and alcohol use, problems at school, etc." (see also Weis, 1986). The scope of information collection by the Gluecks is truly impressive, and the restored data provide a potentially rich data source for reanalysis. At the same time, the multiple sources of information on crime and other misbehavior allow for extensive analysis of the validity of the basic Glueck data. More precisely, both the construct and predictive validity of the Glueck data can be examined through a comparison of the multiple sources of unofficial and official data collected across the similar domains of behavior (Laub et al., 1990).

Construct Validity

Table 3.1 displays the complete list of delinquent conduct and other antisocial behaviors reported by the three types of respondents. The offenses range from the less serious, although important, items such as smoking and drinking to more serious offenses such as stealing or arson. Not only are many types of misconduct reported across varying levels of seriousness, but the domain of behavior studied is often similar for each reporter.[2]

From this original list we first created theoretically relevant scales containing items that were collected for all three groups of reporters. This strategy allowed us to examine the degree of overlap among reporters and address the issue of construct validity. The correlations among parent-, teacher-, and self-reported indicators for several types of crime were all in the expected direction and for the most part statistically significant. The cross-setting validity of misbehaviors that inherently involve both parties (such as truancy) have the strongest relationships. For example, the correlation of teacher-reported truancy with parent- and self-reported truancy is .65 and .73, respectively ($p < .05$). Self- and parent-reported truancy are also highly correlated ($r = .69$, $p < .05$). In a similar fashion, reports of theft and smoking/drinking are

Table 3.1   Self-reported, Parent-reported, and Teacher-reported Items in
             Unraveling Juvenile Delinquency Data

Self-reported	Parent-reported	Teacher-reported
Smoking	Smoking	Smoking
Drinking	Drinking	Untruthfulness
Running away	Running away	Stubbornness
Bunking out	Bunking out	Profanity
Gambling	Gambling	Quarrelsomeness
Late hours	Late hours	Cheating
Truancy	Truancy	Truancy
Stealing rides	Stealing rides	Disobedience
Sneaking admissions	Sneaking admissions	Impudence
Begging	Begging	Disorderliness
Destructive mischief	Destructive mischief	Destroys school materials
Auto stealing	Auto stealing	Stealing
Impulsive stealing (m)	Impulsive stealing (m)	Cruelty, bullying
Impulsive stealing (s)	Impulsive stealing (s)	Tantrums
Planful stealing (t)	Planful stealing (t)	Defiance
Planful stealing (fbg)	Planful stealing (fbg)	
Arson	Arson	
	Lying	
	Stubbornness	
	Vile language	
	Pugnacity	
	Tantrums	

(m) = minor; (s) = serious; (t) = trivial; (fbg) = for big gain.

significantly interrelated among reporters. The divergence that did
emerge concerned items that represent different concepts, like teacher
reports of behavior at school and parental reports of behavior at home
or in the neighborhood.

We then created a composite measure of total unofficial delinquency
from the self, parent, and teacher reports, and a summary measure of
the unofficial reports for each particular offense (for example, truancy
as reported by parents, teachers, and self). Scales were also constructed
that reflected the total amount of delinquency (all crime types) reported
by a particular source; these were designated as "self-report total,"
"parent-report total," and "teacher-report total." In constructing these
scales we restricted the items to standard delinquent behaviors that
were measured consistently across all reporters. Hence, we eliminated
incorrigibility (stubbornness, vile language, lying, and so forth) and
other behaviors that were only asked of one reporter (for example,

Table 3.2   Pearson Correlation Coefficients among Official and Unofficial
Summary Delinquency Measures (N = 1,000)

A. Unofficial Crime-specific Measures	Total Unofficial Delinquency	Official Delinquency	Number of Convictions
Truancy (s + p + t)[a]	.87*	.80*	.65*
Runaway (s + p)	.85*	.72*	.57*
Theft (s + p + t)	.85*	.79*	.66*
Smoke/drink (s + p + t)	.75*	.60*	.53*
Vandalism (s + p + t)	.59*	.47*	.38*
Car-hop (s + p)	.82*	.66*	.59*
Auto-theft (s + p)	.46*	.41*	.35*
Incorrigible (p + t)	.43*	.41*	.31*
Self-reported total	.94*	.82*	.69*
Parent-reported total	.89*	.76*	.62*
Teacher-reported total	.70*	.54*	.51*

B. Unofficial Summary Measures by Source	Self	Parent	Teacher
Self-reported total	—	.72*	.60*
Parent-reported total		—	.55*
Teacher-reported total			—

a. s = self-reported; p = parent-reported; t = teacher-reported.
*$p < .05$.

teacher-reported destruction of school materials). As such, the unofficial scales reflect common delinquency as measured by parents, teachers, and the boys themselves.[3]

In establishing the validity of our measures across settings, we can
compare both unofficial and official reports for the same individuals.
Because of the rich nature of the Glueck data, we can compare these
two sources not only in general, but by specific crime types as well. In
Table 3.2A we display the correlations among the specific types of
unofficial delinquency and three different summary measures of delinquency—the total number of unofficial delinquencies, whether or not
the boy had an official police record, and the total number of convictions
at time of selection for the study. All of the correlations among our
crime-specific unofficial measures and total unofficial and official delinquency are highly significant, illustrating a high degree of concurrent
validity. Truancy and theft have the largest correlations with both
official and unofficial total delinquency. Even rare offenses like auto
theft show consistent positive correlations regardless of whether official
or unofficial validation criteria are used.

Table 3.2B displays the cross-setting convergence of the total reports of delinquency for each unofficial source. The reports of the boys themselves and their parents were somewhat more likely to agree than those between the boys and their school officials or the school officials and the parents. Overall, though, the data in Table 3.2B indicate substantial agreement across sources of measurement. Because our self, parent, and teacher measures correlate so well with each other, we rely throughout this book mostly on the *Total-reported* scale, which combines the self, parent, and teacher reports of delinquency and other misconduct. This summary measure, ranging from 1 to 26, facilitates a parsimonious comparison of official and unofficial measures of delinquency. The total unofficial measure also represents the best overall indicator of the diversity, breadth, and extent of delinquent involvement.

OTHER METHODOLOGICAL CONCERNS

Another issue of concern pertains to the nature of data collection in the Gluecks' study. Some have argued (for example, Blumstein et al., 1988b: 66; McCord and McCord, 1959: 96; Wilkins, 1969: 733) that the Gluecks' procedures—especially in the cross-sectional *UJD*—suffer from "retrospective bias." Namely, the interviewers who conducted the social investigations knew whether a family included a delinquent or a nondelinquent sample member. Some of the questions in the interview schedule also relied on subjective ratings by the interviewers, and in certain instances, an evaluative coding scheme was used.

Moreover, during data collection at the initial wave of the study, most of the delinquents had not been in the classroom and under the observation of teachers for some months (that is, since their commitment to a correctional facility). The nondelinquents were also currently known to their teachers (Glueck and Glueck, 1950: 149). Taken together, these facts raise the possibility of retrospective bias and a possible "halo" effect. Kerlinger (1973: 549) has defined a halo effect as "a tendency for the rating of one characteristic to influence the ratings of other characteristics." If teachers knew the subject under discussion was incarcerated, how did this knowledge affect their reporting of behavioral characteristics concerning school conduct for that subject while he was in school? Conversely, if it was known that the Gluecks were inquiring about nondelinquents in the school setting, did this knowledge affect reporting practices among teachers?

Although a double-blind approach would have been the optimal design, we reiterate that the Gluecks' strategy of data collection focused on multiple sources of information that were *independently* derived. For example, in the first wave of data collection the Gluecks made use of detailed interviews with the boy chosen for the study, his parents, and his teachers.[4] In addition to these interviews, the Gluecks' research team also conducted a field investigation through a meticulous culling of information from records of both public and private agencies that had any involvement with the family. The same data collection strategy was adopted for waves 2 and 3. The basic Glueck data represent the comparison, reconciliation, and integration of these multiple sources of data.

In addition, information appearing as subjective ratings by interviewers or that which relies on evaluative coding schemes was, in fact, corroborated by specific accounts of behavior as recorded in the several sources of records examined and as gathered through reports during the home interview (see also Vaillant, 1983: 245–247). Our preliminary analyses, in addition to results presented in the following chapters, also revealed considerable variation in the social variables (for example, family discipline, parental rejection, school attachment) *within* both the delinquent and the nondelinquent group.[5] And, as shown above, the delinquency variables meet conventional criteria for construct validation. On balance, then, retrospective bias cannot be ignored, but it is unpersuasive as an argument against the basic quality of the cross-sectional and longitudinal data collected by the Gluecks.

Further Validation

As part of a larger project, we tried to locate and interview the original members of the Gluecks' research team from the *UJD* study. We were able to conduct detailed oral history interviews with three members of the team—Sheila Murphrey, a secretary for the Gluecks for 30 years, Mary Moran, a case investigator, and Richard LaBrie, a computer programmer. We also talked with several of the original interviewers from the project, including Mildred Cunningham, George McGrath, and John Burke, although we were unable to conduct detailed interviews with these team members. These oral histories describe in some detail the day-to-day workings of the *UJD* project, give an overview of the actual implementation of methodology used, and provide a glimpse of the personalities of the Gluecks themselves. In the Appendix, we present excerpts from these interviews that relate to issues of methodology and data quality. We believe that these oral history data offer further validation regarding data collection procedures and the basic integrity of the *UJD* project.

Perhaps the ultimate test of validity, however, is to be found in the degree to which our analyses of the data comport with expectations derived from past research and theory. This test—involving the relationship of delinquency with theoretically defined variables—in fact constitutes the bulk of our book. Before we present our analyses bearing on predictive relationships and the validity of independent variables, we discuss the remaining components of our efforts to restore and supplement the data.

RECONSTRUCTING AND SUPPLEMENTING CRIMINAL HISTORIES

Criminal history data for each subject were gathered from extensive record checks of police, court, and correctional files and cover the period from first arrest to age 32. Some of the information available includes the number of arrests, the number of convictions, correctional experiences over time, the types of dispositions, offense-specific arrest sequences, and the length of all correctional experiences as well as the number of probation/parole revocations (see Glueck and Glueck, 1950, 1968).

Unfortunately, coding decisions by the Gluecks prohibited key analyses of the criminal histories of the Glueck men. For instance, the Gluecks did not code the exact number of arrests by specific crime type across all three age periods. Moreover, the Gluecks coded the number of offenses by category (for example, 5–6) and only coded up to 13 arrests in each wave, thus artificially truncating the upper end of arrest history distribution. They also provided a checklist of only the overall nature of these offenses, and they did not code any dates of arrests or of dispositions (for instance, the dates of incarceration). Thus no information is available on the sequence of arrest events and dispositions in the criminal history, which precludes the precise estimation of "time free" when calculating individual rates of offending.

All of this information was available in the original case records, and hence another component of our research strategy became the recoding of raw data into a more useful format. Specifically, over approximately a two-year period, we reconstructed and validated a hierarchical data file of complete criminal histories for 480 of the original delinquents from first arrest to age 32.[6] The Glueck men generated more than 6,300 arrest charges during this time period. For each arrest event, we coded

Table 3.3   Descriptive Data on Sample Size and Criminal Involvement of
Delinquent Group, by Age and Type of Crime

A. Glueck Sample Sizes by Average Age at Interview

	Wave 1: Age 14	Wave 2: Age 25	Wave 3: Age 32
Sample size	500	463	438
Deaths	—	17	8

B. Number of Persons Arrested by Type of Crime and Age

Arrests (persons)	Age < 17	Ages 17–25	Ages 25–32
Violent	73	151	76
Property	443	275	124
Robbery	19	61	29
Burglary	329	164	62
Alcohol/drugs	11	152	126
Public order	72	224	159

C. Participation by Type of Crime and Age

% Arrested	Age < 17 (N = 480)	Ages 17–25 (N = 446)	Ages 25–32 (N = 423)
Total	100%	84%	70%
Violent	15%	34%	18%
Property	92%	62%	29%
Robbery	4%	14%	7%
Burglary	68%	37%	15%
Alcohol/drugs	2%	34%	30%
Public order	15%	50%	38%

the date, the specific type of charge or charges,[7] the exact sequence of
arrests, and the dates and types of all criminal justice interventions
including the actual dates of incarceration (if any).[8] We coded close to
60 different offense types and more than 20 various dispositions for the
Glueck men.[9]

Given the strong overlap among offenses, the rarity of many crime
types, the low level of specialization in specific crimes committed by
the Glueck men (Davis, 1992), and our theoretical framework which
does not make crime-specific predictions, the analyses in this book
rely primarily on broad crime categories (for example, total, violent,
property). Table 3.3 gives an overview of *participation* in crime, presenting descriptive data on violent crime, property crime, robbery, burglary,

Table 3.4   Average Raw Charge Frequencies and Annualized Rates of
Charges While Free in the Community, by Age and Type
of Crime

A. Raw Frequencies	Age < 17	Ages 17–25	Ages 25–32
Violent	.215	.538	.296
Property	4.187	2.045	.712
Robbery	.042	.188	.083
Burglary	1.662	.688	.267
Alcohol/drugs	.027	.937	.872
Public order	.198	1.307	1.087
Total	6.485	5.821	3.444

B. Per Year Free	Age < 17	Ages 17–25	Ages 25–32
Violent	.014	.159	.167
Property	.275	.706	.289
Robbery	.003	.069	.082
Burglary	.109	.291	.118
Alcohol/drugs	.002	.165	.160
Public order	.013	.313	.250
Total	.425	1.611	1.026

alcohol/drugs, and public-order offenses across all waves. The general
patterns are consistent with past research. For example, participation
peaks in the age 17–25 category and declines in the age 25–32 period
for all offense types (cf. Hirschi and Gottfredson, 1983).

Table 3.4 displays the *frequency* of involvement in specific crime types
across waves. Panel A shows the annualized number of charges by
wave. To account for opportunities to commit crime, we also created
more refined measures of crime frequency—the number of arrests
divided by the number of days free in the community from birth to age
17, from ages 17 to 25, and from ages 25 to 32. These measures were
then converted to average annual rates for each period (that is, frequency of arrests per year free). By considering only time free in the
community, we were able to obtain more precise measures of crime
frequency for the delinquents than those traditionally used in criminological research. These measures (see Panel B) form one of the major
dependent variables when we analyze in Chapter 7 the adult criminal
careers of the 500 subjects originally in the delinquent group.

As expected, the control-group men did not experience the same rate

Table 3.5   Descriptive Data on Sample Size and Criminal Involvement of
            Control Group, by Age and Type of Crime

A. Glueck Sample Sizes by Average Age at Interview

	Wave 1: Age 14	Wave 2: Age 25	Wave 3: Age 32
Sample size	500	466	442
Deaths	—	5	7

B. Number of Persons Arrested by Type of Crime and Age

Arrests (persons)	Age < 17	Ages 17–25	Ages 25–32
Violent	3	17	11
Property	35	31	12
Robbery	0	2	1
Burglary	8	10	3
Alcohol/drugs	1	53	46
Public order	8	64	49

C. Participation by Type of Crime and Age

% Arrested	Age < 17 (N = 500)	Ages 17–25 (N = 466)	Ages 25–32 (N = 442)
Total	10%	20%	16%
Violent	1%	4%	2%
Property	7%	7%	3%
Robbery	0%	0%	0%
Burglary	2%	2%	1%
Alcohol/drugs	0%	11%	10%
Public order	2%	14%	11%

of later criminal behavior as did the original delinquents. Nevertheless, more than 100 of the controls were arrested in adulthood, and we believe it is important to analyze the factors accounting for the late onset of crime and deviance. To accomplish this task, we coded the complete criminal histories for the control group, including dates of each arrest. Descriptive information on arrests by type of crime and age for the controls is displayed in Table 3.5. These data are analyzed in Chapter 8 as a further test of our theory of informal social control and deviance over the life course.

Crime at Ages 32–45

We were also fortunate to gain access to information that allowed us to supplement the criminal history data collected by the Gluecks' research team. These data were originally collected by Dr. George Vaillant as part of a collaborative effort with the Study of Adult Development on the relationship of alcohol use and motor vehicle offenses (see Vaillant, 1983, for details). The data result from a search of the records housed in the Office of the Commissioner of Probation, the central depository for criminal records in Massachusetts. These records were searched in 1974 and contain all officially recorded court information for the Glueck men up to age 45 (on average).[10]

From these raw court records we then coded criminal history data for ages 32 to 45 for both the original control group and the delinquent group. Because of the nature of the information gleaned by Dr. Vaillant's staff, we were able to code only the number and type of offenses charged for the delinquent and control subjects during ages 32 to 45.[11] If a subject was not arrested and brought to court in Massachusetts during this period, his record does not appear in the files. We also have no information on crimes committed out of state, whether or not the subject died after age 32, and crimes not reported to the police or recorded in the official state records. Nonetheless, these records provide a unique glimpse of criminal behavior in middle adulthood that can be merged with the Gluecks' data to examine crime and deviance over a significant portion of the life course.

HISTORICAL CONTEXT OF THE *UJD* STUDY

The *UJD* subjects were born between 1924 and 1935. This was a period marked by the Great Depression, the rise of Hitler and Nazism, and extraordinary unrest and instability around the world. The Gluecks' research team began gathering data on the subjects for the first wave of the *UJD* study in 1939–1940—the initial stages of World War II. This first wave of data collection continued through 1948. Data collection for waves 2 and 3 continued throughout the 1950s and into the first half of the 1960s, a time of postwar prosperity and unprecedented economic opportunity in the United States.

Table 3.6 shows the key historical events influencing the lives of the subjects in the *UJD* study and anchors these events with respect to age for the oldest and youngest cohort members of the study. Because of the age variation among the subjects, key historical events affected cohort members at different points in the life course. This suggests the importance of considering cohort effects, a main feature of life-course analysis. According to Elder (1974), a cohort analysis is essential to

Table 3.6   Age of Glueck Men by Historical Events

Date(s)	Event	Age of Cohort Members	
		Older birth year (1925)	Younger birth year (1932)
1929–1930	Great Depression, onset	4–5	NA
1933	New Deal launched	8	1
1939–1940	World War II mobilization, initial stage	14–15	7–8
1945	World War II ends	20	13
1950–1953	Korean War	25–28	18–21
1950–1957	First follow-up by the Gluecks	25	25
1957–1964	Second follow-up by the Gluecks	32	32
1973	Vaillant's follow-up of criminal records	49	41

understanding the effect of social change on lives by linking individuals to a specific social context (see also Modell, 1989). Although the Gluecks' study was initiated after the Great Depression and during World War II, these macro-historical events are not even mentioned in their *UJD* publication. The Gluecks wrote several articles on delinquency in wartime prior to the publication of *UJD* (see Glueck and Glueck, 1964 for details), but it appears that they did not consider these historical events of major relevance in their own research project (either in data collection or data analysis).

Elder and Caspi (1990) have argued that birth year sets an individual in history and that "historical influence takes the form of a cohort effect when social change differentiates patterns of successive cohorts" (Elder and Caspi, 1990: 210). Of particular importance is the "life-stage principle," which states that the effect of historical events will vary depending upon the stage of life when the event is experienced (Elder and Caspi, 1990: 219). To illustrate this point with respect to adolescence, Elder, Caspi, and Burton write:

> The difference between growing up in the depressed 1930s and in war-mobilized America of 1940–45 was literally a difference between two worlds of adolescence . . . Hard times in the Great Depression influenced the lives of adolescents through economic and job losses of parents, and also through its effects on the lives of grandparents who often moved in for a time. For young people during World War II, the distinctive features

of adolescence included the war-related employment of parents from sun-up to sun-down, the military service and war trauma of older brothers, and the mobilization of school children for civil defense and the war effort. (1988: 151–152; see also Elder, 1980)

Of course, the analysis of cohort effects is not without problems, especially with respect to interpretation. For instance, individual cohort members are not uniformly exposed to historical events, and important variation exists *within* specific cohorts (see Elder and Caspi, 1990: 212). Moreover, in certain instances, cohort effects are difficult to distinguish from period effects (see Farrington, 1990; Gottfredson and Hirschi, 1990). Finally, the exact meaning of cohort effects is subject to various interpretations given the unlimited number of potential explanatory variables (Gottfredson and Hirschi, 1990: 226; for an overview see Glenn, 1981).

As indicated above, the subjects of the Gluecks' study were born between the years 1924 and 1935. Since very few men were born in 1924, we chose 1925 as the birth year for the oldest cohort members. On the other hand, since few sample members were born between 1932 and 1935, we chose 1932 as the birth year for the youngest members of the sample (see Table 3.7). A man born in one of the early cohorts (for example, 1925) grew up during the Great Depression (1929–1933), experienced adolescence during World War II (1941–1945), and had his early adulthood during the Korean War (1950–1953). Moreover, this individual was already in his mid-twenties during the expansion of economic opportunities after World War II. In contrast, a man born in one of the later cohorts (for instance, 1932) completely missed the Great Depression, but experienced World War II as part of his middle childhood (ages 8 to 12) and was 18 at the beginning of the Korean War. Significantly, this individual reached adolescence and young adulthood during the expansion of economic opportunities after World War II.

Whether or not these age distinctions make any difference is, of course, an empirical question. In Table 3.7 we present some descriptive data relating to the timing of key life events for selected birth cohorts from the *UJD* study. Given differences in the delinquent and nondelinquent groups over time (see Glueck and Glueck, 1968), plus the fact that we are using the cohort data as illustrative of a larger theoretical idea, we have restricted our examination of cohort effects within the delinquent group. The life events include school exit, entry into the

Table 3.7   Descriptive Data on Birth Cohorts and Timing of Social Events
for Delinquent Group

A. Frequency and Percent Distribution by Birth Year

Birth Year	Number	Percent
1924	43	9.0
1925	71	14.8
1926	88	18.3
1927	79	16.5
1928	60	12.5
1929	43	9.0
1930	28	5.8
1931	28	5.8
1932	23	4.8
1933	11	2.3
1934	4	.8
1935	2	.4

B. Timing of Selected Social Events by Birth Year

	Birth Year	
Social Events	1924–1925	1929–1935
Age at first enlistment	18.3	17.8
Age at first employment	16.6	16.0
Age first left school	15.6	15.4
Age at first marriage	21.4	21.0
Age at first arrest	12.4	11.0
	(N = 114)	(N = 139)

military, entry into the labor force, age at first marriage, and age at first arrest. The median birth year for the delinquent subjects in the Gluecks' study was 1927. In light of the distribution by year of birth, we divided subjects into three birth cohorts—1924–1925, 1926–1928, and 1929–1935—representing 24 percent, 47 percent, and 29 percent, respectively, of the total sample of delinquent subjects. We then compared the timing of key events for the early birth cohort (1924–1925) with the late birth cohort (1929–1935).

As revealed in Panel B of Table 3.7, there is little difference in the timing of key life events by birth year among the delinquent subjects in the *UJD* study. For instance, the average age of first employment was 16 for both cohorts, and the age at first marriage was 21.4 for the early cohort and 21.0 for the late cohort. The only exception is that the younger cohort experienced a first arrest somewhat earlier than the older cohort—a difference that may be artifactual because of changing police practices. As in Featherman, Hogan, and Sorenson's (1984) analysis of cohort effects, the two cohorts we have examined here are too similar in terms of historical experience to provide much difference with respect to life-stage experiences. Indeed, the vast majority (over 70 percent) of the Gluecks' delinquents were born within four years of one another. As a result, cohort differences do not appear to represent a substantial threat to our analyses.

Nonetheless, we come back to the larger issue of history (period influences) and cohort differences in later analyses and also in Chapter 10, where we discuss the significance of our results for the study of crime in the present. We believe that the historical context in which the Glueck data were collected is a positive feature and serves as a baseline to identify areas where research findings are consistent across time, and, equally important, to identify areas where contemporary research differs.

CONCLUSION

This chapter has briefly summarized our major efforts in recasting the Glueck data. More complete details can be found in our other published work (Laub and Sampson, 1988; Sampson and Laub, 1990) and in the chapters that follow. Having set the backdrop in the first three chapters—theoretically, historically, and now empirically—we begin our life-course analysis with an examination of the origins of delinquency in childhood and adolescence.

THE FAMILY
CONTEXT
OF JUVENILE
DELINQUENCY

4

The Gluecks' research sought to answer a basic, enduring, and even popular question in the study of delinquency—what factors differentiate boys reared in poor neighborhoods who become serious and persistent delinquents from boys raised in the same neighborhoods who do *not* become delinquent or antisocial? Indeed, a classic movie explored this question in 1938 as the Gluecks began planning their study. The movie was *Angels with Dirty Faces* and starred James Cagney, Pat O'Brien, Humphrey Bogart, Ann Sheridan, and, of course, the Dead End Kids. James Cagney played the role of Rocky Sullivan, who was by contemporary definitions a high-rate, chronic offender—in other words, a "career criminal." Pat O'Brien played the role of Jerry Connelly, who became a priest in the local neighborhood parish. Both men were childhood friends, committed petty crime together, and were in fact products of the same slum environment. Yet both obviously had very different life experiences with respect to serious and persistent criminal activity.

Similarly, as a group both the Gluecks' 500 delinquents and the 500 nondelinquents were raised in the same slum environments, yet they too experienced very different outcomes. The fundamental question was, and still is, why? In this chapter we begin to answer this important question from a theoretical perspective on families and informal social control.

THEORETICAL FRAMEWORK

Over the last two decades research in criminology has begun to refocus its attention on the role of the family in explaining delinquency (see, for example, Hirschi, 1969, 1983; Loeber and Stouthamer-Loeber, 1986; Farrington, 1987; Wilson, 1983; Loury, 1987; Laub and Sampson, 1988; Hagan, 1989; Gottfredson and Hirschi, 1990). In what is probably the most comprehensive review to date, Loeber and Stouthamer-Loeber identify four dimensions of family functioning in order to "organize our understanding of child conduct problems" (1986:38). Briefly described, these include the *neglect* paradigm, which examines parent-child and child-parent involvement and parental supervision; the *conflict* paradigm, which analyzes discipline practices and parent-child and child-parent rejection; the *deviant behaviors and attitudes* paradigm, which focuses on parental criminality and deviant attitudes among parents; and the *disruption* paradigm, which looks at marital conflict and parental absence (1986:40).

Loeber and Stouthamer-Loeber's (1986) meta-analysis of available studies shows that all four dimensions of family functioning relate to delinquency, aggressiveness, and other misconduct among juveniles. They argue that "socialization variables, such as lack of parental supervision, parental rejection, and parent-child involvement, are among the most powerful predictors of juvenile conduct problems and delinquency. Medium-strength predictors include background variables such as parents' marital relations and parental criminality. Weaker predictors are lack of parental discipline, parental health, and parental absence" (1986:29). What is especially impressive about the Loeber and Stouthamer-Loeber review is the general consistency of findings across a wide range of studies.

In this chapter we extend these ideas by testing the theoretical model shown in Figure 4.1. Consistent with a theory of informal social control and crime and deviance over the life course, the general organizing principle is that the probability of deviance increases when an individual's bond to society is weak or broken (Durkheim, 1951; Hirschi, 1969; Kornhauser, 1978). In other words, when the social ties (that is, attachment, commitment) that bind an individual to key societal institutions (such as family, school, work) are loosened, the risk of crime and delinquency is heightened. The specific feature of our model involves a two-step hypothesis: structural context influences dimensions of informal social controls by the family, which in turn explain variations in delinquency.

Focusing first on the proximate role of families, we propose that four factors will increase the likelihood of delinquency: (1) erratic, threatening, and harsh/punitive discipline by both mothers and fathers, (2) low parental supervision, (3) parental rejection of the child, and (4) weak emotional attachment of the boy to his parents. Our theoreti-

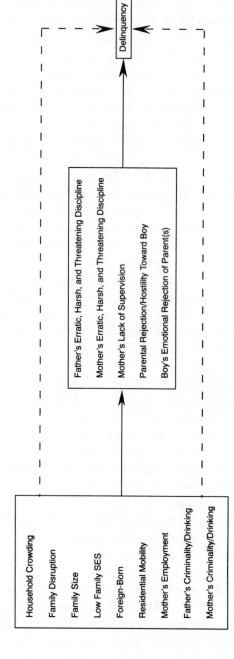

Figure 4.1 ° Theoretical model of structural background factors, family process, and delinquency. Broken line indicates hypothesized weak or insignificant effect; solid line signifies hypothesized strong effect. Because of the *UJD* matching design, age, race/ethnicity, neighborhood SES, and IQ are controlled with respect to delinquency.

cal conceptualization of the family is drawn in part from "coercion theory" as formulated by Patterson and colleagues (1980, 1982). Unlike most theories, coercion theory places a prominent etiological role on *direct* parental controls in explaining delinquency. In particular, the coercion model assumes that less skilled parents inadvertently reinforce their children's antisocial behavior and fail to provide effective punishments for transgressions (Patterson, 1982; see also Gottfredson and Hirschi, 1990: 99). On the basis of research designed to assess this perspective, Patterson describes a set of parenting skills conducive to successful child rearing: "(a) notice what the child is doing; (b) monitor it over long periods; (c) model social skill behavior; (d) clearly state house rules; (e) consistently provide sane punishments for transgressions; (f) provide reinforcement for conformity; and (g) negotiate disagreements so that conflicts and crises do not escalate" (1980: 81). As Patterson further argues, "Parents who cannot or will not employ family management skills are the prime determining variables . . . Parents of stealers do not track; they do not punish; and they do not care" (1980: 88–89).

The emphasis on parent-child interaction in coercion theory has much in common with traditional social control theory (Hirschi, 1969). Patterson's model differs mainly in the mediating mechanisms it emphasizes—that is, direct parental controls as found in discipline and monitoring practices. By contrast, Hirschi's (1969) original formulation of control theory emphasized indirect controls in the form of the child's emotional bond or attachment to parents. Similarly, Hagan (1989: 210–212) refers to attachment as "relational" control. Hirschi (1969) did not view direct parental controls (for example, monitoring) as prominent because they are seemingly inoperative during situations when delinquent activity is a viable possibility (Larzelere and Patterson, 1990: 304). For Hirschi, relational controls embodied by parent-child attachment were thus the most crucial for inhibiting delinquency.

On balance, however, Patterson's model is consistent with social control theory because direct parental controls are likely to be positively related to relational, indirect controls. Antisocial behavior in the presence of parents is also likely to generalize to other situations (Larzelere and Patterson, 1990: 305). Moreover, Hirschi has recently argued that direct controls such as monitoring and surveillance are important despite the short-term calculations and brevity involved in delinquent acts: "If brevity makes surveillance more difficult, immediacy makes it more profitable. The would-be offender can often do what he wants to do in a hurry, but if he is unable to do so, he is unlikely to persist in the effort" (1991: 51). Hirschi thus argues that variations among families in adult supervision of youth have important ramifications for delinquency.

For these reasons, Hirschi (1983, 1991) and Gottfredson and Hirschi (1990) include direct parental controls in a recent statement of control theory that relies heavily on Patterson's coercion model. Their reformulated model of effective parenting entails monitoring the behavior of children, recognizing their misdeeds, and punishing (correcting) those misdeeds accordingly in a consistent and loving manner (Gottfredson and Hirschi, 1990: 97). Similarly, Hagan (1989) incorporates what he terms "instrumental control" (for example, supervision, monitoring) in his power-control theory of common delinquency. In addition, Hirschi (1983) argues that parental affection and a willingness to invest in children are essential underlying conditions of good parenting and, hence, the prevention of misbehavior (see also Gottfredson and Hirschi, 1990: 98).

This view of families corresponds to Braithwaite's (1989) notion of "reintegrative shaming," whereby parents punish in a consistent manner and within the context of love, respect, and acceptance of the child. The opposite of reintegrative shaming is stigmatization, where parents are cold, authoritarian, and enact a harsh, punitive, and often rejecting regime of punishment (1989: 56). When the bonds of respect are broken by parents in the process of punishment, successful child rearing is difficult to achieve.

Given their theoretical compatibility, we combine the central ideas of social control and coercion theory along with the notion of reintegrative shaming into a unified model of informal family social control that focuses on three dimensions—discipline, supervision, and attachment. In our view, the key to all three components of informal family social control lies in the extent to which they facilitate linking the child to family and ultimately society through emotional bonds of attachment and direct yet socially integrative forms of control, monitoring, and punishment. These dimensions of informal family control have rarely been examined simultaneously in previous research. Hence our theoretical model permits assessment of the relative contributions of family process variables to the explanation of delinquency (see also Patterson and Dishion, 1985; Johnson, 1986; Cernkovich and Giordano, 1987; Hagan, 1989).

The second part of our theory posits that structural background factors influence delinquency largely through their effects on family process (see also Laub and Sampson, 1988). Previous research on families and delinquency often fails to account for social structural context and how it influences family life. By contrast, the logic of our model leads to the expectation that structural context will have weak direct effects on delinquency. Thus we hypothesize that the effects of family process mediate or account for the effects of structural background (see Figure 4.1).

Among other benefits, our conception may shed light on the relationship between the criminality of parents and the delinquency of their children. Although such a relationship appears to some as evidence for a genetic or biological link (see Rutter and Giller, 1983: 182), in our informal social control framework, parental deviance influences a child's delinquency through the disruption of social control. More precisely, we argue that parents who commit crimes and drink excessively are likely to use harsh discipline in an inconsistent manner or to be lax in disciplining their children. A central characteristic of deviant and criminal life styles is the rejection of restrictions and duties—especially those that involve planning, patience, and investment in the future (Gottfredson and Hirschi, 1990: 101). Parenting is perhaps the most demanding of conventional roles, and we expect that deviance in the adult world will manifest itself in disrupted styles of child socialization. Namely, supervision and discipline will be haphazard or nonexistent, and the parent-child/child-parent attachments will be tenuous (see Hirschi, 1983: 58–60). According to this conceptualization there is little, if any, need to introduce biological theories of heredity if the direct effect of parental criminality on delinquency is null and instead is mediated by social processes of family functioning.

Our model and data further enable us to examine the direct and indirect effects of such key factors as family disruption, family size, socioeconomic status (SES), household crowding, residential mobility, mother's employment, and birthplace of parents. Although these structural background factors have been associated with delinquency in past research (for a review, see Rutter and Giller, 1983), it is our contention that they will also affect family social control mechanisms. For instance, social control theory suggests that family size, residential mobility, and employment by mothers outside of the home may increase difficulties in supervising and monitoring children. In this regard Hirschi (1991) has argued that despite its empirical power in predicting delinquency, family size is largely ignored in modern criminology. This seems to be a mistake, especially when one considers the influence of family size on occupational achievement and investment in education (Blake, 1989), which themselves may be important for delinquency (see also Chapter 5). Similarly, factors such as family disruption and residential mobility may affect not only the parents' supervisory capacity, but also bonds of attachment and disciplinary practices (Rutter and Giller, 1983: 183; Braithwaite, 1989).

Finally, poverty and poor living conditions (for example, low socio-economic status, household crowding, and foreign-born/immigrant status) have been linked to delinquency in prior studies. We posit that these same variables also have an effect on family social control mechanisms. As Rutter and Giller (1983: 185) state, "Serious socio-economic disadvantage has an adverse effect on the parents, such that parental disorders and difficulties are more likely to develop and good parenting is impeded." In a similar vein, Larzelere and Patterson (1990: 307) have recently argued that many lower social status couples are marginally skilled as parents, in part because they experience more stress and have fewer resources than do middle-class parents. From this viewpoint the effect of SES and disadvantaged social status on delinquency is mediated through parental discipline and monitoring practices.

The theoretical model depicted in Figure 4.1 combined with the unique nature of the Glueck data contributes to the literature on families and delinquency in other specific ways as well. First, our study contains measures of attachment in both directions—parent to the child and child to the parent. Gove and Crutchfield (1982) note that most of the research on families and delinquency collects data from juveniles, and thus focuses solely on the child's perception of attachment to the parent (for example, Hirschi, 1969). Gove and Crutchfield (1982) use a measure of attachment that relies on the parent's perception, but few studies have both. The Gluecks obtained information from both parents and juveniles, and their data were derived from independent interviews with both parties. Therefore, we were able to construct two measures of attachment, parent-child and child-parent, allowing for a fuller speci-fication of the attachment variable.

Second, we begin by assessing the differential effects of mothers and fathers separately for key variables like parental criminality and style of discipline. Loeber and Stouthamer-Loeber (1986) argue that little is known about the effects of fathers as parents. It is thus important to explore whether the behavior of mothers and that of fathers have similar or different effects on their children.

Third, on the basis of the information available, we combine the factor of excessive alcohol use by parents with the criminality of parents to determine more fully the effect of parental deviance on intervening variables like attachment, discipline practices, and supervision. Although few studies consider parental alcoholism (see McCord, 1979), it is potentially as important as parental criminality in an examination of family functioning (cf. Robins, 1966).

EMPIRICAL MEASURES

On the basis of theoretical guidance, the family process literature reviewed above, and preliminary evidence from our earlier research (Laub and Sampson, 1988), we identified a set of structural background factors relevant to an empirical assessment of both family functioning and delinquency. Recall that age, race/ethnicity, neighborhood socioeconomic status, and general intelligence are controlled in the matching design. Independent of these matching factors, we examine the following structural variables: household crowding, family disruption, family size, socioeconomic status, nativity (foreign-born status), residential mobility, and mother's employment outside of the home. Our earlier research (Laub and Sampson, 1988) utilized a subset of dichotomous variables from the original *Unraveling* study to specify an initial model of families and delinquency using several of these background factors. This chapter extends this model with new measures of structure, family process, delinquency, and early childhood misbehavior.

The variables in the model are drawn from our recoding and computerization of the Gluecks' *Unraveling* data and are a mixture of categorical, ordinal, and interval-level measures. The initial set of these family and delinquency variables is displayed in Table 4.1, along with their descriptive statistics. *Household crowding* is composed of three categories: comfortable (parents one room, children own room), average (two persons per bedroom), and overcrowded (more than two persons per bedroom excluding infants). *Family disruption* is coded one when the boy was reared in a home where one or both parents were absent because of divorce, separation, desertion, or death.[1] *Family size* is the number of children in the boy's family and ranges from one to eight or

Table 4.1 Descriptive Statistics on Initial Set of Structural Background Factors, Intervening Family-process Variables, and Delinquency

Variable	Mean	S.D.	Min.	Max.	Valid N
Structural Background					
Residential mobility	6.75	4.72	1	16	999
Family size	5.08	2.21	1	8	999
Crowding	2.17	.61	1	3	995
Family disruption	.47	.50	0	1	1,000
Mother's employment	.40	.49	0	1	993
Family SES[a]	.00	1.64	-3.4	3.6	998
Foreign-born	.60	.49	0	1	987
Father's deviance	2.00	.86	1	3	1,000
Mother's deviance	1.45	.68	1	3	1,000
Family Process					
Father erratic/harsh	2.53	.93	1	4	876
Mother erratic/harsh	2.52	.95	1	4	968
Mother's supervision	1.97	.86	1	3	989
Parental rejection	1.56	.69	1	3	963
Attachment to parent	2.26	.75	1	3	997
Delinquency					
Official status	.50	.50	0	1	1,000
Self-reported unofficial	5.02	3.79	1	14	1,000
Parent-reported unofficial	2.70	2.76	0	13	1,000
Teacher-reported unofficial	.72	.89	0	4	1,000
Total unofficial	8.44	6.67	1	26	1,000

a. Standardized scale based on z-scores.

more. *Family socioeconomic status* is a standardized scale composed of the average weekly income of the family and a measure of the family's reliance on outside aid. This variable captures whether the family was living in comfortable circumstances (having enough savings to cover four months of financial stress), marginal circumstances (little or no savings but only occasional dependence on outside aid), or dependent circumstances (continuous receipt of outside aid for support). The indicator of *foreign-born* indexes whether one or both parents were born outside the United States. *Residential mobility* is an interval-based measure of the number of times the boy's family moved during his childhood and ranges from none or once to 16 or more times. *Mother's employment* is a dichotomous variable where housewives were coded zero and working mothers (full time or part time) were coded one (see Glueck and Glueck, 1950 for further details).

The remaining two structural background variables combine the criminality and drinking habits of mothers and fathers to form general indicators of deviance. *Criminality* was determined by official records of arrest or conviction (excluding minor auto violations and violation of license laws). *Alcoholism and/or drunkenness* refers to intoxication and includes frequent, regular, or chronic addiction to alcohol, and not to very occasional episodes of over-drinking in an atmosphere of celebration (Glueck and Glueck, 1962: 217). The resulting deviance variable for both mother and father ranges from 1 to 3. Our major theoretical goal is to examine whether adult deviance (that is, criminality and drunkenness) influences delinquency of children through the intervening processes of family functioning.

The five intervening family process variables are father's and mother's style of discipline, parent-child and child-parent attachments, and parental supervision. Information for these variables was gathered through interviews with parents and the delinquent or nondelinquent child in conjunction with extensive record checks of social service and criminal justice agencies. The behaviors we are calling family process variables (for example, attachment, supervision, and discipline practices) were not directly observed by the Gluecks' research team (cf. Patterson, 1982), but rather were inferred from the interview materials and the record checks mentioned above. (For more details, see Glueck and Glueck, 1950: 41–53.)

Parenting style was measured by combining three variables tapping the discipline and punishment practices of the mother and father. The first constituent variable concerns the use of physical punishment by the parent and refers to rough handling, strappings, and beatings eliciting fear and resentment in the boy—not to casual or occasional slapping that was unaccompanied by rage or hostility. The second constituent variable measures threatening and/or scolding behavior by mothers or fathers that elicited fear in the boy. Both these types of punishment relate to Braithwaite's (1989) notion of stigmatization. The third component taps erratic and harsh discipline—that is, if the parent was harsh and unreasoning, if the parent vacillated between strictness and laxity and was not consistent in control, or if the parent was negligent or indifferent about disciplining the boy (Glueck and Glueck, 1962: 220). Hence, the threatening/erratic ordinal scales comprise four categories (1 to 4) and measure the degree to which parents used inconsistent disciplinary measures *in conjunction with* harsh, physical punishment and/or threatening or scolding behavior. In Braithwaite's (1989) scheme, these variables tap the sort of punitive shaming and negative labeling that are likely to increase delinquency.

Parental supervision is defined as suitable if the mother provided supervision over the boy's activities at home or in the neighborhood. If unable to supervise the boys themselves, mothers who made arrangements for other adults to watch the boy's activities were assigned a "suitable" classification. "Fair" supervision refers to partial supervision. Supervision was considered "unsuitable" if the mother left the boy on his own, without guidance, or in the care of an irresponsible person (Glueck and Glueck, 1962: 219).[2] *Parental rejection* is an ordinal scale tapping whether parents were openly hostile to the child or did not give the child much emotional attention or bonding. *Attachment to parent* is also an ordinal indicator of whether the boy had a warm emotional bond to the father and/or mother as displayed in a close association with the parent and in expressions of admiration for the parent (Glueck and Glueck, 1962: 220). This is directly analogous to Hirschi's (1969) conceptualization of attachment.

As Elder has noted, the foremost problem in archival work centers on matters of measurement (1974: 326). In addition to using multiple indicators of our key concepts and composite scales (whenever possible and theoretically appropriate), we took numerous steps to ensure the quality of measures. This analysis demonstrated that the family variables were related both concurrently and predictively in a manner consistent with theory and past research. For example, erratic and threatening styles of parenting by mothers and fathers are related to parental rejection of the child ($r = .31$ and $.30$, respectively, $p < .05$). Conversely, where erratic and threatening discipline is low, attachment of the boy to the parent (as reported by the youth) is high ($r = -.29$ and $-.24$, $p < .05$). The mother's supervision was positively related to parental attachment ($.38$, $p < .05$) but negatively related to erratic discipline of both mothers and fathers ($-.47$ and $-.42$, $p < .05$) and to parental rejection ($-.47$, $p < .05$). And, as expected, in families where the mother exhibited disrupted parenting in the form of harsh, threatening discipline, so did the father ($.52$, $p < .05$). These significant correlations, all in the predicted and expected direction, support standard criteria for construct validation (see, for example, Cook and Campbell, 1979; Hindelang et al., 1981). Moreover, the correlations are not so high as to suggest problems with discriminant validity or multicollinearity. That is, the evidence shows that the family constructs correlate among themselves in a theoretically consistent manner, yet are sufficiently independent to support discriminant validity and allow assessment of independent effects.

We also reemphasize that the Glueck data are different in kind from survey research and questionnaires where measurement error, especially on attitudes such as moral beliefs (see, for example, Matsueda, 1989), is large. Namely, the Glueck data by nature represent the integration of multiple sources of information even for individual items; moreover, our items refer almost exclusively to behavior (discipline, rejection, supervision) and not to attitudes. Considering the additional fact that many of the dependent and independent variables are skewed and hence violate assumptions of multivariate normality, we thus do not rely on covariance structure models (such as LISREL).[3]

Other Methodological Concerns

It is possible that differences in family patterns (for instance, marital breakup, income levels, parental criminality) influenced processing by the juvenile justice system. For example, juvenile justice officials may consider a delinquent's home life in deciding whether to refer an alleged delinquent to court (Hirschi, 1991). Family effects may thus be confounded to some unknown extent with responses by agents of official social control at that time.

We address this issue through systematic comparison of unofficial (self, parent, and teacher reports) and official delinquency for the 1,000 boys in the study. Extending the empirical validation strategy in Chapter 3, we assess construct validity by testing our theoretical model using alternate measures of the key dependent variable. As Hindelang, Hirschi, and Weis (1981: 112) argue: "One . . . test of validity involves comparison of alternative measures of the same concept when they are correlated with outside variables. If two variables are measures of the same concept, they should be correlated with other variables to substantially the same extent" (see also Campbell and Stanley, 1963). Having coded and incorporated the relevant information, we are therefore able, unlike our earlier efforts (Laub and Sampson, 1988), to construct unofficial delinquency measures that are compared with results from the official record dichotomy. The descriptive statistics on the unofficial delinquency measures are shown in the lower third of Table 4.1. Following the logic of convergent validation noted by Hindelang and colleagues (1981), if our results converge we can have increased confidence in the validity of the data.

Causal ordering and reciprocal effects also surface as a potential problem because the wave 1 data are inherently cross-sectional. In particular, it is possible that childhood delinquency and antisocial behavior may have disrupted patterns of family social control (Patterson, 1982; Lytton, 1990). Recent research also suggests that school attachment and delinquency may generate feedback effects (Liska and Reed, 1985).

Upon first consideration it seems unlikely that delinquency is responsible for family processes of child rearing by adults (such as supervision, discipline, and attachment) that are known to be stable over long periods (Patterson, 1982; Gottfredson and Hirschi, 1990). Disrupted parenting does not just pop up suddenly; as in other dimensions of the life course, there is substantial continuity in adult behavioral styles including but not limited to parenting (Caspi et al., 1987, 1988, 1989). Moreover, much of the Gluecks' information on family processes, although retrospective, referred to several years before the onset of official delinquency. For example, family discipline was determined by parental reports, psychiatric interviews, and reports from social workers who had known the family over a long time (Glueck and Glueck, 1950: 133). Similarly, emotional ties between parent and child were measured as far back as the boys' early life experiences (5 to 8 years old). It is also quite unlikely if not logically impossible that delinquency of the child determined the structural background factors we analyze (for example, parental criminality, foreign-born status, poverty, mobility).

In accordance with most previous research and theory in delinquency, we therefore begin by specifying structural background and family process as exogenous in the explanation of delinquency (see Figure 4.1).[4] Once the key parameters of family process are identified, we then consider the role of early childhood misbehavior as a possible confounding factor in understanding patterns of informal social control. That is, we investigate the possibility that difficult children themselves cause disrupted parenting. We do so by taking advantage of some unique measures in the Glueck data on misbehavior that occurred well before the onset of official delinquency. By subjecting the family model to a strict test, we thus provide a means to validate the major empirical results flowing from the original assumptions of the theory as portrayed in Figure 4.1.

INITIAL RESULTS

We begin in Table 4.2 with an overview of the bivariate association between family process and delinquency as measured by official records and total unreported delinquency. The magnitude and direction of relationships support the underlying social control model. Namely, all relationships are in the expected direction, all are quite large, and all maintain regardless of the method of delinquency measurement. For example, both official and unofficial delinquency increase monotonically as the mother's and father's erratic/harsh discipline increases (gammas = .64/.69, and .52/.54, respectively). The percentage differences are not only consistent across categories of discipline, but they represent differentials anywhere from 7 to a factor over 30.

The bottom part of Table 4.2 shows that delinquency declines monotonically with increasing levels of supervision and attachment. In fact, 83 percent of those in the low supervision category were delinquent compared to only 10 percent of those in the high category, an eightfold difference (gamma = -.84). The unofficial criterion shows an even greater ten-fold differential. Parental rejection and attachment are also substantially related to both official and unofficial delinquency.

Having demonstrated the strong connection between family process and delinquency, we now step back and consider the extent to which family processes of informal social control are in fact endogenous and hence potentially mediate the effect of more distal, structural factors. To accomplish this, Tables 4.3 and 4.4 display the results of ordinary least squares (OLS) models of family process variables regressed on structural background factors. Overall, the results vindicate the theoretical prediction that structural background factors have substantial effects on family processes of social control. For example, in Table 4.3 columns 1 and 2 of data show that household crowding, large families, father's deviance (that is, criminality/drunkenness), low family socioeconomic status, and foreign-born status contribute significantly ($p < .05$) to the father's erratic use of harsh/punitive discipline and punishment.[5] The largest effect by far is that fathers who were alcoholic or criminal were, all else being equal, much more likely (by a factor of two) to use force and inconsistent discipline on their sons than fathers

Table 4.2 Bivariate Association between Family Process and Delinquency

	Father's erratic/ harsh discipline				Mother's erratic/ harsh discipline			
	Low	Medium		High	Low	Medium		High
	(147)	(244)	(362)	(123)	(158)	(309)	(343)	(158)
% Officially delinquent	7	39	66	74	2	42	65	80
Gamma =			.64*				.69*	
% Unofficially delinquent[a]	3	27	48	52	1	30	43	61
Gamma =			.52*				.54*	

	Mother's supervision			Parental rejection			Attachment to parent		
	Low	Medium	High	Low	Medium	High	Low	Medium	High
	(382)	(252)	(355)	(539)	(311)	(113)	(186)	(363)	(448)
% Officially delinquent	83	58	10	31	70	91	78	61	30
Gamma =		-.84*			.74*			-.60*	
% Unofficially delinquent	60	39	5	19	54	66	53	44	20
Gamma =		-.72*			.62*			-.48*	

a. Percent unofficially delinquent refers to the (trichotomized) "high" category.
*p < .05.

Table 4.3   OLS Linear Regression of Family Process Variables Relating to Discipline and Supervision on Structural Background Factors (N = 814)

Background Factors	FAMILY PROCESS: DISCIPLINE AND SUPERVISION					
	Father erratic/harsh		Mother erratic/harsh		Mother's supervision	
	β	t-ratio	β	t-ratio	β	t-ratio
Residential mobility	.07	1.66	.07	1.78	-.22	-6.19*
Family size	.10	2.72*	.08	2.25*	-.12	-3.66*
Crowding	.11	3.03*	.12	3.26*	.01	.44
Family disruption	-.04	-1.11	.01	.41	-.05	-1.64
Mother's employment	.04	1.20	.04	1.15	-.22	-7.60*
Family SES	-.12	-3.22*	-.14	-3.65*	.12	3.59*
Foreign-born	.14	4.37*	.13	3.88*	-.08	-2.67*
Father's deviance	.26	6.68*	.17	4.34*	-.16	-4.49*
Mother's deviance	.02	.61	.10	2.64*	-.18	-5.47*
	$R^2 = .20$		$R^2 = .19$		$R^2 = .37$	

*$p < .05$.

with no record of alcoholic or criminal deviance ($\beta = .26$). This pattern is supportive of Hirschi's (1983) notion that parental deviance contributes to family dysfunction. It also suggests the possibility that some, if not all, of the effect of the father's criminality on the son's delinquency may be attributable to family discipline.

The same pattern generally holds true for the mother's use of erratic and harsh discipline as well. In fact, father's deviance has the largest effect on mother's disrupted parenting—almost double that of mother's deviance. By contrast, the effect of mother's deviance on father's erratic/harsh discipline is nil ($\beta = .02$), suggesting that mothers disproportionately carried the burden of child care and family discipline. Still, the mother's parenting style, like the father's, is disrupted by large family size, crowding, foreign-born status, and poverty.

The results for mother's supervision are also supportive of our general social control framework—again, both mother's and father's drinking/criminality are important in reducing effective monitoring of the boy by the mother. So too are residential mobility, employment by mothers, large family size, low family socioeconomic status, and foreign-born status.[6] The largest effects on parental supervision result from residential mobility and mother's employment outside of the home, followed

Table 4.4 OLS Linear Regression of Family Process Variables Relating to Emotional Ties on Structural Background Factors (N = 814)

| Background Factors | FAMILY PROCESS: EMOTIONAL TIES | | | |
| | Parental rejection | | Attachment to parent | |
	β	t-ratio	β	t-ratio
Residential mobility	.19	5.08*	−.10	2.59*
Family size	−.02	−.60	−.01	−.38
Crowding	.02	.68	.01	.43
Family disruption	.25	7.28*	−.15	−3.98*
Mother's employment	.05	1.71	−.02	−.64
Family SES	−.12	−3.26*	.15	3.84*
Foreign-born	.09	2.86*	−.10	−3.06*
Father's deviance	.10	2.69*	−.12	−3.08*
Mother's deviance	.12	3.56*	−.06	−1.59
	$R^2 = .30$		$R^2 = .16$	

*$p < .05$.

by rather substantial negative effects for parental deviance. There has been much debate about the effect of mother's employment outside of the home on delinquency, but relatively little on how supervision might mediate this background factor (see Hoffman, 1974; Maccoby, 1958; H. Wilson, 1980). In the Gluecks' data and time period (circa 1940), employment by mothers outside of the home appears to have had a significant negative effect on mother's supervision.[7] This is exactly the pattern supportive of the social control framework and confirmed by other empirical research (see, for example, Maccoby, 1958; H. Wilson, 1980). It remains to be seen whether employment outside of the home by mothers has any direct effect on delinquency. It is also worth noting that the mother's employment has no discernible effect on the father's or mother's use of erratic/harsh discipline.

In Table 4.4 we turn to an examination of the relational dimension of family social control—emotional attachment between parent and child. The data in columns 1 and 2 show that family disruption, residential mobility, poverty, foreign-born status, and both father's and mother's deviance have significant effects on parental rejection of the child. These results suggest that in families with only one parent, frequent moves, disadvantaged financial/ethnic position, and a pattern of devi-

Table 4.5 OLS Linear and ML Logistic Regression of Official Delinquency Status on Structural Background Factors and Family Process (N = 814)

| | OFFICIAL DELINQUENCY STATUS | | | |
| | OLS Linear | | ML Logistic[a] | |
Full Model	β	t-ratio	b	t-ratio
Residential mobility	.04	1.36	.03	1.19
Family size	.08	2.81*	.15	2.72*
Crowding	−.06	−2.15*	−.32	−1.75
Family disruption	.04	1.31	.36	1.50
Mother's employment	−.01	−.56	−.11	−.48
Family SES	−.05	−1.74	−.12	−1.68
Foreign-born	−.00	−.00	.00	.01
Father's deviance	−.01	−.11	−.06	−.44
Mother's deviance	.01	.44	.15	.84
Father erratic/harsh	.12	3.81*	.48	3.47*
Mother erratic/harsh	.12	3.81*	.45	3.35*
Mother's supervision	−.38	−10.68*	−1.24	−8.16*
Parental rejection	.12	3.94*	.65	3.60*
Attachment to parent	−.08	−2.89*	−.38	−2.66*
	OLS R^2 = .49		ML model χ^2 = 491, 14 d.f.	

a. Entries for ML Logistic "b" are the raw maximum-likelihood logistic coefficients; "t-ratios" are coefficients divided by S.E.

*$p < .05$.

ant parental conduct, parents are more likely to exhibit indifference or hostility toward their children. Interestingly, these effects are rather substantial and larger than those associated with the factors of household crowding, family size, and working mothers. Except for the factor of maternal deviance, the results for boy's attachment to parents (columns 3 and 4) mirror those for parental rejection.

Table 4.5 displays results from the full model of the effects of structure *and* family process on delinquency. The first two columns contain the results from the OLS linear regression of official delinquency status on background factors and family process variables. Because the official delinquency criterion violates the assumptions of OLS regression about the distribution of dependent variables, we also estimate the model using maximum-likelihood (ML) logistic regression (see Aldrich and Nelson, 1984).

In general, the results are invariant across method and support the causal model in Figure 4.1. Note that all but two of the structural background factors have no direct effect on delinquency, but instead operate through the family process variables. The main exception is family size, which has a direct positive effect in both the OLS and ML models. Crowding has a small negative effect in the OLS model only, suggesting that, all else being equal, crowded homes *reduce* delinquency. As a result, crowding appears subject to a suppressor effect—it has an indirect positive effect on delinquency through disrupted parenting (see Table 4.3) and a negative direct effect when family process is controlled. These counterbalancing effects are suppressed if we simply consider the total effect of crowding on delinquency (β = .00). In any case, were this result to hold up upon further scrutiny, it might mean that, all else being equal, guardianship and surveillance are facilitated by overcrowding. Perhaps this occurs because of inadvertent monitoring by nonparental family members who are most directly affected by overcrowding (for instance, siblings who must share a bedroom).

On the other hand, all the family process variables maintain significant effects on delinquency in the same theoretical direction as Table 4.2, and several of these effects are quite large. The effect of parental supervision on delinquency is especially noteworthy (β = −.38, ML t-ratio = −8.16). At the same time, both mother's *and* father's erratic/punitive discipline have independent positive effects on delinquency of the same magnitude. The data also reveal that the affective dimension of family process is important too. In this regard, parental rejection of the child has a direct positive effect on delinquency, whereas boy's attachment to parent inhibits delinquency. Independent of both background variables and family discipline factors, emotional ties of child to parent and parent to child thus appear to distinguish serious, persistent delinquents from nondelinquents.

As noted, the ML logistic regression verifies the OLS regression. Indeed, the pattern and relative magnitude of effects are essentially identical, and hence all substantive conclusions remain the same. Probably because of the even split of delinquents and nondelinquents, the dichotomous nature of the *Unraveling* data is quite robust to alternative methodological tests of the theoretical model (see also Laub and Sampson, 1988).[8]

The initial results clearly support the theoretical model in Figure 4.1. Namely, when an intervening variable mediates the effect of an exogenous variable or variables, the direct effects of the latter should disappear. Except for family size and crowding, that is exactly what is seen in Table 4.5. Moreover, when OLS and ML logistic regression models are estimated without the hypothesized mediating variables, most structural background factors have large, significant effects on delinquency in the expected manner. For example, the reduced-form ML t-ratios for the effects of family size, foreign-born, mother's employment, family disruption, crowding, SES, mobility, father's deviance, and mother's deviance on delinquency are 3.93, 1.64, 2.97, 1.90, .10, −4.41, 5.56, 3.80, and 4.48, respectively. But, as seen in Table 4.5, only family size retains a consistent significant (albeit reduced) effect on delinquency when the family dimensions of discipline, supervision, and attachment are controlled. Not surprisingly, the calculation of indirect effects (see Alwin and Hauser, 1981) reveals that of the total effect of all structural background factors on delinquency, 73 percent is mediated by family process. Therefore, the results demonstrate the importance of considering indirect effects of structural background.

Other Criteria of Delinquency

It is possible that our finding of family effects is in part the result of differential official processing by the juvenile justice system (for example, disproportionate referral of youth from dysfunctional families). We examine this hypothesis using the unofficial measures of delinquency collected by the Gluecks' research team. The first three columns of data in Table 4.6 show the standardized effects of structural variables and family process factors on measures of delinquency and other misconduct reported by the respondent, parent, and teacher. Although our basic theoretical model is supported even with these unofficial measures of delinquency, some different results do emerge for certain structural background factors. For example, family disruption along with family size and crowding are significantly related to self-reported delinquency, and residential mobility is significantly related to both self- and teacher-reported delinquency. Also, depending upon the particular reporter, some of the family process variables are no longer significantly related to delinquency (for example, mother's use of erratic and inconsistent discipline is not significantly related to self-reported delinquency). On balance, however, the majority of background factors are mediated by intervening processes of family social control. In this regard, mother's supervision has the largest negative effect on all indicators of unofficial delinquency, as it did on official delinquency in Table 4.5.

Column 4 displays the results for the summary measure of unofficial

Table 4.6   OLS Linear Regression of Unofficial Delinquency Reports on
Structural Background Factors and Family Process (N = 814)

	UNOFFICIAL DELINQUENCY			
	Self-reported	Parent-reported	Teacher-reported	Total reported
Full Model	β	β	β	β
Residential mobility	.07*	.06	.10*	.07*
Family size	.10*	.06	.05	.09*
Crowding	−.07*	−.05	−.04	−.07*
Family disruption	.06*	.10*	−.02	.08*
Mother's employment	−.03	.01	−.01	−.02
Family SES	−.05	−.04	−.06	−.05
Foreign-born	−.04	−.03	−.03	−.04
Father's deviance	.01	−.02	.04	.00
Mother's deviance	.04	.01	−.05	.02
Father erratic/harsh	.09*	.15*	.12*	.13*
Mother erratic/harsh	.06	.11*	.11*	.09*
Mother's supervision	−.39*	−.23*	−.29*	−.35*
Parental rejection	.09*	.14*	.02	.11*
Attachment to parent	−.10*	−.06	−.02	−.08*
	R^2 = .47	R^2 = .36	R^2 = .27	R^2 = .49

*$p < .05$.

delinquency that combines the self, parent, and teacher reports. This measure provides a comprehensive and reliable indicator of the extent of unofficial delinquency. The data show that although five of the nine structural background factors have direct effects on total unofficial delinquency, all of the beta coefficients are less than .10 in magnitude. More important is that the results for family process variables are replicated. In fact, the pattern of effects for total unofficial delinquency in Table 4.6 is virtually identical to the prior results for official delinquency.

Even when the summary delinquency measure is broken down into distinct offense types (truancy, theft, smoking/drinking, running away, and so forth), the same general pattern emerges (data not shown). Consistent with Tables 4.5 and 4.6, for example, mother's supervision has the largest effect on truancy, running away, larceny, smoking/drinking, vandalism, "car-hopping," motor-vehicle theft, and even a general measure of "conduct disorder." This is hardly surprising, since a long line of research has demonstrated the lack of specialization in particular crime types and a strong positive covariation among delinquency items (Gottfredson and Hirschi, 1990; Osgood, 1990).

In short, all five family process variables show significant and predicted effects of similar magnitude and rank order for the two key measures of delinquency. Family social control thus sharply distinguishes delinquents from nondelinquents in the Gluecks' sample regardless of whether official or unofficial delinquency is used. As far as we can determine from the data, then, our major findings do not appear to be the result of differential processing by formal agents of social control.

DIFFICULT CHILDREN:
A RECONSIDERATION OF FAMILY EFFECTS

To this point in our analyses, the data suggest that family processes of informal social control have important inhibitory effects on adolescent delinquency. Although this seems intuitively plausible and conforms to our theoretical expectations, recent research raises questions regarding unidirectional models that attribute the development of delinquency to parental influence. In particular, Lytton (1990) has argued that both child and parent are sensitive to the behavior of the other and have certain levels of tolerance for each other's behavior (see also Anderson et al., 1986). As a result, parent and child display constant reciprocal adaptation to each other's behavior level. For example, when a child's behavior has reached the upper limit of the parent's tolerance (through overactivity or aggressiveness), the parent's "upper limit control" reactions, such as control and restriction, are activated (Lytton, 1990: 683). To the extent that parents' behavior is a reaction to troublesome childhood predispositions, our models may be misspecified.

In this section we therefore explore the consequences of early childhood misbehavior for parental styles of discipline and emotional attachment. We are guided by two related streams of evidence. The first is empirical research establishing the early onset of many forms of childhood misbehavior (West and Farrington, 1973; Earls and Jung, 1987; Robins, 1966; White et al., 1990). In one of the most sophisticated studies to date, White and colleagues (1990) examined the predictive power of behavior measured as early as age 3 on antisocial outcomes at ages 11 and 13. They found that teacher- and/or parent-reported behavioral measures of hyperactivity and restlessness in a young child (age 3), difficulty in management of the child at age 3, and early onset of problem behaviors at age 5 predicted later antisocial outcomes. This research by White and colleagues (1990) is impressive because it shows the extent to which later delinquency is foreshadowed by very early misbehavior and general difficulty among children. Their finding cannot be explained away by retrospective bias because the study involved the prospective follow-up of an unselected (that is, total) birth cohort to age 15. When styles of parenting are a direct reaction to these early behavioral dispositions of the child, assumptions regarding family social control are called into question.

Our second motivation stems from consideration of recent research in psychology that provides an empirical and theoretical basis for the importance of early childhood. Lytton (1990) has written an excellent overview of this complex body of research, which he subsumes under the theoretical umbrella of "control systems theory." In brief, control systems theory assumes that parent and child display reciprocal adaptation to each other's behavior level (Anderson et al., 1986). In accordance with this assumption, Lytton begins with the fact of early childhood deviance, such as that noted above by White and colleagues. These behavioral styles of children in turn are hypothesized to have what Lytton calls "child effects" on parents.

One reason for these child effects is that reinforcement does not work in the usual way for conduct-disordered children. As Lytton (1990: 688) notes, there is evidence suggesting that conduct-disordered children "may be underresponsive to social reinforcement and punishment." Hence, normal routines of parental punishment and child rearing become subject to disruption because of early antisocial behavior—that is, children themselves differentially engender parenting styles likely to exacerbate antisocial behavior. This reciprocal pattern is the essence of control systems theory.

The behavior that prompts parental frustration is not merely aggressiveness or delinquency, however. Much as White and colleagues argue, some children show what Lytton (1990: 690) refers to as "difficult behavior" such as whining, restlessness, inadaptability to change, and strong-willed resistance from early on in the life course. These tendencies are often subsumed under the label "temperament," and are considered early emotional characteristics of the child that are relatively stable over time (Earls and Jung, 1987; Tonry et al., 1991). We do not need to resolve the controversy over the origins of temperament and early childhood difficulty (see Earls and Jung, 1987: 497) to recognize that parental styles of discipline may be endogenous with respect to individual differences in temperament. Or as Lytton argues, "It could well be earlier difficultness in the child that provokes later parental rejection" (1990: 685).

To support this contention, Lytton (1990: 690) reviews evidence showing a connection between a child's being rated as difficult in preschool and the child's delinquency as an adolescent, a relation that holds independent of the quality of parents' child-rearing practices. For example, Olweus (1980) showed by a longitudinal path analysis that mothers of boys who displayed a strong-willed and hot temper in infancy later became more permissive of aggression, which in turn led to greater aggressiveness in middle childhood. There was also a direct path from early temperament to later aggressive behavior. As Lytton argues, "It is reasonable to assume that it was the strong pressure of the infant's temperament that made mothers back off from very strict control of aggressive behavior" (1990: 690). Moreover, there is intriguing experimental evidence that when children's inattentive and non-compliant behavior is improved by administering certain stimulant drugs (for instance, Ritalin), their mothers become less controlling and mother-child interaction patterns are nearly normalized (1990: 688). All of this speaks to the idea that parenting, at least in part, must be considered an endogenous reaction to children.

Further evidence in favor of "child effects" from the criminology literature is found in West and Farrington's (1973) well-known longitudinal study. They showed that boys' "troublesomeness" assessed at ages 8 and 10 by teachers and peers was a significant predictor of later delinquency independent of parental supervision, parental criminality, and family size. However, the reverse was not true—parental effects on delinquency disappeared once early troublesomeness was taken into account. As Lytton observes, this finding "suggests the primacy of child effects" (1990: 690).

In short, there is a theoretical and empirical basis for reconsidering our model by introducing early childhood effects. Lytton's review in fact suggests just such a strategy to ascertain the relative importance of parent and child influences. Namely, one can test the effects of early childhood factors on later delinquency, with parent factors held constant, against the prediction of parents' effects on delinquency, with early childhood factors held constant. The relative strength of each set of variables would be an index of the importance of the main independent variables—child or parent (1990: 694). Put more simply, from our perspective the key question is whether our family model holds up once we consider early childhood dispositions. If the parenting or family effects on delinquency observed earlier are spurious, then our model should collapse once childhood difficulty is controlled. On the other hand, if control systems theory is correct, we are liable to see both child *and* parent effects on the outcome of adolescent delinquency.

Measuring Childhood Selection Effects

To provide the strictest test possible, we replicate our key family process model by controlling for three indicators of early childhood predisposition toward disruptive behavior that have face validity—difficult child, early onset, and tantrums. Although the Gluecks' *UJD* data are not longitudinal, there are retrospective interview data on patterns of these types of childhood behavior. From the parent's interview we created a measure of *child difficulty* from a dichotomous variable distinguishing those children who were overly restless and irritable as children from those who were not. The restlessness question was asked of parents about the early developmental period of the youth's life. The measure labeled *tantrums* reflects the extent to which a child engaged in violent temper tantrums and was predisposed to aggressiveness and fighting. The Gluecks attempted to collect data only on habitual tantrums—when tantrums were "the predominant mode of response" by the child to difficult situations growing up (Glueck and Glueck, 1950: 152). This measure also corresponds closely to one used by Caspi (1987).[9]

The third variable is labeled *early onset* and is constructed from self-reports of the age of onset of misbehavior. The age of onset of unofficial behavior rather than official reaction is thus at issue here. On the basis of theoretical concerns in conjunction with the distribution of age of onset, we created a dichotomous variable where a one indexes an age of onset earlier than age 8. Those who had a later age of onset *and* those who reported no delinquency (and hence no age of onset) were assigned a zero. Thus, there is variation in the early onset measure within both the delinquent and the nondelinquent groups.

We have no way to establish conclusively the validity of these three measures. Nevertheless, preliminary analysis did suggest considerable evidence of construct and predictive validity. As to the latter, all three measures predict official delinquency as a juvenile. For example, 66 percent of the children rated difficult in early childhood were arrested in adolescence as compared to 37 percent of those rated not difficult (phi = .29, $p < .05$). Similarly, 86 percent of those boys with tantrums were arrested before reaching adulthood, compared to 40 percent of those with no evidence of early tantrums (phi = .38, $p < .05$). The respective figures for unofficial early onset are 95 percent and 45 percent, respectively (phi = .25, $p < .05$).

These three childhood measures also predict behavior well into adulthood. Although this issue is taken up in more detail in Chapter 6, it is sufficient to say here that difficult behavior in childhood predicts arrest and other adult deviance even at age 32. For example, 58 percent of those with temper tantrums in childhood were arrested at ages 25–32, 31 percent had excessive drinking problems, and 62 percent were officially charged in the military. The comparable figures for those with no tantrums were 41 percent, 19 percent, and 33 percent (all $p < .05$).

Moreover, all three measures correlate among themselves in the manner expected by theory. Of those children rated difficult in childhood, 34 percent exhibited tantrums compared to 13 percent of those with no history of "difficultness." Similarly, for those with an early onset of misbehavior, 47 percent were identified as having tantrums, compared to 20 percent of those with no early onset (all $p < .05$). On the other hand, the three child dimensions are clearly not redundant since each independently explains variation in later delinquency, and no phi coefficient is larger than .50. There is thus reasonable evidence that the measures of early childhood misbehavior and difficult temperament satisfy tests of discriminant validity as well as construct, predictive, and face validity.

REPLICATION

We begin the replication models by studying the effects of early childhood on the five dimensions of family process that were considered exogenous in the previous analyses. Table 4.7 displays the standardized direct effects on all five family variables. The results indicate that childhood "difficultness" has significant effects on measures of direct parental controls. Substantively, for example, the results suggest that children who were rated difficult, who habitually engaged in violent tantrums,

Table 4.7 Replication of OLS Regression Model of Family Process and Structural Background Factors, Controlling for Early Childhood Difficulty and Disruptive Antisocial Behavior (N = 729)

Structural and Childhood Factors	FAMILY PROCESS				
	Father erratic/harsh β	Mother erratic/harsh β	Mother's supervision β	Parental rejection β	Attachment to parent β
Residential mobility	.02	.03	-.19*	.14*	-.11*
Family size	.14*	.09*	-.15*	-.02	-.04
Crowding	.10*	.10*	.02	.02	.03
Family disruption	-.07	.01	-.03	.22*	-.11*
Mother's employment	.07*	.05	-.24*	.05	-.02
Family SES	-.12*	-.14*	.08*	-.13*	.16*
Foreign-born	.12*	.14*	-.08*	.08*	-.11*
Father's deviance	.23*	.15*	-.15*	.10*	-.11*
Mother's deviance	.00	.08*	-.18*	.13*	-.07
Early onset	.06	.09*	-.07*	.05	-.03
Difficult child	.17*	.07*	-.07*	.06	-.06
Tantrums	.09*	.12*	-.11*	.09*	-.04
	$R^2 = .25$	$R^2 = .23$	$R^2 = .40$	$R^2 = .31$	$R^2 = .18$

*$p < .05$.

and who exhibited early misbehavior had lower levels of supervision imposed by their mothers. Perhaps more intriguing, and consistent with a control systems perspective, is the fact that childhood difficulty significantly predicts the inconsistent and harsh use of discipline by both mothers and fathers. Childhood difficulty has an especially large effect on father's harsh/punitive reactions.

On the other hand, childhood conduct and temperamental problems do not have much of an effect on the emotional bonds between parent and child. This makes sense from the perspective of control systems theory, since the focus is on the reciprocity of behaviors. It is quite plausible that parents become frustrated with unruly children and respond with harsh discipline and attenuated supervision even as they continue to love them. Tantrums may thus spark parental rejection, but overall the relational (Hagan, 1989) or affective dimensions of family social control are relatively independent of the child's early propensity toward disruptive behavior.

These results appear to confirm Lytton's (1990) arguments regarding the endogeneity of parental styles of discipline and control of their children, especially direct controls. Simply put, parents appear responsive to early behavioral difficulties—angry, temperamental children who misbehave provoke in their parents a disrupted behavioral style of parenting and control. On the other hand, it is still possible that the observed results stem from simultaneity—parental behavior may reciprocally shape child temperament and the likelihood of tantrums.

We should also not overlook the basic integrity of our family model, which remains largely intact. Indeed, the rationale for introducing child effects was not to establish conclusively the validity of control systems theory, but rather to provide a strict test of the validity of our own theoretical conceptions about the direct and indirect effects of families on adolescent delinquency. In this regard note that structural background factors, independent of childhood effects, continue to exert powerful effects on family processes of informal social control. For example, the largest determinants of mothers' lowered supervision are employment, residential mobility, mother's deviance, father's deviance, and family size, followed by tantrums. Similarly, factors such as parental deviance and poverty have larger effects than childhood predispositions on erratic/harsh discipline. Therefore, the data support a model wherein structural background factors explain patterns of family social control, even controlling for childhood temperamental styles and early

Table 4.8   Full OLS Linear and ML Logistic Regression of Delinquency on Structural Background Factors, Family Process, and Early Childhood Difficulty and Disruptive Antisocial Behavior (N = 729)

Full Model	OFFICIAL DELINQUENCY STATUS (0, 1) ML Logistic[a]		UNOFFICIAL DELINQUENCY REPORTS (1–26) OLS Linear	
	b	t-ratio	β	t-ratio
Residential mobility	.01	.33	.06	1.92
Family size	.21	3.36*	.12	4.11*
Crowding	−.56	−2.63*	−.09	−3.11*
Family disruption	.26	.95	.07	2.43*
Mother's employment	.06	.20	.01	.46
Family SES	−.13	−1.53	−.03	−.86
Foreign-born	−.05	−.20	−.04	−1.35
Father's deviance	−.09	−.52	−.00	−.14
Mother's deviance	.26	1.31	.02	.81
Father erratic/harsh	.38	2.49*	.10	2.87*
Mother erratic/harsh	.47	3.09*	.08	2.37*
Mother's supervision	−1.15	−6.78*	−.32	−8.68*
Parental rejection	.73	3.58*	.11	3.29*
Attachment to parent	−.35	−2.25*	−.08	−2.68*
Early onset	1.86	2.73*	.10	3.95*
Difficult child	.88	3.73*	.08	2.98*
Tantrums	1.38	4.68*	.14	4.90*
	ML model χ^2 = 493, 17 d.f.		OLS R^2 = .53	

a. Entries for ML Logistic "b" are the raw maximum-likelihood logistic coefficients; "t-ratios" are coefficients divided by S.E.

*$p < .05$.

disruptive behavior. We now complete the picture by assessing the outcome criterion of adolescent delinquency.

Table 4.8 displays two "full" models of structural background, family process, and childhood effects on delinquency. The first two columns list the ML logistic results for the official delinquency criterion. Columns 3 and 4 list the OLS results for the total measure of unofficially reported delinquency. By comparing these two behavioral outcomes—one official and one unofficial—we should be in a position to assess the overall validity of our basic theoretical model.

The results are strikingly consistent and yield three substantive conclusions. First, as in earlier models, structural background factors again influence delinquency largely through their effects on mediating dimensions of family process. For example, only crowding and large family size have consistent effects across the two indicators of delinquency—the former reducing and the latter increasing delinquency. Second, and as expected, the measures of early onset, childhood difficulty, and tantrums *all* have significant direct effects on delinquency that are unaccounted for by family process and structural background. Disruptive and unruly children are significantly more likely to be arrested and engage in extensive delinquent behaviors. Third, and most important from our perspective, are the robust results regarding family process: despite controlling for three measures of early childhood propensities, the dimensions of parental discipline, attachment, and supervision all continue to influence delinquent conduct in the manner predicted by our theoretical model. In fact, mother's supervision has by far the largest effect on delinquency, with a beta coefficient more than double the largest child effect (that is, tantrums).

Table 4.9 completes our analysis of family and child effects with reduced or trimmed models of delinquency. These models were estimated by successively eliminating predictors that were not significant at $p < .10$ from the model in Table 4.8. The reduced model for unofficial delinquency indicates that mobility, large families, family disruption, low crowding, parental erratic/harsh discipline,[10] parental rejection, weakened attachment to parent, early onset, difficult children, and tantrums all significantly explain variations in the breadth of involvement in adolescent delinquent behavior. The model for official delinquency is identical except that the effects of residential mobility and family disruption are fully mediated by family process variables. Apparently, mobility and family disruption have direct effects on the breadth and extent of unofficial delinquency that are not reflected in the official criterion.

On balance, our family model thus remains intact, surviving a strict test for three dimensions of early childhood antisocial behavior/temperament. In fact, one way of interpreting Table 4.9 is that changes in adolescent delinquency (that is, variations unexplained by early propensity to deviance) are directly explained by informal processes of family social control in adolescence. The magnitude of the family effects is especially noteworthy—for example, independent of all other factors

Table 4.9   Trimmed Models of Official and Unofficial Delinquency, Key
            Structural Background Factors, Family Process, and Early
            Childhood Difficulty/Antisocial Behavior (N = 742)

| | OFFICIAL DELINQUENCY STATUS (0, 1) | | UNOFFICIAL DELINQUENCY REPORTS (1–26) | |
| | ML Logistic[a] | | OLS Linear | |
Significant Predictors	b	t-ratio	β	t-ratio
Residential mobility	NI		.09	2.79*
Family size	.23	3.97*	.13	4.53*
Crowding	-.47	-2.30*	-.09	-3.02*
Family disruption	NI		.08	2.64*
Parents erratic/harsh	.41	4.89*	.15	4.81*
Mother's supervision	-1.21	-8.07*	-.31	-9.33*
Parental rejection	.87	4.55*	.11	3.51*
Attachment to parent	-.40	-2.63*	-.08	-2.79*
Early onset	1.84	2.77*	.10	4.01*
Difficult child	.87	3.82*	.08	3.10*
Tantrums	1.48	5.01*	.14	5.21*
	ML model χ^2 = 496, 9 d.f.		OLS R^2 = .53	

a. Entries for ML Logistic "b" are the raw maximum-likelihood logistic coefficients;
"t-ratios" are coefficients divided by S.E.
NI = not included in model specification.
*p < .05.

including childhood antisocial behavior, a one-unit increase in mother's
supervision (on a three-point scale) is associated with a 54 percent
decrease in official delinquency.[11] The magnitudes of the standardized
effects on unofficial delinquency paint the same picture (for example,
β = -.31 for mother's supervision). Therefore, while child effects are
clearly present, supporting an "ontogenetic" model (see Dannefer,
1984), the "sociogenic" model of family has larger effects and confirms
earlier patterns. It appears that knowledge of childhood propensities is
not a sufficient condition for explaining delinquency.

Further Tests

We performed a series of additional tests to assess the robustness of
results. The first involved a re-estimation of models using procedures
to determine whether missing data biased the results. Although missing

data were not a problem overall, the final model in Table 4.9 was estimated after the elimination of over 200 cases with incomplete information on relevant variables. Loss of data is of particular concern in the replication analyses using "child effect" measures (for example, compare N of cases in Table 4.8 to Table 4.5). Therefore, we estimated mean-substitution and pairwise-deletion models in which we entered a dichotomous variable for missing cases. Specifically, we assigned a one to those persons who had missing data and were thus excluded from the earlier results; those included were assigned a zero. This strategy permits an examination of whether those with missing data were systematically different, and whether their exclusion biases the results.

When these alternative estimation procedures were invoked, the major results remained remarkably intact. In particular, our reduced model of delinquency in Table 4.9 looked similar whether pairwise deletion was used or whether all 1,000 cases were analyzed on the basis of assigned mean values for otherwise missing cases. The largest predictor of delinquency remained mother's supervision, and all other family effects remained significant and of the same relative magnitude. More important, the dummy variable for missing cases had an insignificant effect on official delinquency, and was weakly correlated with exogenous variables.

The second series of tests involved re-estimating the explanatory models with additional control variables that are not central to our theoretical model, but that may nonetheless confound the results. For example, although the Gluecks matched subjects case by case on age and IQ, there were some residual matching differences that conceivably might affect multivariate results (cf. Reiss, 1951b). The other variables examined were mesomorphy and extroversion, two "constitutional" variables emphasized by the Gluecks in *Unraveling*. Despite controlling for these individual difference constructs, all family effects retained their significant predictive power.[12] And once again mother's supervision had the largest of all effects on delinquency, whether official or unofficial.

SUMMARY AND CONCLUSIONS

A major finding of our analysis is that family process variables are strongly and directly related to delinquency in the direction predicted by our theoretical model. The results thus support our integrated theory of informal social control derived from Hirschi (1969, 1983), Gottfredson and Hirschi (1990), Patterson (1980, 1982), Hagan (1989), and Braithwaite (1989), and they confirm the recent meta-analysis by Loeber and Stouthamer-Loeber in which they found that socialization variables, "aspects of family functioning involving direct parent-child contacts," are the most powerful predictors of delinquency and other juvenile conduct problems (1986: 37, 120). Interestingly, these family process variables—supervision, attachment, and discipline—were identified by the Gluecks as the most important family correlates of serious, persistent delinquency (1950: 261). Although we expanded their work considerably by constructing theoretically specified scales of family social control, by developing unofficial measures of self-, parent-, and teacher-reported delinquency, and by conducting extensive multivariate analyses, our research essentially confirms an important substantive theme explicated by the Gluecks over 40 years ago.

Another major finding is that, except for family size and crowding, none of the structural background factors had a consistent direct effect on measures of delinquency.[13] Instead, family process mediated approximately 75 percent of the effect of structural background on delinquency. The data thus support the social control theory depicted schematically in Figure 4.1. We believe that this model has significance for future research by explaining how it is that key background factors influence delinquency. A concern with only direct effects conceals such relationships and leads to erroneous conclusions. More generally, families do not exist in isolation but instead are systematically embedded in social structural contexts.

Our conceptualization also suggests the importance of previously neglected variables in criminological research—especially alcoholism and criminality of parents. Parental deviance of both mother and father strongly disrupts family processes of social control, which in turn increases delinquency.

The data further point to the complex role of social selection and social causation in the genesis of delinquency. Although difficult children who display early antisocial tendencies do appear to self-select or sort themselves into later states of delinquency, family processes of informal social control still explain the largest share of variance in adolescent delinquency. Our results therefore suggest that no matter how good the prognostic device currently available for predicting delinquency (cf. White et al., 1990), delinquency in adolescence is explained largely by exogenous family factors that also occur in adolescence. Put differently, child effects may exist, but they are hardly sufficient for explaining delinquency, especially when compared with the socializing influence of the family.

Given the overall nature of our results, it is troubling that many sociological explanations of crime ignore the family. This neglect has generated a marked divergence between both empirical findings and the conventional wisdom of the general public—especially parents—and the views of social scientists who study criminal behavior. As Hirschi has noted: " 'Modern' theories of crime . . . assume that the individual would be noncriminal were it not for the operation of unjust and misguided institutions. 'Outdated' theories of crime assume that decent behavior is not part of our native equipment, but is somehow built in through socialization and maintained by the threat of sanctions" (1983: 54). In fact, the "modern" view has a venerable history and can be found in the 1938 movie referred to at the beginning of the chapter. At the beginning of the film the young boys, James Cagney (Rocky Sullivan) and Pat O'Brien (Jerry Connelly), break into a box car to steal some pens. The police come and both boys run to avoid getting caught. One boy, Jerry, is a little quicker and gets away. Rocky, slower of foot, gets caught. Of course, Rocky does not squeal on his best friend, and he is the one who turns out to be a criminal later in life. The explanation offered in the film is that "reform school made a criminal out of Rocky," "there but for the grace of God go I," and "Rocky was a good kid gone bad." At the end of the film, after Rocky Sullivan is executed for several homicides, Pat O'Brien in the role of Jerry Connelly sadly remarks: "Let's say a prayer for a boy who couldn't run as fast as I could."

Although labeling and luck may play a role in crime causation (see especially Chapters 7 and 8), our research suggests that family life is far more important in understanding persistent criminal behavior in the early adolescent years. Although not developed in the film, this theme could easily have been applied to Rocky Sullivan and Jerry Connelly too. At one point in the movie, Rocky says to Jerry that his father will not miss him while he is in reform school and he is "better off without him." Jerry, on the other hand, talks of the fact that his mother always wanted him to be a priest and the influence that had in his career decision. Thus, differences in family life along the lines suggested by our research could have been used to portray why these two boys grew up differently. We must admit, though, that empirical reality lacks the interest, the entertainment, and indeed the drama that is found in the film as it currently exists. Good stories seem to have more appeal than empirical facts, even to social scientists.

THE ROLE OF
SCHOOL, PEERS,
AND SIBLINGS

5
—
—

As should be clear by now, one of the distinguishing character-istics of what we have identified as the "Glueck perspective" was a focus on the family life of delinquents and nondelinquents (see also Laub and Sampson, 1991). Although interest in the family was to become unfashionable in sociological criminology during the 1950s and 1960s, it was one of the main staples of the Gluecks' research agenda. As noted earlier, the Gluecks developed a prediction scale of delin-quency in *Unraveling Juvenile Delinquency* that centered on family vari-ables—especially disciplinary practices, supervision by parents, and child-parent attachment. Those families with lax discipline combined with erratic and threatening punishment, poor supervision, and weak emotional ties between parent and child were found to generate the highest probability of delinquency (Glueck and Glueck, 1950: 261). This family model was largely confirmed in the previous chapter.

Perhaps because of their intense focus on the importance of family, the Gluecks limited their interest in other variables relevant to child-hood and adolescence. In particular, the only school-related variable used by the Gluecks in their various attempts to predict delinquency was school misconduct in the form of truancy (Glueck and Glueck, 1959). Moreover, without any empirical justification, the Gluecks con-cluded that "school attainment itself cannot be regarded as a causal factor" (Glueck and Glueck, 1950: 276). This assertion is surprising because even though many boys at that time dropped out of school, the Gluecks did find school-related differences between delinquents and nondelinquents. In fact, the Gluecks found that "delinquents ex-pressed a violent dislike for school, resentment at its restrictions, lack of interest in school work" (Glueck and Glueck, 1950: 153). Nonethe-less, the Gluecks failed to incorporate school factors in their overall perspective and made no effort to examine systematically the effects of school along with family functioning.

In a similar manner, the Gluecks did not examine in any depth their data on peer group relations and the onset of serious delinquency. Their data showed that while virtually all of the delinquents had delinquent friends (98 percent), only 7 percent of the nondelinquents had delinquent companions (Glueck and Glueck, 1950: 164). Recall that the delinquent and nondelinquent subjects in the Glueck study were all drawn from neighborhoods of low socioeconomic status in central Boston. The Gluecks concluded from their data that "birds of a feather flock together" and that "this tendency is a much more fundamental fact in any analysis of causation than the theory that accidental differential association of nondelinquents with delinquents is the basic cause of crime" (Glueck and Glueck, 1950: 164). Thus, as with school factors, the Gluecks made no effort to examine the role of peers in generating delinquent behavior relative to family functioning.

In this chapter we seek to correct the Gluecks' imbalance by analyzing the effects of non-family factors like schools and delinquent peer-group attachment on delinquency. At the same time, we incorporate the important findings presented in the previous chapter on family differences between delinquents and nondelinquents. Moreover, we believe that the role of siblings in facilitating the onset of delinquency has been a neglected aspect in current research on delinquency. Thus, the role of siblings and peers will be examined along with family and school variables.

As in the previous chapter, we are theoretically and empirically interested in the joint effects of structure and process on delinquency. Our strategy in this chapter is therefore as follows. First, we present data on what we term "school process" along with several traditional structural variables so that we can assess the extent to which school processes mediate the effect of structural background factors on delinquency. Second, we present data exploring the effects of peer and sibling factors on delinquency, also allowing for structural background effects. For both sets of analyses we then incorporate the role of early childhood antisocial behavior as a potential confounding variable. Our basic motivation, similar to our strategy in Chapter 4, is to identify the effects of school process, delinquent peer attachment, and delinquent sibling attachment independent of both structural background and early childhood predispositions.

Finally, we present a model that contains all process variables (family, school, peers/siblings) and all structural background variables that had a consistent effect on delinquency. This refined model will allow us to look at the independent effects of both school and companions/siblings on serious delinquency in conjunction with family social control variables.

SCHOOL AND DELINQUENCY

From a social control perspective, the school, like the family, is an important socializing institution in the prevention of delinquent behavior. In fact, Gottfredson and Hirschi (1990: 105) argue that in comparison to the family, the school may be better equipped to provide social control. For one thing, it can in principle more efficiently monitor behavior than the family, with one teacher overseeing many children at a time. Second, in contrast to many parents, teachers generally have no difficulty recognizing deviant or disruptive behavior. Third, compared to the family, the school has such a clear interest in maintaining order and discipline that it can be expected to do whatever possible to control disruptive behavior. Finally, like the family, the school has the authority and the means to punish lapses in self-control (Gottfredson and Hirschi, 1990: 105).

Although the school rarely realizes its full potential as a socializing institution, there does exist a large body of research showing that as school attachment increases, the likelihood of delinquency declines (for example, Hirschi, 1969; Kornhauser, 1978; Wiatrowski et al., 1981). Wiatrowski, Griswold, and Roberts (1981) identified four major dimensions of the concept "school attachment"—school performance, educational aspirations and expectations, involvement in school activities, and school-related satisfactions and ties of affection. In a review of the literature on schools and delinquency, Kercher (1988: 303) found that of these four dimensions, "school performance generally displays the strongest association with illegal behavior." Several researchers have found that poor educational achievement and school failure are strongly and consistently related to juvenile offending (see Hirschi, 1969; West and Farrington, 1973; Jensen, 1976; Loeber and Dishion, 1983; Gottfredson and Hirschi, 1990).[1]

The theoretical model we will examine in this chapter with respect to schools is shown in the top part of Figure 5.1. The mediating constructs of school processes are hypothesized to have the strongest effects on delinquency. Specifically, based on the reasoning given above, we

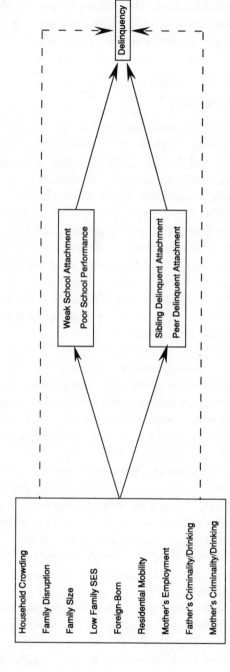

Figure 5.1 Theoretical model of structural background factors, school process, peers/siblings, and delinquency. Broken line indicates hypothesized weak or insignificant effect; solid line signifies hypothesized strong effect. Because of the *UJD* matching design, age, race/ethnicity, neighborhood SES, and IQ are controlled with respect to delinquency.

hypothesize that weak attachment to school and poor school performance will increase delinquency.

The second component of our model posits that structural background factors influence delinquency through their effects on school process. Thus, as in the previous chapter, we expect structural context to have weak direct effects on delinquency. For example, factors related to socioeconomic disadvantage such as poverty and household crowding have been linked to educational deficiencies (Rutter and Giller, 1983: 185–186). Similarly, with respect to factors like family disruption, it is believed that "children reared in such circumstances show increased problems in educational attainment" (Rutter and Giller, 1983: 107).

Perhaps more important, Blake (1989) has recently provided strong evidence for the general proposition that large family size is a risk factor in the educational attainment process. Apparently, even independent of income differences (for example, human capital), individual differences in ability (for instance, measured IQ), and family disruption, children in large families suffer diminished prospects for educational advancement. Presumably this occurs through a reduction in parental social capital, such as individual involvement and time spent with each child (see also Coleman, 1988). To the extent that social capital is more salient than structural features such as income and family disruption, large family size should emerge as a key risk factor for delinquency through its negative effect on school attachment and performance.

The logic of our social control model also suggests that the structural factors of residential mobility and parental deviance will disrupt bonds of attachment between the child and school. In regard to the former, frequent moving would seem theoretically to be a prime risk factor that attenuates ties that might bind a child to the school (cf. Braithwaite, 1989) and increases difficulties in learning (Dunn, 1988: 230). As for deviance, we hypothesize that parents who are offenders and/or have serious drinking problems will have a difficult time monitoring and supervising homework as well as instilling long-range academic goals (Gottfredson and Hirschi, 1990: 100–101). In light of the logic developed above regarding parental recognition of delinquent behavior itself, we would go further and suggest that parents who are themselves deviant would have trouble recognizing, or might even recognize but deny the importance of, educational failure and detachment from school.

Regardless of theoretical predictions, it is still the case that the structural variables examined here are more clearly linked to family process than school process. Better structural indicators relevant to school might be characteristics like classroom crowding, school crime rates, and student ethnic composition.[2] Since these measures were not available, we incorporated our major structural background factors in this chapter even though in all likelihood their influence on school process will be less in comparison to family process. Moreover, we may well find that our structural variables maintain a direct effect on delinquency independent of school context.

PEERS, SIBLINGS, AND DELINQUENCY

Empirical research on peer groups and delinquency is extensive and consistent on the basic facts. Kercher's (1988: 304) recent review of the extant literature says it well: "Association with criminal others is consistently the strongest predictor of illegal behavior." In fact, Elliott, Huizinga, and Ageton (1985) have concluded that bonding to delinquent peers is the most important proximate cause of delinquency. Numerous other studies find a strong link between delinquency of friends and a youth's own delinquency (see, for example, reviews by Johnson, 1979; Agnew, 1991).

Despite the volume of research, the causal effect of peers on delinquency is subject to much debate. The dispute is in part definitional and in part concerns the appropriate temporal ordering of delinquent friends and delinquency. Farrington (1987) has noted that the major problem of interpretation follows from the fact that most delinquent acts are committed in groups, and hence those who commit such acts will almost inevitably have delinquent friends. Thus self-reports of offending and of delinquent peers may, almost by definition, be measuring the same underlying theoretical construct of delinquent behavior (Gottfredson and Hirschi, 1987: 598). There is also no clear demonstration in the literature that association with delinquent peers precedes or facilitates offending, although this may well be true (Farrington, 1987: 37–38). The peer-delinquency correlate could arise from simple selection effects, where "birds of a feather flock together" (see Glueck and Glueck, 1950; S. Glueck, 1956; Gottfredson and Hirschi, 1987).

Somewhat neglected in the peer-delinquency debate is the fact that delinquency is associated with delinquency among siblings and, as shown in Chapter 4, with criminal activity of parents (Farrington et al.,

1975; Robins et al., 1975). It is particularly surprising that the role of siblings has not attracted much attention in criminological research (but see Patterson, 1984, 1986; Rowe, 1985). Robins has forcefully argued that sibling influences on delinquency should be stronger than the influences of peers. Her rationale is rather convincing: "A child's associates outside the family are chosen not only on the basis of propinquity but also on the basis of common interests or by default, because children in the neighborhood desired as associates refuse their friendship. If 'differential association' were a powerful determinant of sociopathy, the siblings' behavior ought to be an even more potent predictor than friends', since association with siblings is more constant and less avoidable" (1966: 180). Robins's finding that siblings' behavior was not related to sociopathy while friends' behavior was led her to conclude that "the 'bad companion' phenomenon is a product of mutual choice between two antisocial children, not merely the result of the excess availability of antisocial children in some neighborhoods" (1966: 180). Robins's insights have important implications for research design, suggesting that a comparison of peer and sibling delinquent influence will go a long way toward distinguishing between social selection and social causation as an explanation of the peer-delinquency relationship.

Following Robins's logic, we therefore examine the joint effects of delinquent companions and siblings on delinquent behavior. The theoretical model of delinquent associations is shown in the bottom part of Figure 5.1. As even differential association theory hypothesizes (see, for example, Sutherland and Cressey, 1978), it is not random or fleeting contacts with delinquent associates that are criminogenic, or even delinquent friends per se. Rather, what is crucial are contacts characterized by frequency, duration, and intensity of association with the delinquent peers. In this regard, Agnew (1991: 49) argues that intensity is closely related to Hirschi's bond of attachment—"the affection and respect the adolescent has toward others." Thus, the critical test involves attachment to peers and siblings who are themselves delinquent.

The model also posits that in the same manner as certain structural background factors (such as parental criminality, family size, mobility) weaken family social control, they will foster attachment to delinquent peers and siblings. Hence, structural background in our model should be linked to delinquency in part through its effects on peer and sibling delinquent attachment, which in turn increases delinquency. In addition, we will assess self-selection or "birds of a feather" processes by testing the effects of peers and siblings on delinquency relative to social control processes of family and school. If social control theorists are right, the effects of family and school should remain large even when delinquent associations are introduced in the model. Weak ties in one setting, such as the family, may spread to other settings, such as peers (Hirschi, 1969: 131, 201), possibly rendering spurious the association between delinquent peer attachment and delinquency.

EMPIRICAL MEASURES

The structural background variables in this chapter are the same nine variables used in Chapter 4, where they are fully described: household crowding, family disruption, family size, mother's employment outside of the home, family socioeconomic status, foreign-born status, residential mobility, and father's and mother's criminality/alcoholism.

School Variables

There are two school process variables in our analysis. The first, labeled "attachment to school," is a standardized z-score measure (range = −2.41 to 2.80) that combines the boy's attitude toward school and the boy's academic ambition. These two constituent variables are highly correlated ($r = .72$, $p < .05$). The source information for this composite measure was derived from the self-report interview with each boy. The second process variable, labeled "school performance," is also a z-score measure (range = −3.46 to 1.85) that combines last year's grades along with the number of times the boy was not promoted to the next grade ($r = -.40$, $p < .05$).[3] This information was culled from the social investigations by the Gluecks' research team, which included interviews with the boy's teachers as well as an examination of all school records.

As expected theoretically, school attachment is positively related to school performance ($r = .56$, $p < .05$), providing evidence of construct validity. However, there is still sufficient independent variation (discriminant validity) so we can reliably establish the separate effects of each construct. In addition, recall that all subjects were matched on general intelligence (IQ). By design, then, measured IQ cannot differentiate delinquents from nondelinquents. Rather, our purpose is to examine school performance independent of IQ.

Peer/Sibling Variables

To establish the role of peers and siblings in delinquency, we examined several variables in the preliminary analysis. With regard to siblings,

Table 5.1   Cross-tabulation of Sibling Delinquency by Attachment to
             Siblings, and Delinquency of Peers by Attachment to Peers

A.		Attachment to Sibling(s)	
	Low	Medium	High
Delinquent Sibling(s)			
No	(62)	(375)	(33)
	38%	55%	57%
Yes	(101)	(312)	(25)
	62%	45%	43%
		Gamma = −.26, p < .05	

B.		Attachment to Peer(s)	
	Low	Medium	High
Delinquent Peer(s)			
No	(40)	(131)	(273)
	34%	49%	57%
Yes	(77)	(135)	(206)
	66%	51%	43%
		Gamma = −.25, p < .05	

we first ascertained whether or not the boy had any brothers or sisters
who were involved in delinquent activity. The second variable of interest was a measure of the boy's relations to his siblings, ranging from
strong attachment to hostile feelings. The information for these measures was derived from the home interview by the Gluecks' research
team, which was supplemented by record checks of various agencies.

We then created a variable that attempts to measure sibling delinquent influence by assigning a one to those boys who had medium or
high levels of attachment to delinquent siblings (N = 337). Those who
had no delinquent siblings or low attachment to siblings were assigned
a zero (N = 571).[4] Our main analysis focuses on the composite measure
since it captures the most appropriate theoretical contrast. This contrast
can be seen visually in the cross-tabulation of delinquency of siblings
by attachment to siblings in Panel A of Table 5.1 (cells 5 and 6 versus
cells 1 to 4). Although there is a moderate negative relationship
between the two source variables (gamma = −.26), what is at issue
theoretically is the combination of high attachment and sibling delin-

quency. (Nevertheless, our analysis below reports on results when constituent measures are individually introduced.)

Our second major construct is peer influence. The Gluecks' research team asked both the parents and the boys themselves about delinquent companions. Unfortunately, the bivariate relationship between delinquency of the subject and delinquent friends is so high that it suggests a tautology, especially when considered in conjunction with the Gluecks' research design. For parental reports, the phi is .80; for self-reports, the phi is .77. The combined parental and self-report measure of delinquency and delinquent friends reveals a phi of .91. Thus, the available measures of delinquent companions are virtually coterminous with delinquency and do not help us address the issue of causal ordering at all. In other words, the correlation tells us nothing that we did not already know from scores of prior studies—delinquents tend to associate with and commit delinquent acts with other delinquents.

To deal with this problem, we constructed a proxy variable for delinquent peer attachment by using the same logic employed for delinquent sibling attachment. The relations of the boy to his schoolmates were measured by the Gluecks on a three-point scale ranging from strong attachment to hostile feelings. Information on delinquent friends was derived from the self-report interview, and adjustment to schoolmates was culled from teacher reports. The latter measure is crucial for many reasons, not the least of which is that little work has been devoted to the *quality* of friendships among boys in delinquent groups (Campbell, 1980: 377; Giordano et al., 1986).

Although attachment to peers and delinquency of peers are negatively related as predicted by control theory, the key cell of interest once again for delinquent influence is that defined by high level of attachment to peers and delinquency of peers (see Panel B, Table 5.1). Therefore, we created a dichotomous measure that taps whether or not the boy had any companions who were involved in any delinquent activity *and* to whom the boy was also highly attached. Some 206 boys met this criterion. Those with no delinquent peers and those with low levels of attachment to peers regardless of their delinquency were assigned a zero.

To be sure, the resulting indicators of sibling and peer delinquent attachment suffer limitations. First, information on the number and sex of companions and siblings is not available in a computerized format. Nor do we know the proportion of peers/siblings involved in delinquent activity.[5] Second, we do not have available the exact ages of each sibling or each companion.[6] Third, and most crucial, delinquents still could have systematically sought out and attached themselves to other delinquents; in this case the association between delinquency and delinquent peer attachment would be noncausal.

Despite these limitations, our peer and sibling measures in conjunction with the research design allow us to counteract many of the pitfalls of previous research. Hirschi (1969: 159) has argued that delinquents are weakly attached to delinquent friends, undermining the logic of differential association and learning theory, which paints a picture of warm and supportive relations among delinquent peers (see also Rowe, 1985: 224). But, by restricting the scoring of our indicator so that we focus on those who are in fact highly attached to delinquent peers (and there are over 200 boys who fit this bill), we come closer to the theoretical construct envisioned by learning theory. We can also compare the effects of delinquent peer attachment with delinquent sibling attachment. As Robins (1966) has argued, if sibling delinquency has no effect relative to delinquent peers, the evidence suggests self-selection and a diminished causal role for the influence of peers.

Even if the delinquent attachment indicators are flawed, our research design provides a strict test of a social control model. Namely, we can assess the effects of peers and siblings relative to social control processes of family and school. If social control theory is right, the effects of family and school should remain large despite introducing controls for attachment to delinquent associates. By contrast, if the direct effects of family and school social control processes remain when peer and sibling delinquent attachments are controlled, then the hypothesis stemming from learning theory that delinquent associations mediate all prior effects on delinquency is not supported (see Matsueda, 1982). On balance, then, the Glueck data permit further refinement of our basic theoretical model through the consideration of rival interpretations.

SCHOOL PROCESS AND DELINQUENCY

Table 5.2 presents the OLS multiple regression results of the effects of the nine background characteristics on two dimensions of school process—attachment to school and school performance. The data show that family size, residential mobility, mother's employment outside of the home, and father's crime and drinking have significant negative

Table 5.2   OLS Linear Regression of School Process Variables on Structural
Background Factors (N = 907)

| Background Factors | SCHOOL PROCESS | | | |
| | Attachment | | Grades | |
	β	t-ratio	β	t-ratio
Residential mobility	−.13	−3.46*	−.08	−1.97*
Family size	−.16	−4.57*	−.08	−2.29*
Crowding	.02	.50	−.05	−1.36
Family disruption	−.03	−.98	−.02	−.47
Mother's employment	−.09	−2.79*	−.05	−1.46
Family SES	.15	4.00*	.07	1.86
Foreign-born	−.01	−.26	−.09	−2.66*
Father's deviance	−.09	−2.39*	−.04	−.97
Mother's deviance	−.07	−1.95	−.10	−2.80*
	R^2 = .16		R^2 = .08	

*$p < .05$.

effects on the boy's attachment to school. Furthermore, the data reveal that family socioeconomic status has a fairly large positive effect on school attachment (β = .15). Overall, then, the data suggest that large families, economic disadvantage, weak ties to the community, and parental deviance all weaken a boy's attachment to school.

The results for school performance in columns 3 and 4 yield a fairly similar pattern to that found for school attachment. Family size, mobility, and mother's deviance depress grades. On the other hand, foreign-born status has a negative effect and parental SES an insignificant effect on performance. Although the effects of structural background factors on school performance are less than the effects on attachment to school as evidenced by the R^2 statistics, overall the findings support the idea that structural variables have important effects on the schooling and educational process—especially family size (Blake, 1989).

The full structural equation results for official delinquency are presented in Table 5.3. Both the OLS and ML regression estimates show that attachment to school has a very large negative effect on delinquency (OLS β = −.44), whereas there is no significant effect for school performance. The lack of an effect for school performance may be the result of the Gluecks' sampling design (that is, matching on IQ), but Olweus (1983) also found no relationship between poor grades and

Table 5.3   OLS Linear and ML Logistic Regression of Official Delinquency
Status on Structural Background Factors and School Process
(N = 907)

| Full Model | OFFICIAL DELINQUENCY STATUS | | | |
| | OLS Linear | | ML Logistic[a] | |
	β	t-ratio	b	t-ratio
Residential mobility	.14	4.42*	.10	3.99*
Family size	.03	1.16	.04	1.01
Crowding	.02	.86	.22	1.27
Family disruption	.05	1.76	.36	1.73
Mother's employment	.05	1.93	.39	1.97*
Family SES	−.08	−2.86*	−.18	−2.77*
Foreign-born	.04	1.54	.31	1.56
Father's deviance	.07	2.41*	.26	2.05*
Mother's deviance	.10	3.49*	.54	3.44*
School attachment	−.44	−13.84*	−.68	−10.77*
School grades	−.04	−1.26	−.06	−.94
	OLS R^2 = .45		ML model χ^2 = 494, 11 d.f.	

a. Entries for ML Logistic "b" are the raw maximum-likelihood logistic coefficients;
"t-ratios" are coefficients divided by S.E.
*$p < .05$.

aggression. The results also indicate that although many of the structural background factors have no effect on delinquency, residential
mobility, SES, and mother's and father's deviance all reveal consistent
direct effects in the expected theoretical direction. Apparently, school
process does not mediate structural background in the same manner as
does family informal social control. As noted earlier, this result makes
sense given the nature of the structural variables available for analysis.

One interesting pattern does deserve emphasis, however. For both
the OLS and ML results, the family size effect on delinquency—which
was unmediated by family social control—appears to be accounted for
by school attachment. Apparently, large families foster lower school
attachment (cf. Blake, 1989; Coleman, 1988), which in turn increases
delinquency. The effects of other background variables like residential
mobility and family SES on delinquency are only partially mediated by
school attachment in the direction predicted by our theoretical model.

As in Chapter 4, we examined the same model using a series of

Table 5.4   OLS Linear Regression of Unofficial Delinquency Reports on
            Structural Background Factors and School Process (N = 907)

	UNOFFICIAL DELINQUENCY			
	Self-reported	Parent-reported	Teacher-reported	Total reported
Full Model	β	β	β	β
Residential mobility	.14*	.11*	.13*	.14*
Family size	.07*	.04	.01	.06*
Crowding	−.01	.04	.01	.01
Family disruption	.06*	.09*	−.02	.07*
Mother's employment	.04	.05	.01	.05
Family SES	−.05	−.04	−.09*	−.06
Foreign-born	−.01	.02	−.01	−.01
Father's deviance	.07*	.07*	.08*	.08*
Mother's deviance	.09*	.08*	.03	.09*
School attachment	−.49*	−.35*	−.31*	−.47*
School grades	.01	−.04	−.12*	−.03
	R^2 = .46	R^2 = .32	R^2 = .29	R^2 = .47

*$p < .05$.

alternative measures—self-reported, parent-reported, teacher-reported, and a summary measure of unofficial delinquency and other misbehavior. These results are displayed in Table 5.4. In general the basic results are replicated: the strongest effect on delinquency regardless of reporter is attachment to school. And again, except for teacher-reported delinquency, the effect of school performance on unofficial delinquency is nil.

With regard to the background factors, we find that consistent direct effects appear across all measures for two variables—mobility and father's criminality/drunkenness. Supportive of social control theory, disruption of community ties and father's deviance appear linked to delinquency both directly and indirectly through the weakening of school-based attachment. Family disruption and mother's criminality/drunkenness also show significant direct effects for self- and parent-reported delinquency. The main difference from Table 5.3 is that family size shows a small positive effect on self- and total-reported delinquency. Generally speaking, though, using unofficial measures of delinquency does not change the basic substantive findings.

We now turn to a replication of the major results by considering the

Table 5.5   Replication of OLS Regression Model of School Process and
             Structural Background Factors, Controlling for Early Childhood
             Difficulty and Disruptive Antisocial Behavior (N = 804)

| | SCHOOL PROCESS | | | |
| | Attachment | | Grades | |
Structural and Childhood Factors	β	t-ratio	β	t-ratio
Residential mobility	−.11	−2.78*	−.06	−1.46
Family size	−.19	−5.18*	−.10	−2.52*
Crowding	.04	1.25	−.03	−.89
Family disruption	−.01	−.30	−.01	−.26
Mother's employment	−.07	−2.22*	−.02	−.66
Family SES	.08	2.18*	.02	.61
Foreign-born	.00	.18	−.07	−1.89
Father's deviance	−.07	−1.85	−.02	−.57
Mother's deviance	−.06	−1.72	−.09	−2.32*
Early onset	−.10	−3.09*	−.06	−1.65
Difficult child	−.08	−2.48*	−.07	−2.16*
Tantrums	−.20	−5.94*	−.19	−5.38*
	$R^2 = .22$		$R^2 = .12$	

*$p < .05$.

role of early childhood antisocial behavior in explaining patterns of schooling and delinquency. As even the Gluecks remarked many years ago (1964: 23), poor school attachment may be a consequence of misbehavior more than a cause. Teachers may be particularly sensitive to unruly and difficult children, leading to rejection of the child or at least a strained teacher-student relationship. All of this undermines the attachment of the child to the school, and indeed the child's performance in the school. A similar argument for reciprocal effects has been made more recently by Olweus (1983) and Liska and Reed (1985).

We cannot estimate simultaneous equations, but we can examine what may be more relevant—the potential confounding role of child self-selection via early misbehavior. To accomplish this, we show in Table 5.5 the effects of child tantrums, early onset, and childhood difficulty on school process, controlling for structural background. The results suggest a substantial role for "child effects" not just in the family (Lytton, 1990) but in school as well. In particular, all three child variables have significant negative effects on school attachment—those boys with a difficult temperament, violent tantrums, and early onset

Table 5.6   Replication of OLS Linear and ML Logistic Regression of
Delinquency on Structural Background Factors, School Process,
and Early Childhood Difficulty and Disruptive Antisocial
Behavior (N = 804)

| | OFFICIAL DELINQUENCY STATUS (0, 1) | | UNOFFICIAL DELINQUENCY REPORTS (1–26) | |
| | ML Logistic[a] | | OLS Linear | |
Full Model	b	t-ratio	β	t-ratio
Residential mobility	.07	2.44*	.12	3.69*
Family size	.08	1.43	.08	2.89*
Crowding	.13	.70	−.02	−.61
Family disruption	.30	1.27	.06	2.13*
Mother's employment	.49	2.18*	.06	2.35*
Family SES	−.20	−2.61*	−.04	−1.51
Foreign-born	.16	.72	−.01	−.50
Father's deviance	.24	1.73	.06	2.09*
Mother's deviance	.52	2.95*	.09	3.08*
School attachment	−.64	−9.17*	−.42	−12.81*
School grades	−.02	−.22	−.00	−.04
Early onset	2.52	3.13*	.12	4.57*
Difficult child	.95	4.49*	.10	3.91*
Tantrums	1.36	4.64*	.13	4.72*
	ML model χ^2 = 502, 14 d.f.		OLS R^2 = .52	

a. Entries for ML Logistic "b" are the raw maximum-likelihood logistic coefficients; "t-ratios" are coefficients divided by S.E.

*p < .05.

were less likely to bond to the school and, although the results are somewhat weaker, to perform well.

It is perhaps surprising then to observe that our basic structural model holds up—despite the strong child effects, school attachment is still influenced by structural features such as mobility, employment, SES, and especially family size. Indeed, family size continues to exert a relatively large negative effect on school attachment. Although early patterns of childhood misconduct do seem to disrupt the schooling process, the effects of structural background largely retain their salience.

Table 5.6 displays the full model of school process, child effects, and structural background on official delinquency status and the total measure of unofficial delinquency. As in Chapter 4, all measures of early childhood difficulty/misbehavior have significant and rather substantial effects on delinquency. Independent of these child effects, however, school attachment again has the largest effect on delinquency. This basic result maintains regardless of how delinquency is measured. Moreover, the results are unchanged even if we substitute early onset of truancy for early onset of general misbehavior (data not shown).[7]

Therefore, we tentatively conclude that school attachment, but not school performance, is a salient inhibitory force in delinquency causation, independent not only of structural background but childhood effects as well.

THE EFFECTS OF PEERS AND SIBLINGS

We now turn to a consideration of peers and siblings in the explanation of delinquency. We begin by asking the question: what background factors explain attachment to delinquent peers and siblings? Table 5.7 provides an initial and fairly straightforward answer about the struc-

Table 5.7   ML Logistic Regression Models[a] of Peer and Sibling Delinquent Attachment on Structural Background Factors

| | DELINQUENT ATTACHMENT | | | |
| | Peers (N = 836) | | Siblings (N = 889) | |
Background Factors	b	t-ratio	b	t-ratio
Residential mobility	−.01	−.88	.01	.89
Family size	.16	3.66*	.39	8.61*
Crowding	−.04	−.26	−.25	−1.75
Family disruption	.14	.76	−.04	−.23
Mother's employment	.27	1.52	.46	2.73*
Family SES	−.09	−1.48	−.03	−.59
Foreign-born	−.09	−.52	.70	4.12*
Father's deviance	.24	1.99*	.45	4.05*
Mother's deviance	.18	1.32	.38	2.86*
	ML model χ^2 = 40.56, 9 d.f.		ML model χ^2 = 178.47, 9 d.f.	

a. Entries for ML Logistic "b" are the raw maximum-likelihood logistic coefficients; "t-ratios" are coefficients divided by S.E.

*p < .05.

tural sources of delinquent associations. Namely, large families and parental deviance significantly increase the log-odds of being attached to either a delinquent peer or a delinquent sibling. The positive effect of family size on sibling delinquency is expected, but the large effect on peer delinquency is somewhat surprising. The effect of parental deviance is also intriguing; apparently, crime runs not just in large families, but in those where the parents are criminal as well.[8] Paternal deviance even increases the odds of a youth being attached to delinquent peers, suggesting a general process of family effects.

Table 5.8 explores the effect of both peer and sibling delinquent attachment on delinquency. As in earlier models, we focus on the official delinquency criterion (ML logistic coefficients, columns 1 and 2) and total unofficial delinquency (OLS β's, columns 3 and 4). When only structural background is controlled, the results are quite straightforward: sibling delinquent attachment has an insignificant influence

Table 5.8　OLS Linear and ML Logistic Regression of Delinquency on Structural Background Factors and Peer/Sibling Delinquent Attachment (N = 762)

	OFFICIAL DELINQUENCY STATUS (0, 1)		UNOFFICIAL DELINQUENCY REPORTS (1–26)	
	ML Logistic[a]		OLS Linear	
Full Model	b	t-ratio	β	t-ratio
Residential mobility	.12	4.83*	.20	5.30*
Family size	.14	2.65*	.12	3.39*
Crowding	−.12	−.17	−.03	−.99
Family disruption	.30	1.43	.06	1.73
Mother's employment	.34	1.64	.04	1.33
Family SES	−.18	−2.63*	−.07	−2.12*
Foreign-born	.04	1.78	.01	.37
Father's deviance	.07	2.71*	.13	3.52*
Mother's deviance	.48	2.88*	.11	3.25*
Delinquent peer attachment	2.43	8.85*	.31	10.42*
Delinquent sibling attachment	.39	1.89	.02	.76
	ML model χ^2 = 330, 11 d.f.		OLS R^2 = .34	

a. Entries for ML Logistic "b" are the raw maximum-likelihood logistic coefficients; "t-ratios" are coefficients divided by S.E.
*$p < .05$.

on delinquency whereas attachment to delinquent peers has a large positive effect. Taking a simple learning theory approach, we might conclude that delinquent associates cause delinquency. But, if this were the case, why doesn't attachment to delinquent siblings also increase delinquency? As Robins (1966) argued many years ago, to the extent that sibling delinquency has no influence relative to peers, the data suggest homogamy in friendship selection (that is, flocking based on similarity in behavior and attitudes). After all, one cannot in a meaningful sense be said to select one's siblings; moreover, contact with siblings is generally quite frequent and perhaps unavoidable. Robins's position is given further credence by the fact that if we substitute sibling delinquency regardless of the degree of attachment (that is, a measure of simple exposure), it still has no effect once relevant factors are controlled (data not shown). For example, controlling for child effects, family process, school attachment, and delinquent peer attachment, sibling delinquency has a beta of only .03 ($p > .20$) on the total measure of a youth's unofficial delinquency.

We also examined numerous models in which the interaction of delinquent peers/siblings and attachment was considered. In general, interaction terms did not improve the fit of models. Moreover, we re-estimated all models for the subgroup of boys who were not highly attached to delinquent peers (by definition, there is no variation in attachment among those boys assigned a 1 for delinquent attachment). For boys with medium to low attachment to delinquent peers, sibling delinquency still had no effect ($\beta = -.04$) on total unofficial delinquency as compared to a large effect of peer delinquency alone ($\beta = .34$, $p < .05$). Once again, the finding that sibling delinquency has no effect relative to peer delinquency—even among those boys who are not closely attached to delinquent peers—suggests self-selection and the group nature of delinquency rather than a causal effect of peers.

In short, neither having nor being attached to delinquent siblings appears to increase the likelihood of delinquency independent of structural background and peer delinquency. This pattern raises questions about delinquent influence as a causal force. Note further that Table 5.8 does not even control for what may account for deviant peer selection in the first place—delinquent predispositions and informal family social control. Indeed, given the theoretical concerns about birds of a feather flocking together (self-selection), it is desirable to control for early childhood antisocial behavior in peer influence models. What is more crucial, what happens when family social controls are considered simultaneously with delinquent peer attachment? Does delinquent peer attachment mediate the effect of family social control on delinquency?

FINAL MODELS AND VALIDATION

In an attempt to provide final resolution of these questions, we turn to specification of a refined model that allows us to consider key dimensions of social structural background, child effects, and the intervening constructs of family social control, school attachment, and peer delinquency. To simplify the presentation, we estimated a series of "trimmed" models that eliminated factors that were consistently unrelated to delinquency in full models (see also Chapter 4). For intervening variables, these included sibling delinquency and school performance. For structural background, the factors of family disruption, mother's employment, SES, and parental deviance also exhibited insignificant direct effects on delinquency once informal family process was controlled. It should be reiterated, though, that just because a factor has an insignificant direct effect does not mean it is unimportant. On the contrary, we have already demonstrated the indirect role of structural background in understanding delinquency.

Table 5.9 displays the final trimmed models that represent the significant "direct-effect" predictors of delinquency. These factors are classified under the general dimensions of child effects, social structure, and social process. We see consistent positive effects of childhood predispositions toward antisocial behavior on later delinquency. Specifically, those boys who had an early onset of misbehavior, a difficult temperament as a child, and violent tantrums were more likely to be both officially committed as delinquents and to have high levels of unofficial delinquency. These findings again underscore the importance of early onset and conduct disorder on adolescent delinquency (Loeber and LeBlanc, 1990; Lytton, 1990).

Variations in adolescent delinquency not accounted for by child effects are nonetheless strongly related to social processes and to some extent to structural background. Note that crowding has a consistent negative effect on delinquency regardless of measurement source. All else being equal, crowded homes apparently are more conducive to delinquency control. Mobility has a direct effect on unofficial delinquency (Braithwaite, 1989), while family size has a small but not

Table 5.9   Final Best-fitting Models of Official Delinquency Status and Unofficial
Delinquency Reports Regressed on Key Structural Factors, Family and
School Process, Early Childhood Difficulty/Antisocial Conduct, and Peer
Delinquent Attachment (N = 595)

| Final Model | OFFICIAL DELINQUENCY STATUS (0, 1) | | UNOFFICIAL DELINQUENCY REPORTS (1–26) | |
| | ML Logistic[a] | | OLS Linear | |
	b	t-ratio	β	t-ratio
Child Effects				
Early onset	1.48	2.00*	.07	2.84*
Difficult child	.94	3.03*	.05	2.04*
Tantrums	1.28	3.47*	.10	3.83*
Structure				
Residential mobility	NI		.10	3.50*
Family size	.17	2.11*	NI	
Crowding	−.62	−2.23*	−.06	−2.44*
Social Process				
Parent erratic/threatening	.47	4.36*	.13	4.41*
Mother's supervision	−1.05	−5.06*	−.21	−6.17*
Parental rejection	1.18	4.42*	.12	4.18*
School attachment	−.52	−5.86*	−.30	−10.29*
Delinquent peer attachment	2.99	7.04*	.23	8.67*
	ML model χ^2 = 514, 10 d.f.		OLS R^2 = .62	

a. Entries for ML Logistic "b" are the raw maximum-likelihood logistic coefficients; "t-ratios" are
coefficients divided by S.E.
NI = not included in model specification.
*p < .05.

inconsequential effect on official delinquency. Proportional change estimates (see Petersen, 1985) reveal that for each additional family member, the risk of official delinquency increases by 8 percent.

Without much doubt, however, the strongest and most consistent
effects on delinquency flow from the social processes of family, school,
and peers. Erratic, threatening, and harsh discipline, low levels of supervision, and parental rejection all independently contribute to delinquency. In addition, school attachment has large negative effects on
delinquency independent of family social control. And attachment to
delinquent peers exerts a significant positive effect on both indicators

of delinquency, regardless of family and school process.[9] Its magnitude is quite large—having delinquent friends increases the probability of becoming officially delinquent by 90 percent. The OLS models show similar relative magnitudes: school attachment, mother's supervision, and delinquent peer attachment all have t-ratios greater than 5. Exclusive of other factors, the largest effect is school attachment ($\beta = -.30$).

As in Chapter 4, we examined alternative models and procedures to assess the basic validity of results. This involved a re-estimation of all models using both mean substitution and pairwise deletion of missing values, with a dummy variable distinguishing those cases that were missing in the original models. Again, the results were substantively identical, even though there are some 400 cases missing in Table 5.9. For example, in the mean substitution model (N = 1,000) the standardized effects of school attachment, supervision, and delinquent peer attachment on unofficial delinquency were –.31, –.23, and .20, respectively (cf. Table 5.9). Not only were the results virtually identical, but the dummy variable for missing data was weakly related to the dependent and independent variables. In fact, the missing data indicator was correlated at less than –.10 with all variables. Therefore, the final model of Table 5.9 does not appear biased by the exclusion of missing data.

Following the strategy used in Chapter 4, we also re-estimated the final delinquency models with additional controls for age, IQ, mesomorphy, and extroversion. Once again the results were largely invariant regardless of the introduction of these individual-difference constructs. School attachment, mother's supervision, and delinquent peer attachment continued to exert the strongest effects on unofficial and official delinquency.[10] School attachment had significant negative effects on delinquency even when the analysis was repeated in three different age groups (< 14, 14–15, 15 and older). We examined the potential interaction with age because any potential reciprocal effect of delinquency on school attachment (cf. Liska and Reed, 1985) would arguably be less likely in the early grades. The evidence revealed a consistent negative effect for each age group.

Finally, as a strict test we repeated the key analyses *within* the group of official delinquents. Although the variance in official delinquency status is by definition eliminated, we can still examine variations in unofficial delinquency. By controlling official delinquency status, we eliminated any retrospective biases that occurred because raters knew the boy was a delinquent. Potential effects of incarceration on the independent variables were also addressed (see Hirschi and Selvin, 1967) by controlling for the exact number of days each delinquent boy was incarcerated as a juvenile.

The within-group results confirmed the predictive power of our major variables. Controlling for incarceration time, the largest predictors of unofficial delinquency among the official delinquents were school attachment (β = −.24), supervision (β = −.13), parental rejection (β = .13), and delinquent peer attachment (β = .12). All these variables were significant at $p < .05$. Considering the restricted variation in delinquency and the controls for incarceration time (itself correlated with delinquency), the results provide surprisingly strong support for the final model in Table 5.9. In particular, retrospective bias and incarceration time do *not* account for the effects of informal family and school social controls on delinquency. If anything, retrospective biases appear to contaminate childhood effects—tantrums, childhood difficulty, and early onset all had insignificant direct effects on unofficial delinquency among official delinquents in models where incarceration time was controlled.

CONCLUSIONS

We interpret the final model in Table 5.9 and attempts to challenge it as providing basic support for our general theoretical conception. First, the results are largely consistent across methods of delinquency measurement, alternative model specifications, and treatments of missing data. Second, as argued throughout this book, the effects of structural background are mostly indirect and hence mediated by intervening sources of social control. Third, child effects remain significant, but they do not undermine the importance of social control. Fourth, among the dimensions of informal social control processes, the family and school appear most important.

Of course, delinquent peer attachment cannot be ignored since it has significant and rather substantial direct effects on both official and unofficial delinquency. On the other hand, Table 5.9 clearly shows not only early "child effects" on delinquency that cannot be explained by social learning from peers, but also that the effects of family and school attachment are large and direct. In addition, further analysis reveals that the mother's supervision has the largest effect on attachment to delinquent peers (data not shown). This finding is expected from the perspective of social control theory, wherein family bonds are presumed to be causally prior to the formation of peer attachment. Combined with the knowledge that (1) sibling delinquency had little or no effect in prior analysis and (2) the delinquent peer attachment variable may still reflect birds of a feather flocking together, the results do not support a "pure" differential association/learning theory. That is, from the perspective of differential association theory, family, school, and other effects are fully mediated by learning in delinquent groups (see especially Matsueda, 1982).[11]

We therefore conclude that the basic tenets of our integrated theory of informal social control and delinquency are supported by the evidence. Substantively, the results suggest that when the bonds linking a youth to society—whether through the family or school—are weakened, the probability of delinquency is increased. Family ties—discipline, supervision, and attachment—are especially important; this supports the basic framework of Hirschi (1969), Gottfredson and Hirschi (1990), and Patterson (1982), not to mention the Gluecks themselves (1950). The results also support Braithwaite's linkage of labeling theory with the theory of reintegrative shaming, in that what seems particularly criminogenic is harsh, unreasoning, and punitive discipline combined with rejection of the child. Stigmatizing punishment, by the family as well as the State (see Chapter 7), appears to backfire.

CONTINUITY
IN BEHAVIOR
OVER TIME

6

n this chapter we explore the continuity between childhood misbehavior and later adult outcomes covering a variety of life domains. As reviewed in Chapter 1, there is considerable evidence favoring the proposition that individual differences in antisocial and criminal behavior emerge in childhood and remain stable across the life course (Olweus, 1979; Loeber, 1982; Huesmann et al., 1984; Gottfredson and Hirschi, 1990). Even as long as 50 years ago the Gluecks confirmed "the early genesis of antisocial careers" (1930: 143). Findings regarding behavioral continuity are thus supported by a rich body of empirical research spanning several decades (see also Robins, 1966, 1978; West and Farrington, 1977; Wolfgang et al., 1987).

Criminological research usually focuses on *homotypic continuity*—the continuity of similar behaviors or phenotypic attributes over time (Caspi and Bem, 1990: 553). Perhaps more interesting, the linkage between childhood misbehavior and adult outcomes is found across life domains that go well beyond the legal concept of crime. This phenomenon has been defined as *heterotypic continuity* (Caspi and Bem, 1990: 553)—the continuity of an inferred genotypic (that is, latent) attribute presumed to underlie diverse phenotypic (that is, manifest) behaviors. In particular, a specific antisocial behavior in childhood might not predict phenotypically similar behavior in later adulthood but may still be associated with behaviors that are conceptually consistent with that earlier behavior (Caspi and Moffitt, 1992). Although not always criminal per se, adult behaviors falling in this category might include excessive drinking, traffic violations, marital conflict, job instability, and harsh discipline of children. Gottfredson and Hirschi (1990: 91) invoke a similar idea when they refer to adult behaviors "analogous" to crime such as accidents, smoking, and sexual promiscuity that are hypothesized to result from a common factor—lack of self-control. In any case, the essence of heterotypic continuity is that individual characteristics in childhood (for example, ill-tempered behavior) will not only appear across time but will be manifested in a number of diverse situations.

It is presumed that antisocial children replicate their antisocial behavior in a variety of adult realms in part because of the differing reactions that antisocial behavior brings forth (Caspi, 1987). Maladaptive behaviors are "found in interactional styles that are sustained both by the progressive accumulation of their own consequences *(cumulative continuity)* and by evoking maintaining responses from others during reciprocal social interaction *(interactional continuity)*" (Caspi et al., 1987: 313, emphasis added). An example of interactional continuity occurs when a child with temper tantrums provokes angry and hostile reactions in parents and teachers, which in turn feeds back to trigger further antisocial behavior by the child. Cumulative continuity is generated by the negative structural consequences of delinquency for life chances. For example, arrest, official labeling, incarceration, and other negative life events associated with delinquency may lead to the "closing of doors" as far as opportunities go (for example, school failure, unemployment). Delinquent activities are also likely to sever *informal* social bonds to school, friends, and family (Thornberry, 1987).

Evidence for the behavioral coherence implied by heterotypic continuity is found in the study by Huesmann and colleagues (1984) where they report that childhood aggression was related not just to adult aggression but also to marital conflict, drunk driving, moving violations, and severe punishment of offspring. Other studies reporting a similar coalescence of deviant and criminal acts over time include West and Farrington (1977), Robins (1966), and Jessor, Donovan, and Costa (1991). It is interesting that the findings of heterotypic continuity generated largely by psychologists are quite consistent with criminological research showing little or no specialization in crime as people age (Wolfgang et al., 1972; Blumstein et al., 1986; Elliott et al., 1989; Osgood et al., 1988).

Moreover, there is limited although intriguing evidence supporting the cumulative continuity notion that childhood delinquency is linked to adult stratification outcomes—independent of childhood social class. Caspi (1987: 1211) found that the tendency toward explosive, undercontrolled behavior in childhood was recreated over time, especially in problems involving subordination (for example, in education, military, and work settings) and in situations that required negotiating interpersonal conflicts (for instance, marriage and parenting). Children displaying severe temper tantrums in childhood were especially likely to abort their involvement with education, and this in turn fostered problematic outcomes such as unemployment, job instability, and low income. In *Deviant Children Grown Up*, Lee Robins also found strong relations between childhood antisocial behavior and adult occupational status, job stability, income, and residential mobility (1966: 95–102). Robins went so far as to conclude that "antisocial behavior [in childhood] predicts class status more efficiently than class status predicts antisocial behavior" (1966: 305).

Overall, the evidence suggests that delinquent behavior is relatively stable across stages of the life course and that antisocial behavior in childhood predicts a wide range of troublesome adult outcomes. These findings support Hagan and Palloni's (1988: 90) argument that we need to examine how delinquent and criminal events mediate broader life trajectories, both criminal and noncriminal. We follow this reasoning by exploring the direction, magnitude, and diversity of continuity. That is, in this chapter we ask the question: do childhood behaviors have important ramifications in later adult life, whether criminal or noncriminal in form?

Drawing mainly on Caspi (1987), Robins (1966), Gottfredson and Hirschi (1990), and the theoretical framework sketched in Chapter 1, our thesis is threefold. The first hypothesis is that early antisocial behavior (for example, childhood misbehavior, juvenile delinquency) is linked to adult deviant behavior across a variety of settings including charges in the military (for instance, being AWOL), general deviance, alcohol abuse, and official crime. Second, we posit that childhood delinquency is also linked to dimensions of adult social bonding, including economic dependence, educational attainment, attachment to the labor force, and quality of marital experiences. Third, we argue that these outcomes occur independent of traditional sociological and psychological variables such as social class background, ethnicity, IQ, and even the family/school factors found to predict the onset of delinquency. Thus, we propose that crime, deviance, and informal social control are intimately linked over the full life course.

MEASURES OF CHILDHOOD AND ADULT ANTISOCIAL BEHAVIOR

In the analysis that follows we use three measures of antisocial behavior during childhood and adolescence. The first is official delinquency status as determined by the sampling design of the Glueck study. The second measure is the composite of self, parent, and teacher reports of delinquency and other misconduct for each subject in the study. The "total report" variable used in the cross-tabular analysis is a summary measure that we trichotomized into three groupings of involvement in delinquency. This measure captures both unofficial delinquency and incidents known to the police. The third measure—temper tantrums—is the same indicator used in Chapters 4 and 5. Again, this measure reflects the extent to which a child engaged in violent temper tantrums on a frequent basis while growing up. As noted earlier, this measure has been used in prior research on continuity in behavior over the life course (Caspi et al., 1987).

In our analysis of childhood effects on adult behavioral outcomes, we use several indicators of adult crime, deviance, and problematic adjustment to work, military service, and family relations. Descriptive information on most of these outcome measures is available in Glueck and Glueck (1968: 71–141).

Crime and Deviance

From the detailed criminal history information collected by the Gluecks' research team, we created a variable assessing whether or not the subject had an official arrest during the follow-up periods (ages 17–25 and 25–32). As reported in Chapter 3, we also coded the criminal histories of each subject from age 32 until age 45. A dichotomous variable was created to reflect an arrest for any crime in this period, excluding minor nonmoving auto violations (such as expired license/registration). The raw data came from the archives maintained by George Vaillant at Dartmouth College, and are based on official record searches in Massachusetts (see Chapter 3).

Using information derived from interviews conducted by the Gluecks' research team at each wave, we also created a measure of specific deviance focusing on excessive use of alcohol and/or drugs as well as a composite measure of general deviance that reflects frequent involvement in gambling and engagement in illicit sexual behavior (for example, use of prostitutes).

Military Service

Given the time period during which the Glueck study was conducted, a majority of the men served in some branch of the military (67 percent overall). Data were collected on the military experience for each of these subjects during the wave 2 investigation (age 25). The sources of information that were used included records from the specific branch of military service in question, Selective Service, State Adjutant General, Veterans Administration, and Red Cross in conjunction with interviews with the subject himself.

In this context, we are especially interested in the criminal and deviant behavior of the men while serving in the military (for example, in connection with desertion, AWOL, theft). Our dichotomous measure captures conduct that came to the attention of military authorities during military service. We also have available a measure of *frequent offending* (more than one official charge) and *serious offending* (felonies) while serving in the military. In addition, we were able to assess other important outcomes with respect to military service, namely, rank achieved and type of discharge.

School, Work, and Family Life

Eleven behavioral domains spanning economic, educational, employment, and family status were chosen to investigate continuity between childhood delinquency and a variety of adult outcomes during the age 17–25 and age 25–32 periods. Three refer to objective structural conditions of school, work, and family life—high school graduate, economic dependence, and divorce—and were derived from home interviews as well as record checks (Glueck and Glueck, 1968: 75, 81, 92, 100). The remaining measures refer to the quality or strength of social ties in adulthood—job stability, attachment to spouse, and commitment to occupational attainment. Described more fully in Chapter 7, information for these latter measures was also collected during the home interview and corroborated whenever possible by record checks. Descriptive statistics on key source variables collected during each follow-up period for both delinquent and control groups are found in Glueck and Glueck (1968: 71–130).

PATTERNS OF CONTINUITY

The data in Table 6.1 display the results of our examination of the continuity between delinquency and antisocial behavior in childhood and adult crime and deviance. The pattern is quite remarkable—all relationships are statistically significant ($p < .05$), in the direction pre-

Table 6.1 Relationships between Delinquent and Antisocial Behavior in Childhood (Up to Mean Age of 14) and Later Adult Crime and Deviance (Ages 17–45)

| | Childhood Antisocial Behavior | | | | | | |
| | Official Delinquency[a] | | Self-Parent-Teacher-reported Delinquency | | | Early Tantrums | |
	No	Yes	Low (0–3)	Medium (4–13)	High (14–30)	No	Yes
Adult Crime and Deviance							
% Arrested (17–25)	20	76	15	48	80	41	72
% Arrested (25–32)	14	61	10	36	66	32	58
% Arrested (32–45)	16	55	13	34	57	31	49
% Excessive alcohol/drug use (17–25)	11	41	7	23	47	22	37
% Excessive alcohol/drug use (25–32)	9	35	6	19	40	19	31
% General deviance (17–25)	5	25	5	15	24	11	29
% General deviance (25–32)	6	30	5	18	30	14	33

Note: All relationships are significant at $p < .05$.
a. Official delinquency status matched case-by-case on age, IQ, ethnicity, and neighborhood SES.

dicted, and substantively large. Arrests during the age 17–25 and age 25–32 periods are three to four times greater for those delinquent in childhood compared to nondelinquents. More impressive, the homotypic continuity of delinquency and crime extends well into middle adulthood. More than half of the official juvenile delinquents were arrested during ages 32–45, as compared to only 16 percent of the controls. Continuity in official criminal behavior is thus found over a 30-year period.

These results are replicated with the unofficial (that is, parent, teacher, self) reports of delinquency and early temper tantrums and with the unofficial reports of adult misbehavior. With respect to reports of excessive drinking and general deviance, delinquents were on average four times more likely than nondelinquents to later abuse alcohol and engage in deviance. In all cases, the relationships are monotonic across categories of unofficial delinquency. Youths reported to have high rates of delinquency in adolescence were more than five times as likely to be arrested at ages 17–25 than those with low reported rates of juvenile misbehavior, and almost seven times as likely to be arrested in young adulthood (25–32). Even temper tantrums in childhood exhibit a strong relationship with adult criminality, although to a lesser extent than official and unofficial delinquency. Regardless of which measure of delinquency or antisocial behavior in childhood is used, childhood misbehavior thus has a powerful relationship with adult crime and deviance.

The basic results in Table 6.1 were replicated using a wide variety of alternative measures and tests for magnitudes of relationship. For example, specific crime types in adulthood were examined along with specific crime types in adolescence. In general, this did not lessen the picture of stability painted in Table 6.1. As expected based on our earlier results (and much previous research), the lack of specialization in criminal activity serves to yield similar results over a wide range of crime measures. We also calculated RIOC (relative improvement over chance) measures of association for all 2 by 2 tables (see Farrington and Loeber, 1989). RIOC measures adjust for the base rate of delinquency; given the 50 percent base rate in the *Unraveling* research design, the RIOC measures did not tell us anything different than the cross-tabular figures did.

Table 6.2 presents data on the behavior of the Glueck men while in the military. We believe the military is a particularly important area

Table 6.2   Relationships between Delinquent and Antisocial Behavior in Childhood (Up to Mean Age of 14) and Later Adult Behavior in the Military (Ages 18–25)

| | Childhood Antisocial Behavior | | | | | | |
| | Official Delinquency[a] | | Self-Parent-Teacher-reported Delinquency | | | Early Tantrums | |
Adult Military Behavior	No	Yes	Low (0–3)	Medium (4–13)	High (14–30)	No	Yes
% Charged	20	64	18	35	70	33	62
% Frequent offender	4	29	3	12	33	12	25
% Serious offender	4	32	3	12	38	13	30
% Dishonorable discharge	4	30	2	12	34	12	29
% Rank of corporal or higher	64	36	67	46	37	54	41

Note: All relationships are significant at p < .05.
a. Official delinquency status matched case-by-case on age, IQ, ethnicity, and neighborhood SES.

because it represents a relatively homogeneous social environment in which to explore differences in behavior. In addition, World War II provided full employment for delinquents and nondelinquents alike and thus represents a "natural experiment" of the unemployment-crime hypothesis (Gottfredson and Hirschi, 1990: 164). With respect to criminal behavior, over 60 percent of the official delinquents were subsequently charged while in the military as compared to only 20 percent of the controls. The pattern emerges even more strongly when we examine frequency and seriousness of offending in the military: delinquent youths faced a seven-fold greater risk of frequent/serious offending compared to nondelinquents. Delinquents were also more likely to desert or to be absent without leave (AWOL) compared with their nondelinquent counterparts. As the Gluecks themselves noted, "The nature of the offenses with which the men were charged suggests that the same difficulty in adjusting satisfactorily to the discipline of parents and teachers and the demands of behavioral codes . . . persisted in the former juvenile delinquents when they were faced with the demands of adult life" (Glueck and Glueck, 1968: 136–137).

This general pattern is confirmed when unofficial delinquency is used as the measure of childhood misbehavior. For instance, 70 percent of those with reports of high unofficial offending in childhood were charged with offenses in the military, while only 18 percent of those with low unofficial offending reports were so charged. Those subjects who had engaged in severe temper tantrums as a child were about twice as likely to be charged in the military.

Not surprisingly, the delinquents were also more likely to later experience dishonorable discharges from the military than were the nondelinquents (30 percent versus 4 percent, respectively). A related finding is that those with delinquency in their childhood were far less likely to achieve the rank of corporal or higher in the Army (or the equivalent rank of seaman, first class, or higher while in the Navy) compared with their nondelinquent counterparts (36 percent versus 64 percent, respectively). Both of these patterns hold for unofficial delinquency as well as for temper tantrums. Overall, then, delinquent subjects did not fare nearly as well in the military as their nondelinquent counterparts. Regardless of the particular measure of childhood misbehavior used, the continuity of childhood misbehavior to adulthood thus emerges even while under military service.

Probably the most intriguing long-term correlates of child misbehav-

Table 6.3 Relationships between Delinquent and Antisocial Behavior in Childhood (Up to Mean Age of 14) and Later Adult Outcomes Relating to School, Work, and Family (Ages 17–32)

| | Childhood Antisocial Behavior | | | | | | |
| | Official Delinquency[a] | | Self-Parent-Teacher-reported Delinquency | | | Early Tantrums | |
	No	Yes	Low (0–3)	Medium (4–13)	High (14–30)	No	Yes
Adult School, Work, and Family Outcomes							
% High school graduate	34	2	39	13	2	22	3
% Weak occupational commitment (17–25)	39	74	35	55	77	51	71
% Weak occupational commitment (25–32)	34	64	33	43	69	43	65
% Economically dependent (17–25)	6	29	5	17	31	14	29
% Economically dependent (25–32)	11	39	8	21	44	19	43
% Low job stability (17–25)	19	47	16	32	51	27	50
% Low job stability (25–32)	16	50	12	29	56	27	51
% Divorced/separated (17–25)	5	22	5	9	26	12	21
% Divorced/separated (25–32)	12	27	10	15	33	16	32
% Weak attachment to spouse (17–25)	14	49	12	26	56	26	54
% Weak attachment to spouse (25–32)	22	52	18	35	57	31	56

Note: All relationships are significant at $p < .05$.
a. Official delinquency status matched case-by-case on age, IQ, ethnicity, and neighborhood SES.

ior are found in a wide range of later adult domains not typically considered by criminologists. Table 6.3 displays data for several such behaviors spanning educational, economic, employment, and family domains in an effort to illustrate the generality of the link between childhood delinquency and adult behavior. The Glueck data show that delinquents (official and unofficial) were much less likely than nondelinquents to finish high school by age 25. The same is true for those who engaged in temper tantrums as a child.

With respect to employment, for both delinquency measures delinquent boys were at least three times more likely than nondelinquents to generate a history of unstable employment at ages 25–32. For those delinquent in childhood, about half at each wave experienced job instability as an adult. Similarly, delinquency in childhood is related to economic dependence (for example, receiving welfare) in young adulthood (ages 17–25) and later adulthood (ages 25–32).

In terms of family life as an adult, delinquents were roughly three to five times more likely to get divorced or separated from their spouses as were nondelinquents. A similar pattern emerges when total reported misbehavior is used in addition to early tantrums. In fact, the percentage of men who became divorced was twice as high among those with a history of temper tantrums compared to those with no temper tantrums. We also found that half or more of those delinquent in childhood (whether official or unofficial) had weak attachment to their spouses, compared to less than 25 percent of the control group sample. Even the occurrence of early tantrums in childhood is related to weak attachment to the spouse as an adult (54 percent versus 26 percent at wave 2 and 56 percent versus 31 percent at wave 3).

MULTIVARIATE PREDICTIONS

To this point the data clearly underscore the continuity of delinquent behavior from adolescence to adulthood. However, an interesting question remains: what is the role of informal social controls and early "child effects" in understanding continuities? As we have shown in Chapters 4 and 5, through their effects on delinquency, there is an association of family factors and child effects (such as erratic parenting, lack of supervision, difficult temperament) with later adult crime. For example, the gammas reflecting the relationship between trichotomized measures of mother's supervision, attachment to parent, and parental rejection (see Table 4.2) and arrest at ages 17–25 are –.60, –.40, and .52, respectively (all $p < .05$). The corresponding gammas for arrest at ages 25–32 are –.51, –.34, and .46 (again, all $p < .05$). Moreover, the percentage of boys with erratic and harsh/threatening parents who were later arrested as adults was approximately double that of boys whose parents used consistent, warm, and nonphysical forms of punishment.

The unknown is whether adolescent delinquency mediates the long-term relationship between family factors and adult crime. If it does so fully, then family factors should have no effects on adult crime once delinquency is controlled. Our theoretical framework combined with the extensive analyses in earlier chapters of the origins of delinquency

Table 6.4   ML Logistic Coefficients and *T*-ratios Predicting Arrest in Adulthood (Ages 17–25, 25–32, 32–45) within Delinquent and Control Group Samples by Unofficial Delinquency, Child Effects, and Major Family Social Control Factors in Adolescence

A. Child/Juvenile Factors	Adult Delinquent-group Arrests					
	Ages 17–25		Ages 25–32		Ages 32–45	
Unofficial delinquency	.10	(3.06)*	.08	(2.70)*	.08	(2.79)*
Supervision	.08	(.36)	–.11	(–.58)	–.12	(–.67)
Erratic parenting	–.12	(–1.12)	–.02	(–.20)	.15	(1.51)
Parental rejection	.24	(1.27)	–.01	(–.06)	.00	(.02)
Attachment to parent	.10	(.56)	.03	(.16)	–.06	(–.39)
Early onset	.28	(.63)	.09	(.24)	.09	(.25)
Difficult child	–.20	(–.75)	.08	(.35)	.39	(1.64)
Tantrums	.42	(1.48)	.30	(1.20)	–.03	(–.12)
Model χ^2, 8 d.f.	17.6		11.8		18.1	

B. Child/Juvenile Factors	Adult Control-group Arrests					
	Ages 17–25		Ages 25–32		Ages 32–45	
Unofficial delinquency	.25	(4.56)*	.27	(4.59)*	.16	(2.91)*
Supervision	–.26	(–1.23)	.04	(.14)	–.41	(–1.62)
Erratic parenting	.18	(1.90)	–.02	(–.17)	–.16	(–1.49)
Parental rejection	–.35	(–.98)	–.40	(–.90)	–.35	(–.84)
Attachment to parent	–.02	(–.09)	.20	(.68)	–.03	(–.10)
Early onset	–5.86	(–.46)	–4.91	(–.38)	.34	(.26)
Difficult child	–.90	(–2.54)*	–.30	(–.79)	–.26	(–.71)
Tantrums	.45	(.88)	.43	(.74)	–.78	(–.98)
Model χ^2, 8 d.f.	44.6		24.8		14.5	

*$p < .05$.

provides a clear research strategy to assess this issue. We first conduct analyses separately within each sample, which controls for original position on official delinquency. Then, within each group we examine the multivariate predictive effects on adult crime of unofficial delinquency and the key family and individual-difference constructs that distinguished delinquents from nondelinquents in previous analysis (see the factors in Table 4.9). This research strategy allows us to determine whether family social control factors have a direct effect on adult crime or whether they are mediated by delinquency.

The answer, as Table 6.4 shows, could not be any clearer. For both the delinquent and the control group samples, unofficial delinquency up to age 14 has significant positive effects on arrest at ages 17–25, 25–32, and 32–45. On the other hand, family and individual-difference constructs have, for all intents and purposes, no effect on adult crime. Indeed, 41 out of 42 coefficients reflecting the effects of seven family/individual factors on six adult crime outcomes are insignificant. The lone exception is the "difficult child" factor for age 17–25 crime among the control group members, and this effect is *negative* (the more difficult the child, the less likely is crime at ages 17–25). We do not place much confidence in this result, since it does not maintain over time. Therefore, the major message conveyed by these data is that the relationship of early family and child factors to adult crime is accounted for by individual differences in adolescent delinquency.

DISCUSSION

We have demonstrated that delinquent behavior in childhood has significant and substantial relationships with a wide range of adult criminal and deviant behaviors, including charges initiated by military personnel, interview-based reports of involvement in deviance and excessive drinking, and arrest by the police up to 30 years later. This conclusion holds regardless of the measure of delinquency, and the predictive power of unofficial delinquency within the delinquent and control groups accounts for the prior effects of informal family social control.

Perhaps more important, the same childhood antisocial behaviors predict educational, economic, employment, and family status up to eighteen years later. These results also hold regardless of the particular measure of delinquency used, and, because of the matched design of the Gluecks' study, they cannot be explained by original differences between delinquents and nondelinquents in age, IQ, neighborhood

SES, and ethnicity—variables often associated with stratification outcomes.

Overall, then, the original delinquents and nondelinquents in the Gluecks' study exhibited behavioral consistency—both homotypic and heterotypic—well into adulthood (see also Glueck and Glueck, 1968). These findings confirm prior research (see especially Robins, 1966; Farrington, 1989) and seem to suggest the existence of a stable tendency toward criminality and other troublesome behavior. Robins and Ratcliff, for example, have argued that "there exists a single syndrome made up of a broad variety of antisocial behaviors arising in childhood and continuing into adulthood" (1980: 248). Similar arguments underlie Gottfredson and Hirschi's (1990) general theory of crime, where they suggest that "low self-control" can account for the positive correlations of crime over time as well as the relationships among crime and noncriminal acts (such as accidents or alcohol use). As Nagin and Paternoster (1991) point out, Gottfredson and Hirschi's theory posits that continuity in deviant behavior over time is generated by population heterogeneity in an underlying propensity for crime that is established early in life and remains stable over time. From this viewpoint, the varied outcomes correlated with childhood antisocial behavior are all expressions of the same underlying trait or propensity.

Continuity may be fueled by more than just early differences in propensity, however. As noted earlier, interactional and cumulative continuity may sustain antisocial behavior in a variety of adult realms in part because of the differing reactions and consequences that antisocial behavior brings forth. In particular, delinquency may interfere with successful adult development through the cumulative continuity of lost opportunity, above and beyond that generated by early propensity (or low self-control) and interactional continuity (Caspi et al., 1987). The notion of cumulative continuity is consistent with the original contentions of labeling theory that reactions to primary deviance may create problems of adjustment that foster additional crime in the form of secondary deviance (Lemert, 1951; Becker, 1963). A good example is the negative effects of arrest and incarceration on future employment chances (Bondeson, 1989; Freeman, 1992). Of course, deterrence theory argues that criminal justice sanctions (such as arrest and imprisonment) may have a negative effect on future offending. Either way, the essential point according to what Nagin and Paternoster (1991) label the *state dependence* argument is that the relationship between past and future crime is causal in nature (that is, crime has a genuine behavioral influence on the probability of committing subsequent crimes).

If we extend further the logic of what might be termed a structural version of labeling theory and state dependence, the connection between official childhood misbehavior and adult outcomes may be accounted for in part by the structural disadvantages and diminished life chances accorded institutionalized and stigmatized youth. The stigma of conviction may even extend across generations, explaining the effects of parental conviction on sons' delinquency regardless of family background and early propensity to crime (Hagan and Palloni, 1990). Hagan's (1991) recent research also suggests that the deleterious effect of adolescent deviance on adult stratification outcomes is greatest among lower-class boys. Middle-class boys, who presumably were better able structurally to avoid the negative consequences of official labeling, did not suffer impairment in adult occupational outcomes as a result of their adolescent delinquency (see also Jessor et al., 1991).

Taken together, these studies suggest that observed continuity in behavior may be partially "illusory" (Farrington, 1986b: 373) and the result of a structural imputation process that begins early in childhood (Hagan and Palloni, 1990). Howard Becker in particular has developed the idea of a *deviant career*—a stable pattern of deviant behavior that is sustained by the labeling process (Becker, 1963: 24–39). The structural disadvantages that delinquency incurs may also lead to the attenuation of adult social bonds that might otherwise counterbalance the effects of early childhood misbehavior.

CONCLUSIONS

Our results in conjunction with prior research and theory suggest that early differences in delinquency manifest themselves in later adult crime in at least two ways. In one process individuals with an early propensity to crime (for example, low self-control) caused by family/ school processes and child effects systematically sort themselves throughout adulthood into states consistent with this trait. According to this view, correlations between adult behaviors (such as unemployment and crime) are thus spurious and should disappear once controls are introduced for prior individual-level differences in criminal propensity (see Gottfredson and Hirschi, 1990: 154–168).

The other process is state dependence, implying a causal role of delinquency in facilitating adult crime. Although this role is potentially direct (see Nagin and Paternoster, 1991), we emphasize a cumulative, developmental model whereby delinquent behavior has a systematic attenuating effect on the social and institutional bonds linking adults to society (for example, labor force attachment, marital cohesion). This raises the further possibility that, in turn, adult social bonds explain variations in adult crime above and beyond those accounted for by early childhood differences. These perspectives are not mutually exclusive, which suggests that both early delinquency and the dimensions of adult social bonding have independent effects on adult crime. We turn now in Chapters 7 and 8 to a full explication and empirical assessment of this central theoretical proposition.

ADULT
SOCIAL BONDS
AND CHANGE IN
CRIMINAL BEHAVIOR

7

The concept of change, together with its measurement and analysis, has not received the same attention in the social sciences as its counterpart. In this chapter we address this imbalance by bringing change to center stage alongside stability. Our orientation recognizes that the two concepts are not mutually exclusive, as is often thought (see Jessor, 1983). On the contrary, intraindividual change and interindividual differences in intraindividual change are both important concerns of developmental research that is longitudinal in design (Jessor et al., 1991: 160). Rather than being irreconcilable, "continuity and change are best seen as two aspects of a single dialectical process in which even major transformations of individuality emerge consequentially from the interaction of prior characteristics and circumstances" (Jessor et al., 1991: 160–161).

A focus on change throughout the life course is also central to a developmental perspective on crime that considers the course of offending in varying social contexts, especially "life transitions and developmental covariates, which may mediate the developmental course of offending" (Loeber and LeBlanc (1990: 451). Integrated with our general concept of social bonding, this line of reasoning suggests that social ties to the adult institutions of informal social control (family, work, community) may serve as links in the chain connecting deviant behavior across the life course. Our research thus seeks to identify the transitions and ties embedded in individual trajectories that relate to adult informal social control. According to our thesis, childhood pathways to crime *and* conformity are significantly modified over the life course by adult social bonds.

THEORY AND HYPOTHESES

Unlike most researchers in the life-course mold, we emphasize the quality or strength of social ties more than the occurrence or timing of discrete life events (cf. Hogan, 1978; Loeber and LeBlanc, 1990: 430–432). For example, we agree with Gottfredson and Hirschi (1990: 140–141) that the structural institution of marriage per se does not increase social control. However, strong attachment to a spouse (or cohabitant) combined with close emotional ties creates a social bond or interdependence between two individuals that, all else being equal, should lead to a reduction in deviant behavior (see also Braithwaite, 1989: 90–91; Shover, 1985: 94). Similarly, employment alone does not increase social control. It is employment coupled with job stability, job commitment, and mutual ties to work (that is, employee-employer interdependence) that should increase social control and, all else being equal, lead to a reduction in criminal and deviant behavior (see also Crutchfield, 1989: 495).[1]

The logic of our argument suggests that it is the social investment or *social capital* (Coleman, 1988) in the institutional relationship, whether it involves a family, work, or community setting, that dictates the salience of informal social control at the individual level. As Coleman (1990: 302) argues, the distinguishing feature of social capital lies in the structure of interpersonal relations and institutional linkages. Social capital is created when these relations change in ways that facilitate action. In other words, "social capital is productive, making possible the achievements of certain ends that in its absence would not be possible" (Coleman, 1988: 98). By contrast, physical capital is wholly tangible, being embodied in observable material form (1990: 304), and human capital is embodied in the skills and knowledge acquired by an individual. Social capital is even less tangible, for it is embodied in the *relations among persons* (1990: 304). A core idea, then, is that independent of the forms of physical and human capital available to individuals (for example, income, occupational skill), social capital is a central factor in facilitating effective ties that bind a person to societal institutions.

Coleman's notion of social capital can be linked with social control theory in a straightforward manner—lack of social capital is one of the primary features of weak social bonds as defined earlier (see also Coleman, 1990: 307). The theoretical task is to identify the characteristics of social relations that facilitate the social capital available to individuals, families, employers, and other social actors. According to Coleman (1990: 318–320), one of the most important factors is the closure (that is, connectedness) of networks among actors in a social system. In a system involving employers and employees, for example, relations characterized by an extensive set of obligations, expectations, and interdependent social networks are better able to facilitate social control than are jobs characterized by purely utilitarian objectives and nonoverlapping social networks. Similarly, the mere presence of a relationship (such as marriage) between adults is not sufficient to produce social capital, and hence the idea of social capital goes beyond simple structural notions of marital status.

According to this theoretical conception, adult social controls are not as direct or external as for juveniles (for example, monitoring, supervision of activities). Rather, adult social ties are important insofar as they create interdependent systems of obligation and restraint that impose significant costs for translating criminal propensities into action. It is unrealistic to expect that adults with a criminal background (or low self-control) can be wholly transformed by institutions (marriage or work), or that such institutions are even capable of imposing direct controls like surveillance. Nevertheless, we believe that adults, regardless of delinquent background, will be inhibited from committing crime to the extent that they have social capital invested in their work and family lives (see also Cook, 1975). By contrast, those subject to weak systems of interdependence (Braithwaite, 1989) and informal social control as an adult (for example, weak attachment to the labor force or noncohesive marriages) are freer to engage in deviant behavior— even if nondelinquent as a youth. This dual premise allows us to explain desistance from crime as well as late onset.

We also emphasize the reciprocal nature of social capital invested by employers and spouses. For example, employers often take chances in hiring workers, hoping that their investment will pay off. Similarly, prospective marriage partners may be aware of a potential spouse's delinquent background but may nonetheless invest their future in that person. This investment by the employer or spouse may in turn trigger a return investment in social capital by the employee or husband. The key theoretical point is that social capital and interdependence are reciprocal and are embedded in the social ties that exist between individuals and social institutions. This conception may help explain how change in delinquent behavior is initiated (for example, an employer may take a chance on a former delinquent, fostering a return investment in that job which in turn inhibits the deviant behavior of the employee).

At first blush, our focus on change may seem at odds with the findings in Chapter 6 that (1) criminal behavior is stable over time and (2) the formation of adult social bonds is negatively related to juvenile delinquency. We reconcile these facts in two ways. First, not only is continuity far from perfect, it refers to the aggregate of interindividual differences and does not capture within-individual change. In this regard, our theoretical framework implies that adult social ties can modify childhood trajectories of crime despite the general stability of between-individual differences.

Second, weak adult social bonds may also serve as a mediating and hence sequential link between early delinquency and adult criminal behavior. As discussed in Chapter 6, the idea of cumulative continuity suggests that delinquency tends to "mortgage" one's future by generating negative consequences for life chances (for example, arrest, official labeling, and incarceration, which in turn spark failure in school, unemployment, weak community bonds). Serious delinquency in particular may lead to the "knifing off" of opportunities (Caspi and Moffitt, 1992; Moffitt, 1991) such that participants have fewer options for a conventional life. The concept of "knifing off" appears to be especially applicable to the structurally constrained life chances of the disadvantaged urban poor (cf. Hagan, 1991).

On the other hand, the absence or infrequency of delinquency—especially encounters with the police and/or institutionalization—provides opportunities for prosocial attachments to take firm hold in adulthood. Thus, nondelinquents are not just more motivated (presumably), but also better able structurally to establish strong social ties to conventional lines of adult activity. If nothing else, incumbency in prosocial roles provides advantages in maintaining the status quo and counteracting negative life events (for example, last hired, first fired). In this sense we emphasize the state-dependence notion (Nagin and Paternoster, 1991) that history matters—where one has been and how long one has been in that state are crucial in understanding adult developmental patterns.

Our theoretical perspective is also consistent with Gottfredson and Hirschi's (1990: 137) argument that the incidence of criminal acts is problematic and varies when self-control is held constant. That is, variations in criminal propensity reflected by early delinquency provide an incomplete explanation of adult crime because the latter's realization is dependent, among other things, on opportunity (for instance, lack of guardianship or surveillance). Ties to work and family in adulthood influence opportunities and hence the probability that criminal propensities will be translated into action. For example, all else being equal, those in stable employment and marital relations are subject to more continuity in guardianship than those in unstable employment or marital roles.

In brief, ours is a dynamic theory of social capital and informal social control that at once incorporates stability and change in criminal behavior. Change is central to our model because we propose that variations in adult crime cannot be explained by childhood behavior alone. We specifically hypothesize that the strength of adult social bonds has a direct negative effect on adult criminal behavior, controlling for childhood delinquency. At the same time our model incorporates the link between childhood delinquency and adult outcomes, implying a cumulative, developmental process whereby delinquent behavior attenuates the social and institutional bonds linking adults to society. As such, adult social bonds not only have important effects on adult crime in and of themselves, but also help to explain the probabilistic links in the chain connecting early childhood differences and later adult crime.

MEASURING ADULT SOCIAL BONDS

Our key independent variables, introduced in Chapter 6, are *job stability*, *commitment*, and *attachment to spouse* at ages 17–25 and 25–32. Information for these measures was collected during the home interview and corroborated whenever possible by record checks. Job stability is measured by a standardized, composite scale of three interrelated variables—employment status, stability of most recent employment, and work habits. Employment status measures whether the subject was employed at the time of the interview; employment stability measures length of time employed on present or most recent job (ranging from less than 3 months to 48 months or more). The work-habits variable consists of a three-point scale: individuals were classified as having poor work habits if they were unreliable in the work setting or if they failed to give any effort to the job; fair work habits were characterized by a generally good job performance except for periodic absences from work or periods of unemployment as chosen by the subject; good work habits were evidenced by reliable performance on the job as noted by the employer as well as instances in which the subject was considered an asset to the organization (see Glueck and Glueck, 1968: 90–94).[2]

An individual's commitment to occupation-related goals may influence job stability. Our measure of commitment at wave 2 is derived from interviews with the subject and significant others and combines three related variables—work, educational, and economic ambitions (Glueck and Glueck, 1968: 124–126). Subjects with low commitment expressed no particular work, educational, or economic aspirations; they had not thought about further schooling or had vague educational ambitions. Subjects with high commitment expressed a strong desire for further schooling (academic, vocational, or professional), and were eager to better themselves and their families (to become a professional, gain more income, and so forth). At wave 3, commitment is a three-point scale representing efforts taken by the subject to improve his work and occupational status between ages 25 and 32. These efforts focus on behaviors beyond working hard or joining a union—for example, additional on-the-job training, taking civil service exams, and participation in special reading and correspondence courses (Glueck and Glueck, 1968: 95).

The third key independent variable in our analysis is attachment to spouse. At wave 2, we use a composite measure derived from interview data describing the general conjugal relationship between the subject and his spouse during the period plus the subject's attitude toward marital responsibility (Glueck and Glueck, 1968: 84–88). Weak attachment was indicated by signs of incompatibility such as a brief period of separation, divorce or separation, or desertion. These individuals were also neglectful of marital responsibilities, financial as well as emotional. In contrast, subjects who were strongly attached displayed close, warm feelings toward their wives, or were compatible in a generally constructive relationship. These individuals assumed marital responsibilities. At wave 3, attachment to spouse is a composite scale derived from interview data describing the general conjugal relationship during the follow-up period plus a measure of the cohesiveness of the family unit. The measure of conjugal relations at wave 3 is the same as for wave 2. Family cohesiveness assesses the extent to which the family unit was characterized by an integration of interests, cooperativeness, and overall affection for each other. This measure was not available at wave 2.

Taken together, these measures capture the quality, strength, and interdependence of an individual's ties to important institutions of informal social control—family, work, and the community at large. They are also reliable: Cronbach's alpha reliabilities at wave 2 and wave 3 are, respectively, .65 and .78 for job stability and .90 and .91 for marital attachment. Commitment at age 25 has an alpha reliability of .68 (age 32 commitment is a one-item measure). In addition to using multiple indicators of key concepts whenever possible and composite scales with good reliabilities, we took other steps to ensure the validity of measures. For example, we investigated the longitudinal and construct validity of both individual items and scales. The results supported the contention that the job stability, marital attachment, and commitment scales were related both concurrently and prospectively in a manner consistent with substantive expectations. When these findings are combined with the results from Chapter 6 showing the predictive relationship between delinquency and later adult social bonds, we have good evidence of reliability and validity.

As noted in Chapter 4, the Gluecks' data differ from conventional survey research where measurement error, especially on attitudes and moral beliefs, is often large (see, for example, Matsueda, 1982; 1989). The Gluecks' data integrate multiple sources of information even for *individual* items. Moreover, the items used here refer almost exclusively to behavioral outcomes rather than attitudes, and where possible we construct multi-item measures. These unique qualities of the Gluecks' data combined with the nature of several outcome variables (for example, dichotomous, count, or time-to-failure) led us to rely principally on logistic, ordinary least squares, and Poisson-based regression models in conjunction with event history analysis.[3]

INITIAL ASSESSMENT OF CHANGE

In Table 7.1 we examine how the social factors of job stability, commitment to educational, work, and economic goals (that is, aspiration), and attachment to spouse among those ever married modify the tendency to persist in deviant and troublesome behaviors over the life span. Because the matched-sample research design maximized differences in delinquency, a within-group analysis controls for original position on delinquency. By definition, the delinquent group sample contains youths who were all delinquent. For them, our goal is to examine the social factors related to subsequent variation in this status.[4]

Table 7.1   Concurrent and Predictive Relationships between Adult Social Bonds and Adult Crime and Deviance within Delinquent Group Sample

Adult Crime and Deviance	Job Stability, Ages 17–25			Commitment, Ages 17–25		Marital Attachment, Ages 17–25	
	Low	Medium	High	Weak	Strong	Weak	Strong
% Excessive alcohol (17–25)	57	24	15*	50	21*	53	17*
% Excessive alcohol (25–32)	53	19	11*	43	16*	47	11*
% General deviance (17–25)	31	13	9*	29	15*	31	8*
% General deviance (25–32)	47	17	8*	37	14*	54	16*
% Arrested (17–25)	91	62	60*	82	64*	87	58*
% Arrested (25–32)	74	47	32*	70	47*	76	34*

Adult Crime and Deviance	Job Stability, Ages 25–32			Commitment, Ages 25–32		Marital Attachment, Ages 25–32	
	Low	Medium	High	Weak	Strong	Weak	Strong
% Excessive alcohol (25–32)	53	19	5*	43	18*	51	6*
% General deviance (25–32)	46	13	4*	39	14*	52	6*
% Arrested (25–32)	80	44	18*	70	40*	78	29*
% Arrested (32–45)	64	48	39*	59	47*	64	43*

*$p < .05$.

Job stability at ages 17–25 has a large inverse relationship with each measure of adult crime and deviance for the delinquent sample.[5] Moreover, young-adult job stability has substantial *predictive* power, exhibiting very large negative effects on alcohol use, general deviance, and arrest in the subsequent 25–32 age period. Subjects with low job stability at ages 17–25 were at least four times more likely to exhibit severe problems with alcohol in later adulthood and at least five times more likely to engage in deviant behavior compared to those with high job stability. Given the predictive nature of findings, it seems unlikely that adult crime itself can account for the patterns observed. And because these relationships obtain within the delinquent group, it is difficult to dismiss the results on the basis of a "stability" or "self-selection" argument that antisocial children simply replicate their antisocial behavior as adults—that delinquents invariably continue their interactional styles in adult life, and hence have incompatible relations with family, work, and other institutions of social control (Caspi, 1987). Rather, it appears that job stability in the transition to young adulthood significantly modifies trajectories of crime and deviance.[6]

A similar pattern is seen for commitment to conventional educational and occupational goals. Delinquent subjects with high aspirations and efforts to advance educationally and occupationally were much less likely to engage in deviant behavior, use alcohol excessively, or be arrested at ages 17–25 and 25–32. The pattern is also consistent for the relationship between attachment to spouse and adult crime among those ever married (approximately 50 percent of the sample). All relationships are in the expected direction, significant, and substantively large. As with job stability and commitment, the influence of attachment to wife at ages 17–25 is salient not only in the concurrent period but in the later 25–32 period as well.

The bottom part of Table 7.1 reveals a congruent pattern for the relationship between social bonds at ages 25–32 and criminal/deviant behavior at ages 25–32 and 32–45. Indeed, all the relationships are in the predicted direction, significant, and substantively important. The effects of job stability and marital attachment on excessive alcohol use and deviance are especially noteworthy. The predictive power of these factors is evident up to age 45—some 13 years after the Gluecks' third follow-up interview. For example, over 60 percent of those with low job stability at ages 25–32 were later arrested in the age 32–45 period, compared to 39 percent of those with high job stability. Marital attachment in middle adulthood shows a similar negative relationship with later crime and deviance.

The evidence thus far suggests that informal social controls in adulthood are significantly and substantially related to adult antisocial behavior, regardless of childhood delinquency. The "ontogenetic" model's emphasis on stability, though partially confirmed in Chapter 6, is insufficient as an explanatory model for the life course. Social bonds to the adult institutions of work, education, and the family appear to exert a powerful modifying influence on adult crime and deviance.

ACCOUNTING FOR EARLY CRIMINAL PROPENSITY

Despite the supportive results in Table 7.1, a further and more important question may be raised—do individual differences in crime *within* the delinquent and control groups confound the results? The most delinquent subjects in the delinquent group may have self-selected themselves into later states of job instability, conflict-ridden marriages, and crime (Caspi, 1987; Gottfredson and Hirschi, 1990), a scenario suggested by Table 6.3 from the previous chapter. Similarly, the control-group subjects were presumably not equally nondelinquent in their behavior even though none had an official record (Glueck and Glueck, 1950: 29).

We address this question here and in Chapter 8 through a multivariate strategy that controls for prior criminal tendencies in three major ways. First, analyses are again conducted separately for the two samples, thereby controlling for official delinquency status and the large differences between delinquents and nondelinquents in family and school experiences and a host of other background factors (the control group is analyzed in Chapter 8). Second, within both samples we control for the frequency of official crimes committed in adolescence. For the delinquent group we use the average number of arrests per year free in the community between birth and age 17. Because this rate adjusts for the opportunity to commit crime (that is, it takes account of incarceration time), it is a good indicator of adolescent criminal "propensity" for the delinquent group (Gottfredson and Hirschi, 1990: 220).

The third and perhaps best strategy to control for prior between-individual differences in criminal propensity is to include our measure of unofficial delinquency. Recall from Chapter 6 that this measure of childhood delinquency predicts later adult crime within both the delinquent and the nondelinquent groups, even controlling for seven family and individual-difference constructs. Moreover, the unofficial delinquency measure combines self, parent, and teacher reports of behaviors that often predate contact with the juvenile justice system (for example, truancy, running away, smoking). This measure meets Gottfredson and Hirschi's (1990: 220) criterion that a measure of criminality should be assessed "before crime is possible" and "constructed from information available in the preadolescent years (and validated by its ability to predict subsequent behavior)." We thus employ a validated measure of early between-individual differences in delinquency that remain stable over time.

Our threefold strategy makes explicit the assumption that delinquency in childhood is a salient and measurable characteristic, one that is observed not just by juvenile justice officials but by parents, teachers, and delinquent youths themselves. In this regard, the argument that delinquent tendencies are somehow "unobservable" appears to be counterfactual (cf. Nagin and Paternoster, 1991) and in many respects counterproductive because it encourages statistical modeling approaches to what are fundamentally data problems. In our opinion the best answer to omitted variable bias is to gather more information and include direct measures of relevant variables. Although our strategy attempts to do just that, we also consider in a later section recent methods that allow for unobserved heterogeneity among individuals in criminal propensity.

In short, the present research design represents a strict test of the effects of adult social ties on adult crime and deviance, and is directly linked to our theoretical goal since it allows examination of change in crime and delinquency. That is, because prior levels of delinquency (both unofficial and official) are controlled and the analysis is conducted separately for each group, the resulting multivariate models permit assessment of the independent effects of adult social ties on changes in adult criminality. We are thus able to examine variations in adult behavior not directly accounted for by deviant childhood "propensities" (Gottfredson and Hirschi, 1990).[7]

MISSING DATA AND SELECTION BIAS

Although the Gluecks' original study involved 1,000 subjects, 12 percent are not included in the follow-up interviews either because of death or because they could not be located at all. Furthermore, some measures were deemed by the Gluecks to be inapplicable among the 880 subjects who were followed to age 32. For instance, the components of job stability and marital attachment were not assessed during the follow-up for men who were in prison or in the military for a significant portion of time, or for those who were vagrant for an extended period of time. Certain alcohol and deviance items were likewise not measured for those men absent from the community during a significant portion of the follow-up. Because we cannot reliably determine the social bonds or criminal careers of long-term prisoners and military personnel, or men who could not be interviewed, it was necessary to exclude cases missing one or more of our key measures. Of the approximately 150 delinquents excluded among those followed up, the majority were institutionalized; the rest (about 40) were excluded because of prolonged military service. In the control group, approximately 50 of the 442 followed to age 32 were put in the "inapplicable" category by the Gluecks; the majority of these exclusions stemmed from military service. Of the cases remaining for analysis, true missing (that is, "unknown") data were not a serious problem, averaging about 10 percent for the delinquent group and 5 percent for the control group.

Unfortunately, the excluded cases do not represent a random sample of the men. Those with lengthy incarceration times had longer criminal records and were thus presumably more prone to crime. We also cannot assume that those who served in the military for long periods reflect the characteristics of the rest of the men. For these reasons, results may be biased because of systematic sample selection bias, undermining both external and internal validity (Heckman, 1979; Berk, 1983). Indeed, selection bias is fundamentally connected to the issue of controlling for early criminal propensity (Smith and Paternoster, 1990). The reason is that the error terms of the substantive outcome of interest (crime) may be correlated with the error terms from the equation that guides the selection of cases observed (for example, sentencing decisions to incarcerate an offender for long periods). Under the process of incidental selection, correlation of error terms may cause inconsistent and biased estimates of ordinary least squares regression parameters (Berk and Ray, 1982: 368–371). What is needed is a procedure to capture the expected values of the disturbances in the substantive equation after the nonrandom selection has occurred (Berk, 1983: 391). That is, with the inclusion of a new (and hence previously omitted) variable that represents the hazard of non-selection, consistent and unbiased estimation is possible.

To address this concern, we used sample selection methods to model the process of missing or excluded cases.[8] Basically, the issue boils down to specification of an equation representing the selection process, followed by a second-stage estimation of the substantive equation of interest (in our case, crime), corrected for sample exclusion risk. To estimate the selection equation we first created a dichotomous variable where a 1 was assigned if a follow-up subject was missing on any exogenous variable in the age 25 and age 32 assessments. Assuming a bivariate logistic distribution of errors (see Berk and Ray, 1982: 387–389), we then estimated a series of logistic regression equations predicting the risk of exclusion in different models at ages 25 and 32.[9] The predictors of exclusion risk were chosen on the basis of our knowledge of the attrition process. As noted above, we have good reason to believe that incarceration and military service are the major determinants of selection. We thus included the length of incarceration (both concurrent and prior), length of military service, and an indicator of whether the subject served overseas in World War II. Also included in the selection equations were two measures of criminal propensity (official and unofficial crime) and the year of birth. The latter was chosen because some of the youngest members of the sample apparently had a lower likelihood of being followed up at age 32 because of strained resources at the end of the Gluecks' project.

Table 7.2 displays the maximum-likelihood (ML) results for the wave 2 and wave 3 follow-up. At ages 17–25 the significant predictors of excluded cases are incarceration at ages 17–25, length of adult military service, and official criminal record as a juvenile. As expected, length of incarceration and military service are the major factors explaining the probability of exclusion at the wave 2 analyses.[10] Panel B of Table 7.2 reveals similar results for exclusion at the age 25–32 period. Again, length of military service significantly increases the risk of exclusion, as does length of incarceration at both ages 17–25 and 25–32. Also similar to the second wave follow-up is the finding that as juvenile delinquency increases, the risk of exclusion at wave 3 decreases. In any case, both models fit the data reasonably well in explaining the selection process of nonapplicable or excluded cases (see model chi-square statistics, both $p < .05$).

Using the equations in Table 7.2, we estimated the predicted probabil-

Table 7.2   ML Coefficients and *T*-Ratios Predicting Probability of Exclusion from Multivariate Substantive Models at Ages 17–25 and Ages 25–32: Delinquent Group Follow-Up

A. Independent Variables	Ages 17–25 Selection Equation (1 = excluded)	
	Coefficient	Coefficient/S.E.
Juvenile (age < 17)		
Arrests per year free	−1.27	−2.55*
Unofficial delinquency	−.04	−1.52
Length of incarceration	−.03	−1.00
Birth year	.53	.09
Adult (age 17 and over)		
Length of incarceration (17–25)	.16	8.00*
Length of military service	.50	3.65*
World War II	−.35	−1.08
Model χ^2, 7 d.f.	98.6 (N = 446)	

B. Independent Variables	Ages 25–32 Selection Equation (1 = excluded)	
	Coefficient	Coefficient/S.E.
Juvenile (age < 17)		
Arrests per year free	−1.92	−2.86*
Unofficial delinquency	−.09	−2.66*
Length of incarceration	−.00	−.00
Birth year	.07	.93
Adult (age 17 and over)		
Length of incarceration (17–25)	.15	5.00*
Length of incarceration (25–32)	.16	6.00*
Length of military service	.44	2.54*
World War II	−.17	−.42
Model χ^2, 7 d.f.	188.6 (N = 423)	

Note: Coefficients for incarceration and birth year were multiplied by 100 to reduce places to right of decimal.
    *$p < .05$.

ity of exclusion at the follow-ups. This "hazard rate" instrument serves as a new regressor in the second-stage substantive equations below (for details see Berk and Ray, 1982). It is important to note that our use of sample selection methods follows a substantively meaningful procedure based on a priori knowledge. Sample selection methods have been criticized because arbitrary variables have sometimes been used to model the selection process (see Stolzenberg and Relles, 1990; Berk and Ray, 1982). As Berk and Ray (1982: 394) argue, "The selection problem and all of its solutions rest fundamentally on one's ability to properly model both the substantive process and the selection process." In our case, we are fortunate to have meaningful variables such as incarceration time and military service that are causally linked to the processes generating missing data—a fact reflected in the explanatory power of the models. By incorporating this information into the substantive equations explaining crime, we counteract concerns about the potential systematic nature of reduced sample sizes for waves 2 and 3.[11]

MODELS OF ADULT CRIME AMONG ORIGINAL DELINQUENTS

Table 7.3 presents results for the delinquent group of multivariate analyses of participation in general deviance, excessive drinking, and arrest at ages 25–32.[12] In model 1 we assess the effects of adult social bonds, controlling for marital status and income in addition to measures of official and unofficial juvenile delinquency.[13] The main picture is rather clear—once other factors are controlled, income and marriage do not predict later adult crime and deviance. On the other hand, job stability shows consistent negative effects for all three indicators of crime and deviance. The coefficients are at least two times their standard errors, and indicate that a one-unit increase in job stability reduces the log-odds of later crime/deviance by at least a factor of .18.

Model 2 in Table 7.3 examines the effect of attachment to wife among men who were (or had been) married. The results suggest that cohesiveness is central rather than marriage per se. Marital attachment has significant negative effects on all measures of crime and deviance, net of other factors. The raw coefficients reveal that being highly attached to a spouse reduces the log-odds of crime by at least a factor of 1.2 compared to those in discordant relationships. Among married men, however, the influence of job stability declines in magnitude and statistical significance ($p < .10$).

Since prior levels of childhood delinquency are controlled, these results may be interpreted in terms of the effect of adult social bonds on change in criminal behavior. Note, for example, that deviance, drinking, and arrest are all predicted by juvenile delinquency (at $p < .10$). Hence, both job stability and attachment appear to promote reduc-

Table 7.3   ML Logistic Coefficients and *T*-ratios Predicting Participation in Crime and Deviance at Ages 25–32 by Juvenile Delinquency and Social Bonds at Ages 17–25: Delinquent Group

Independent Variables	Crime and Deviance, Ages 25–32					
	General Deviance		Excessive Drinking		Arrest	
Model 1 (All men, N = 251)						
Juvenile (age < 17)						
Arrests per year free	1.61	(2.68)*	.65	(1.13)	2.74	(3.57)
Unofficial delinquency	–.03	(–.84)	.12	(3.11)*	.08	(2.10)
Young adult (ages 17–25)						
Exclusion risk	–.12	(–.13)	1.76	(1.90)	2.38	(2.07)
Income	–.14	(–1.22)	–.05	(–.49)	–.13	(–1.17)
Marriage	.27	(.80)	–.06	(–.20)	–.10	(–.31)
Commitment	.06	(.90)	–.17	(–2.54)*	.01	(.18)
Job stability	–.27	(–3.79)*	–.18	(–2.64)*	–.31	(–3.74)
Model χ², 7 d.f.	32.1		49.3		65.9	
Model 2 (Ever-married men, N = 151)						
Juvenile (age < 17)						
Arrests per year free	1.29	(1.68)	.72	(.88)	1.65	(1.92)
Unofficial delinquency	–.04	(–.83)	.12	(2.26)*	.02	(.54)
Young adult (ages 17–25)						
Exclusion risk	2.05	(1.63)	.70	(.55)	1.66	(1.30)
Income	–.10	(–.61)	.08	(.51)	–.07	(–.46)
Commitment	.09	(.91)	–.08	(–.83)	–.06	(.63)
Job stability	–.18	(–1.68)	–.12	(–1.08)	–.22	(–1.68)
Attachment to spouse	–1.52	(–3.09)*	–1.24	(–2.45)*	–1.43	(–3.05)
Model χ², 7 d.f.	37.8		29.4		40.5	

*$p < .05$.

tions in crime that are not explained by the original designation as delinquent or by between-individual differences in official or unofficial delinquency.[14]

We now turn to variations in the *frequency* of offending among the delinquent group members. Our key measure is the number of crimes committed (estimated by arrests) per unit of time free, thereby taking into account "street time" and differential opportunities to commit crime.[15] The OLS frequency results in model 1 of Table 7.4 are largely consistent with the participation results of Table 7.3. Job stability in the transition to young adulthood (ages 17–25) has the largest effect on

Table 7.4   OLS Coefficients and *T*-Ratios Predicting Frequency of Crime
While Free at Ages 17–25 and 25–32 by Juvenile Delinquency
and Young Adult Social Bonds: Delinquent Group

	Arrests per Year Free, Ages 17–25		Arrests per Year Free, Ages 25–32	
Independent Variables	β	*t*-ratio	β	*t*-ratio
Model 1 (All men, N = 246)				
Juvenile (age < 17)				
Arrests per year free	.26	5.18*	.19	3.49*
Unofficial delinquency	.14	2.69*	.10	1.86
Young adult (ages 17–25)				
Exclusion risk	.43	8.12*	.24	4.12*
Income	.02	.39	.02	.31
Marriage	−.00	−.05	.06	1.08
Commitment	−.02	−.31	−.09	−1.51
Job stability	−.28	−4.72*	−.36	−5.67*
R^2	.41		.30	
Model 2 (Ever-married men, N = 150)				
Juvenile (age < 17)				
Arrests per year free	.24	3.49*	.18	2.50*
Unofficial delinquency	.06	.89	.06	.77
Young adult (ages 17–25)				
Exclusion risk	.29	4.02*	.08	1.15
Income	−.00	−.07	−.01	−.12
Commitment	−.02	−.30	−.01	−.16
Job stability	−.18	−2.00*	−.27	−2.98*
Attachment to spouse	−.21	−2.43*	−.26	−2.92*
R^2	.34		.31	

*$p < .05$.

crime frequency at ages 25–32, controlling for prior delinquency and the hazard of exclusion. With regard to the latter, exclusion hazard has a significant positive effect on crime frequency, a result in accord with expectations. This finding underscores the importance of controlling for sample selection bias, at least with respect to official crime frequency (cf. Table 7.3). The number of arrests per year free as a juvenile also has a direct effect on adult crime. Still, job stability continues to have a negative effect on the number of arrests while free as an adult, especially at ages 25–32 where it has the largest overall magnitude.

The results in model 2 of Table 7.4 are more supportive of our theory of informal social control than were the results for the dichotomous indicators of participation. The difference is that job stability now has significant negative effects on frequency of crime within the subsample of married respondents. Apparently, job stability is more important in explaining crime frequency than in distinguishing adult offenders from adult nonoffenders. For marital attachment the results are the same: those with high attachment or close bonds with their spouses were less likely to commit crimes than those weakly attached, regardless of prior delinquency, exclusion hazard, and even job stability. Both job stability and attachment to spouse are thus central explanatory factors net of prior delinquency and other characteristics. On the other hand, occupational commitment has weak or insignificant effects in Tables 7.3 and 7.4 once job stability and attachment are controlled.

To this point we have focused on the role of social bonds during the transition to young adulthood for explaining later crime and deviance. But, as noted in the measurement section, we have measures of job stability, commitment, and marital attachment at ages 25–32 as well. We can thus explore whether the inhibitory effect of social ties on crime extends into a later period of adulthood. Accordingly, Table 7.5 displays the effects of social bonds at ages 25–32 on the frequency of crime— both concurrently and prospectively. For crime at ages 25–32, job stability has a large negative effect ($\beta = -.32$) independent of all other factors. This significant effect maintains in the subsample of married persons where attachment to spouse also has a significant negative effect. The large influence of marital attachment holds for ML models predicting participation in crime, deviance, and excessive alcohol use at ages 25–32 (data not shown). It appears that the influence of social bonds did not diminish as the Glueck men advanced in age.

The results for crime at ages 32–45 yield a somewhat different picture. In model 1 job stability at ages 25–32 has a weaker predictive effect on later crime ($p < .10$), and in model 2 its effect is virtually zero. The effect of marital attachment remains strong at these later ages, with marital attachment having the largest direct effect on crime frequency at ages 32–45 ($\beta = -.36$, t-ratio = -5.30). When prior results are taken into account, it is apparent that marital attachment inhibits crime at all three adult developmental periods.[16]

Despite the important role of adult social bonds, we should not lose sight of the long-term predictive power of childhood behavior—unofficial delinquency in adolescence continues to explain variations in

Table 7.5   OLS Coefficients and *T*-ratios Predicting Frequency of Crime at Ages 25–32 and 32–45 by Juvenile Delinquency and Social Bonds at Ages 25–32: Delinquent Group

Independent Variables	Arrests per Year Free, Ages 25–32		Arrest Frequency, Ages 32–45	
	β	*t*-ratio	β	*t*-ratio
Model 1 (All men, N = 330)				
Juvenile (age < 17)				
Arrests per year free	.14	3.36*	.03	.56
Unofficial delinquency	.07	1.68	.16	3.18*
Adult (ages 25–32)				
Exclusion risk	.33	7.34*	.23	4.14*
Income	.06	1.15	−.02	−.25
Marriage	−.17	−3.79*	−.09	−1.72
Commitment	−.10	−2.10*	−.07	−1.14
Job stability	−.32	−5.93*	−.12	−1.87
R^2		.45		.18
Model 2 (Ever-married men, N = 258)				
Juvenile (age < 17)				
Arrests per year free	.25	5.21*	.10	1.83
Unofficial delinquency	.08	1.68	.24	4.32*
Adult (ages 25–32)				
Exclusion risk	.38	7.20*	.27	4.42*
Income	.10	1.69	−.00	−.07
Commitment	−.05	−.99	−.01	−.17
Job stability	−.18	−2.77*	.06	.73
Attachment to spouse	−.32	−5.46*	−.36	−5.30*
R^2		.48		.30

*$p < .05$.

crime some 30 years later. More generally, in the majority of models in Tables 7.3 to 7.5, juvenile delinquency has significant effects on adult crime. As hypothesized earlier, then, both stability and change appear to be simultaneously present.

Event Count Models for Arrest Distributions

Although the delinquent group generated over 5,000 arrests in adulthood—with approximately 10 percent of the men generating 10 or more arrests at ages 25–32 alone—the distribution of arrest counts is nonetheless positively skewed. There is also a significant number of zero arrests, especially at ages 32–45 (45 percent had no arrests during this period). We addressed this issue earlier by creating annualized rates of arrests per day free and taking natural logarithms. To assess the robustness of OLS estimation procedures on these rates, we now consider an alternative approach well suited to the distributional properties of arrest frequencies.

One procedure for handling non-negative event counts is the Poisson regression model (King, 1988; Hagan and Palloni, 1990: 295). The basic Poisson parameter is modeled by: $\ln(\text{lambda}_i) = BX_i$, where B is a vector of parameters, X_i is a vector of exogenous variables for the ith observation, and lambda is the parameter to be estimated for the ith observation.[17] In the Poisson regression model the probability of an event occurring is assumed to be constant over time and independent of the prior history of the process. The result is that the conditional mean and variance of Y_i in the Poisson model are constrained to be equal. The Poisson model also assumes that there is no unobserved heterogeneity in propensity to crime among the subjects. These assumptions are questionable in our data. To relax them, a second parameter—an error term—may be added to the Poisson model. Following Cameron and Trivedi (1986), the error term has a gamma distribution with mean one and variance denoted by alpha. This model is termed the *negative binomial* and is estimated with a maximum-likelihood procedure using the Poisson regression estimates as starting values (see Greene, 1989: 253–254). The negative binomial procedure also permits a test of whether the data violate the Poisson regression assumption. Specifically, the t-value of alpha measures the rate of overdispersion in the data (that is, that the mean and variance are unequal).

Employing first the Poisson and then the negative binomial models, we replicated all OLS regression findings. Not surprisingly, the results suggested that the negative binomial provided a better fit to the data because there was significant heterogeneity and hence overdispersion in the original Poisson models. Table 7.6 thus presents key negative binomial models for the frequency counts of crime at ages 25–32 and 32–45 as predicted by lagged social bonds and control variables. As the t-ratios for alphas indicate, there is significant overdispersion (that is, the t-ratios are all over 5, meaning that the simple Poisson model is highly suspect). The negative binomial estimates for arrest frequency at ages 25–32 indicate that, similar to the findings in Table 7.4, job

Table 7.6   ML Negative Binomial Regression Coefficients and *T*-ratios Predicting Frequency Counts of Arrest at Ages 25–32 and 32–45 by Juvenile Delinquency and Social Bonds at Ages 17–25/25–32: Delinquent Group

Independent Variables	Arrest Frequency, Ages 25–32		Arrest Frequency, Ages 32–45	
	Coefficient	Coefficient/S.E.	Coefficient	Coefficient/S.E.
Model 1 (All men)				
Juvenile (age < 17)				
Arrests per year free	.79	1.60	.23	.61
Unofficial delinquency	.05	2.24*	.06	2.58*
Adult (ages 17–25/25–32)[a]				
Exclusion risk	1.31	2.50*	1.41	3.20*
Income	−.05	−.71	−.04	−.52
Marriage	.35	2.02*	−.53	−2.23*
Commitment	−.04	−1.07	−.28	−1.38
Job stability	−.22	−5.57*	−.07	−1.28
Log-likelihood		−556.0		−661.6
T-ratio for alpha		7.06*		8.94*
Number of cases		250		332
Model 2 (Ever-married men)				
Juvenile (age < 17)				
Post-interview arrests	.90	1.18	.64	1.34
Unofficial delinquency	.02	.61	.08	2.95*
Adult (ages 17–25/25–32)[a]				
Exclusion risk	.79	.93	1.70	2.83*
Income	−.09	−.87	−.02	−.28
Commitment	.06	.92	−.13	−.54
Job stability	−.16	−2.47*	.04	.47
Attachment to spouse	−.99	−3.76*	−.32	−5.16*
Log-likelihood		−317.4		−483.7
T-ratio for alpha		5.17*		7.78*
Number of cases		151		258

a. In explaining arrest frequency at ages 25–32, the exogenous variables pertain to the transition to young adulthood (ages 17–25). For arrest frequency at ages 32–45, the exogenous variables pertain to ages 25–32.

*$p < .05$.

stability and marital attachment both significantly inhibit crime. For crime at ages 32–45, the data once again suggest a weaker effect of job stability among the delinquents (cf. Table 7.5). On the other hand, marital attachment continues to have a large negative effect on the number of arrests at ages 32–45, independent of prior crime and other controls.[18]

In short, modeling the raw arrest frequencies with a negative binomial distribution produces results quite similar in substantive import to the OLS regression models of arrest rates while free. The reason for the similarity is tied to the fact that arrests among delinquents, though not a perfect normal distribution, are still sufficiently numerous to approximate a normal distribution when transformed into rates per unit of time free and then logged. This is not likely to be the case for the control group, where adult crime is much rarer. Hence, in Chapter 8 the negative binomial model looms larger as an important methodological alternative to OLS regression.

Changing Social Bonds

In previous analyses of these data we examined the dual effects of job stability at ages 17–25 and 25–32 on crime at ages 25–32, controlling for prior levels of crime, income, marriage, and commitment (Sampson and Laub, 1990). That is, by entering both the prior and concurrent (Time 2 and Time 3) measures of social bonds, we estimated their changing effects over time (Plewis, 1985: 56–61). The results for perhaps our most precise indicator of crime—frequency per time free—are shown in Table 7.7. For comparative purposes, this model controls for prior *adult* crime rather than sample selection. Since the effects of prior adult crime may have absorbed some of the effect of job stability at ages 17–25, this model is a conservative test and probably underestimates the latter's impact. On the other hand, the hazard rate and adult crime are quite highly correlated, and hence this difference in model specification should not make much difference.

The expectation of similarity is borne out by the data. Although prior adult crime has a direct effect on crime at ages 25–32 in model 1, both prior and current job stability have significant negative effects as well. Substantively, these results suggest that prior levels *and* relative increases in job stability have negative effects on change in adult crime frequency. By contrast, commitment to conventional occupational goals has no effect on crime frequency as measured by arrests per year free in the community.

Table 7.7   OLS Coefficients and *T*-ratios Predicting Frequency of Crime
While Free at Ages 25–32 by Prior Adult Crime and Social
Bonds at Ages 17–25 and 25–32: Delinquent Group

Independent Variables	Arrests per Year Free, Ages 25–32	
	β	*t*-ratio
Model 1 (All men, N = 231)		
Arrest rate (17–25)	.40	7.55*
Income (17–25)	.03	.50
Married (17–25)	.09	1.76
Commitment (17–25)	−.05	−.92
Commitment (25–32)	−.08	−1.23
Job stability (17–25)	−.16	−2.50*
Job stability (25–32)	−.28	−3.89*
R^2	.47	
Model 2 (Ever-married men, N = 188)		
Arrest rate (17–25)	.38	6.61*
Income (17–25)	.06	1.14
Commitment (17–25)	.01	.32
Commitment (25–32)	−.03	−.45
Job stability (17–25)	−.17	−2.53*
Job stability (25–32)	−.12	−1.41
Attachment to spouse (25–32)	−.31	−4.45*
R^2	.51	

*$p < .05$.

Model 2 in Table 7.7, confined to ever-married males, suggests that
marital attachment at ages 25–32 is a significant and substantively
important explanation of levels of crime in young adulthood.[19] Men
with close ties to their spouses at ages 25–32 had much lower levels of
crime than men with discordant relations, net of other factors including
prior adult crime (β = −.31, *t*-ratio = −4.45). The latter compares to a
standardized coefficient of .38 for prior arrest rate at ages 17–25. Moreover, the ML logistic *t*-ratios for marital attachment are larger than those
for the prior arrest rate in explaining general deviance and excessive
drinking (data not shown). Thus, marital attachment is an important
factor in explaining later adult patterns of crime, independent of prior
levels of crime. Job stability continues to predict the frequency of later
adult crime, even among married men.

We also examined the effect of changes in social bonds on change in crime by allowing our key social bonding measures at ages 17–25 and ages 25–32 to simultaneously predict later frequency counts of crime at ages 32–45 (data not shown). Although this strategy increased somewhat the level of collinearity between marital attachment at Time 2 and Time 3 and reduced the sample size in model 2 (see note 19), it permits estimation of the long-term effects of adult social bonds on crime among men in their thirties and forties.

On the basis of maximum-likelihood negative binomial regression, we found the now-familiar positive effect of juvenile delinquency and exclusion risk on later adult crime in model 1. As implied earlier, hazard risk reflects adult criminal propensity because those with a high risk of exclusion are also those with the greatest likelihood of committing crimes in young adulthood and serving time. Independent of juvenile crime and adult exclusion risk, however, job stability at ages 17–25 had significant lagged effects on adult crime at ages 32–45. Apparently, job stability in the late twenties is less important than job patterns established in the transition to young adulthood. Model 2, on the other hand, indicated that marital attachment at ages 25–32 was the only predictor of later crime (t-ratio $= -2.73$), net of prior crime and exclusion risk. Since marital attachment at time 2 was controlled, these results suggest that relative increases in marital attachment at ages 25–32 lead to later reductions in crime frequency. Also consistent with previous results was the finding that the effect of job stability on later crime was attenuated among married men once marital attachment is controlled.

The data to this point suggest a two-part explanation: for the majority of men, job stability is central in explaining adult desistance from crime. This effect is reduced somewhat among those who were married, in which case attachment to wife assumes greater relative importance. Once marital attachment and job stability are taken into account, the effect of commitment is either weak or insignificant. Because the structural features of marriage and wages were also weak or insignificant, our tentative conclusion is that the results support a theory of informal social capital that focuses on the strength of social bonds linking adults to family and work.[20]

INCARCERATION TIME AND JOB STABILITY

One factor that we have not paid much attention to thus far is formal social control by the State. This is understandable in light of our theoretical perspective, which highlights the role of social bonds to family and work. Nonetheless, it is possible that official criminal justice sanctions have empirical consequences for subsequent criminal behavior that counteract our theoretical model. As classic deterrence theory suggests, imprisonment may deter or at least reduce the frequency of future crime.

In this section we therefore focus on incarceration as a criminal sanction, especially length of confinement in juvenile and adult institutions. In the Gluecks' research design all delinquent youths were incarcerated, so there is no variation in the prevalence of institutionalization that can influence later development. There is, however, considerable variation among the delinquents in the *time* they served, not only in adolescence but in adulthood as well. To assess the relevance of incarceration, we calculated the actual number of days (not sentence length) each subject spent in a custodial institution as a juvenile (under age 17) and at ages 17–25 and 25–32.

As shown earlier, institutionalization was one of the two main factors explaining the likelihood that a delinquent youth would be excluded in the measurement of key social factors at the adult follow-up interviews. By examining the direct effects of incarceration on later crime, controlling for exclusion risk, we are in a position to separate the deterrent or criminogenic effect of imprisonment from its role in sample selection. The other major influence on sample selection was length of time spent in another institution—the military. Hence in estimating lagged incarceration effects we also include length of military service for comparative purposes.

The results in Table 7.8 are consistent in portraying the insignificant effects of detention/prison and military service on later criminal behavior. Consider first the results for crime frequency at ages 17–25 predicted by length of juvenile incarceration, controlling for criminal record (official and unofficial) and our social control dimensions. The net effect of juvenile incarceration is insignificant and close to zero in both models 1 and 2. On the other hand, juvenile delinquency and exclusion risk continue to exhibit positive effects as in the past, and job stability and marital attachment have significant negative effects. Apparently, not only does juvenile incarceration have insignificant direct effects on later crime, but its introduction to the models does not change previous findings.

A similar pattern develops when we consider the frequency of of-

Table 7.8   Replication of Key OLS Models Predicting Frequency of Crime
While Free at Ages 17–25 and 25–32 by Juvenile Delinquency,
Young Adult Social Bonds, and Prior Incarceration:
Delinquent Group

Independent Variables	Arrests per Year Free, Ages 17–25		Arrests per Year Free, Ages 25–32	
	β	t-ratio	β	t-ratio
Model 1 (All men, N = 248)				
Juvenile (age < 17)				
Arrests per year free	.25	4.50*	.06	.54
Unofficial delinquency	.14	2.72*	.08	1.19
Days incarcerated	.04	.62	NI	
Young adult (ages 17–25)				
Exclusion risk	.43	8.03*	.04	.16
Income	.03	.49	.03	.48
Marriage	−.01	−.16	.06	.99
Commitment	−.01	−.11	−.09	−1.60
Length of military service		NI	.02	.14
Days incarcerated		NI	.29	1.09
Job stability	−.28	−4.61*	−.34	−5.27*
R^2		.40		.33
Model 2 (Ever-married men, N = 151)				
Juvenile (age < 17)				
Arrests per year free	.28	3.56*	.10	1.19
Unofficial delinquency	.10	1.46	.06	.83
Days incarcerated	.05	.58	NI	
Young adult (ages 17–25)				
Exclusion risk	.31	4.33*	−.01	−.10
Income	.01	.10	−.00	−.01
Commitment	−.00	−.00	−.01	−.08
Length of military service		NI	−.02	−.31
Days incarcerated		NI	.15	1.17
Job stability	−.18	−2.00*	−.26	−2.91*
Attachment to spouse	−.22	−2.55*	−.26	−2.89*
R^2		.35		.32

NI = not included in model specification.
*$p < .05$.

fending at ages 25–32 as a function of prior incarceration at ages 17–25 (columns 3 and 4). In neither model 1 nor 2 does length of incarceration have a deterrent (or criminogenic) effect on later crime. Although there is some inefficiency in OLS estimation because of collinearity between young-adult (ages 17–25) incarceration and sample exclusion risk (r = .75 in model 1 and .66 in model 2), it does not change the negative effects of job stability and marital attachment on later crime. Moreover, juvenile incarceration is not hampered by collinearity (for example, it is correlated at only .09 with exclusion risk), and its effects are similarly insignificant. Crime frequency at ages 32–45 is also unrelated to variations in incarceration length at ages 25–32 net of control variables, and the long-term effects of juvenile incarceration on crime at ages 25–32 is similarly insignificant (data not shown).

These results would seem to justify the conclusion that incarceration is unimportant in explaining crime over the life course. That is, it appears that in terms of its direct effects, incarceration is not a salient factor in the criminal careers of the Glueck men. As discussed earlier, however, the idea of cumulative continuity suggests a subtler effect—that adolescent delinquency and its negative consequences (arrest, official labeling, incarceration) "mortgage" one's future, especially later life chances molded by schooling and employment. In particular, there is theoretical support for hypothesizing that incarceration has negative effects on job stability and employment in adulthood (see especially Bondeson, 1989; Freeman, 1987, 1992). Arrest and imprisonment are highly stigmatizing, and many jobs explicitly preclude the hiring of ex-prisoners (Glaser, 1969: 233–238). By contrast, the absence or low frequency of institutionalization provides opportunities for prosocial attachments—especially at work—to emerge and solidify in adulthood. As a result, those with lengthy incarceration records face structural impediments to establishing strong social ties to conventional lines of adult activity, regardless of their behavioral predispositions (see also Burton et al., 1987).

In short, the logic of our theoretical perspective points to a possible *indirect* role of incarceration in generating future crime. To assess this possibility, we examined the role of job stability at ages 17–25 and 25–32 as an intervening link between incarceration and adult crime. In doing so it is necessary to control for theoretically relevant factors in the etiology of job stability. As Gottfredson and Hirschi (1990) argue, those individuals with low self-control and tendencies toward crime

Table 7.9 OLS Model Predicting Job Stability at Ages 17–25 by Juvenile Delinquency, Drinking, and Prior Length of Incarceration: Delinquent Group

Independent Variables	Job Stability, Ages 17–25	
	β	t-ratio
Juvenile (age < 17)		
Arrests per year free	−.01	−.20
Unofficial delinquency	−.02	−.44
Days incarcerated	−.22	−3.66*
Late adolescence		
Excessive drinking before age 20	−.13	−2.27*
Young adult (ages 17–25)		
Exclusion risk	−.17	−3.13*
R^2	.11	
Number of cases	306	

*$p < .05$.

are also the same individuals likely to have unstable life histories in employment and other conventional lines of activity. Accordingly, we control for official arrest frequency, unofficial delinquency, and exclusion risk. Moreover, previous research (for example, Robins, 1966; Vaillant, 1983) in conjunction with our qualitative analysis in Chapter 9 reveals the important role of drinking in understanding patterns of job stability. Heavy or abusive drinkers tend either to drift from job to job or to be fired from their jobs at a rate much higher than that of nondrinkers. Excessive drinking that began in adolescence (age 19 or younger) is thus also controlled.[21]

Table 7.9 shows that length of juvenile incarceration has the largest overall effect on later job stability—regardless of prior crime, excessive adolescent drinking, and exclusion risk. Even though all the delinquent boys were incarcerated at some point, those incarcerated for a longer period of time had trouble securing stable jobs as they entered young adulthood compared to delinquents with a shorter incarceration history. Since unofficial propensity to deviance, sample selection bias, drinking, and prior criminal history are controlled (the last factor influencing the length of confinement), it seems unlikely that this result is merely spurious.[22]

Table 7.10 OLS Models Predicting Job Stability at Ages 25–32 by Prior
Crime, Delinquency, Drinking, and Length of Incarceration:
Delinquent Group

A. Independent Variables	Job Stability, Ages 25–32	
	β	t-ratio
Juvenile (age < 17)		
Arrests per year free	.07	1.25
Unofficial delinquency	−.07	−1.42
Days incarcerated	−.13	−2.50*
Young adult (ages 17–25)		
Excessive drinking	−.30	−6.03*
Arrests per year free	−.07	−1.03
Days incarcerated	−.24	−3.52*
R^2	.25	
Number of cases	337	

B. Independent Variables	Job Stability, Ages 25–32	
	β	t-ratio
Arrests per year free (< 17)	.01	.19
Unofficial delinquency (≤ 14)	−.10	−1.90
Excessive drinking (17–25)	−.29	−5.75*
Exclusion risk (25–32)	−.16	−2.17*
Total incarceration (< 25)	−.21	−2.52*
R^2	.26	
Number of cases	337	

*$p < .05$.

Table 7.10 underscores the deleterious role that incarceration may
play in developmental trajectories of employment in later periods of
adulthood as well (ages 25–32). The first model in Panel A examines
incarceration length in both adolescence and young adulthood, controlling for juvenile crime and deviance, adult crime, and excessive drinking
as a young adult (ages 17–25). Here we see that excessive drinking as
a young adult does indeed have a powerful negative effect on later job
stability (β = −.30).[23] Still, length of incarceration in both adolescence
and young adulthood has significant negative effects on job stability at
ages 25–32 (β = −.13 and −.24, respectively). These results are notewor-

thy not only because confounding "propensity" factors are taken into account (such as crime and drinking), but also for the long-term negative consequences of juvenile incarceration independent of adult incarceration. Perhaps the structural disadvantages accorded institutionalized adolescents are so great (for example, dropping out of high school, record of confinement known to employers) that their influence lingers throughout adult development.

In Panel B we extend this idea by considering the cumulative effect of incarceration from adolescence (under age 17) through the transition to young adulthood (ages 17–25).[24] Despite this different model specification, the results paint the same general picture as in Panel A. Drinking and exclusion risk significantly reduce job stability at ages 25–32. But so too does the cumulative experience of incarceration—as time served in juvenile and adult correctional facilities increases, later job stability decreases regardless of prior record, hazard risk, and unofficial deviance.

The data clearly suggest that looking only at the direct effects of official sanctions is misleading. Length of incarceration—whether as a juvenile or an adult—has little direct bearing on later criminal activity when job stability is controlled.[25] This does not imply unimportance, however, for there is evidence in Tables 7.9 and 7.10 that the effect of confinement may be indirect and operative in a developmental, cumulative process that reproduces itself over time (see also Hagan and Palloni, 1990). Consistent with the theoretical idea of cumulative continuity and state (duration) dependence (Nagin and Paternoster, 1991), incarceration appears to cut off opportunities and prospects for stable employment later in life. And, as demonstrated throughout this chapter, job stability in turn has importance in explaining later crime. Therefore, even if the direct effect of incarceration is zero or possibly even negative (that is, a deterrent), its indirect effect may well be criminogenic (positive), as structural labeling theorists have long argued.

Modeling Simultaneity

The lack of a direct effect of incarceration on adult crime is not only consistent with our emphasis on informal social control, it also provides a unique opportunity to assess the simultaneous relationship between adult social bonds and crime. As we noted above, the concurrent effect of social bonding on crime may reflect reverse causality. For example, crime itself may reduce job stability if employers are aware of subjects' criminal activity and refuse to hire them or perhaps even fire them if already employed. One suspects that high levels of crime and drinking are also likely to produce strains on marriage that result in discord and conflict. For these reasons we have emphasized the longitudinal role of adult social bonds in explaining crime.

However, if one assumes that incarceration influences crime only insofar as it attenuates job stability, incarceration may be used as an instrumental variable in assessing the simultaneity of the social bond/crime nexus. Similarly, by assuming that the direct effect of juvenile delinquency on adult job stability is insignificant once the concurrent effect of adult crime is taken into account, we can estimate a full simultaneous model. Employing these assumptions, which appear quite reasonable based on earlier findings and our theory, we estimated two versions of a simultaneous equations model for panel data (see Alwin, 1988 for an excellent discussion of covariance structure models using longitudinal data). The first used the full sample to estimate the simultaneous effects of job stability and crime. The second added a measurement model for both crime and social bonds. Namely, adult crime was specified as a latent construct underlying the covariance between the frequency rate of arrests per year free and a summary measure of the extent of crime participation (see Table 7.3) at ages 17–25. Social bonding was also specified as a latent construct, measured by the observable indicators of job stability and marital attachment within the sample of married men. This latter specification is supported both by our theoretical framework and by the significant positive association between job stability and marital attachment among the delinquents at ages 17–25 ($r = .58$, $p < .05$).

This model allows us at once to examine simultaneity and to estimate the latent effect of social bonds on crime, corrected for measurement error. Maximum-likelihood covariance structure models (LISREL) were used to estimate both the full structural model (all men) and the combined measurement-structural model on the subsample of married men (see Joreskog and Sorbom, 1984; Alwin, 1988). The results were consistent and further confirm the general theoretical picture. First, the instantaneous effect of job stability on adult crime frequency was significant (standardized effect = $-.44$, $p < .10$), whereas the reverse pathway was insignificant and one-third the magnitude (standardized effect = −.15). Second, the simultaneous covariance structure model (see Figure 7.1) also suggests a one-way causal role. The simultaneous standardized effect of the latent construct "social bonding" on crime is −.62 (*t*-ratio = −3.53), whereas the corresponding simultaneous effect of the latent construct "adult crime" on adult social bonding is .00 (*t*-ratio = .00). Consistent with earlier results, the hazard risk of exclusion significantly influences both social bonds (negatively) and adult crime (positively), while incarceration as a juvenile significantly attenuates adult social bonds.[26]

The LISREL results converge in suggesting that both job stability and a latent construct of social bonds at ages 17–25—the latter comprising both job stability and marital attachment—have instantaneous negative effects on adult crime at ages 17–25. The reverse, however, is not true. Therefore, even controlling for simultaneity and correcting for measurement error, the basic results of this chapter remain. Apparently the role of adult social bonds is both instantaneous *and* predictive

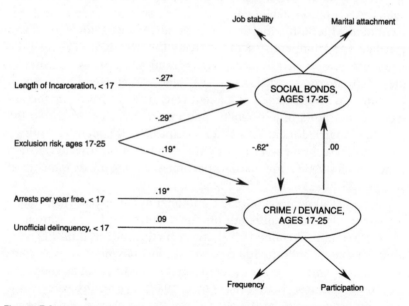

Figure 7.1 Simultaneous covariance structure model of social bonds and crime/deviance at ages 17–25: delinquent group, married men (N = 181). *p < .05; coefficients are standardized.

in nature, independent not only of childhood deviance but of the simultaneous effects of adult crime as well.

EVENT HISTORY ANALYSES

Because of the dynamic nature of the reconstructed Glueck data, they lend themselves naturally to one final and important test. This test involves modeling the exact time to failure (that is, crime) as a function of the exogenous variables defined by our theoretical model. For example, even though two individuals may both experience an arrest in young adulthood, they may differ dramatically in the speed with which such "failure" occurs. Of course, the timing of official *arrest* events may be arbitrary, and any differences may reflect more the characteristics of criminal justice processing at the time of the study than the timing of actual criminal behavior. Nonetheless, if the results of a time-to-failure analysis match in substantive terms the previous findings for participation and frequency, we will have yet another piece of evidence supporting the larger theoretical understanding of crime.

To validate our findings from a dynamic perspective, all models for the delinquent group were replicated using event history analysis. To prepare the data, we constructed the actual number of days until the first arrest of any kind in the age 25–32 period. Because someone can be arrested for different types of events, we also constructed the time until first arrest for property crime, violent crime, and drunkenness. The last factor is examined because of its frequency in the data and also for theoretical reasons discussed in the previous section.

In assessing time to arrest we must account for the fact that many men were incarcerated during adulthood, some for considerable periods. Since an individual is out of the risk pool for arrest while in prison, we calculated the time from jail/prison release until first arrest. Thus, if a person was incarcerated on his 25th birthday, the calculation was from point of later release until first arrest; otherwise the models refer to the hazard of arrest following the age 25 birthday. As it turns out, few men were actually incarcerated at age 25, so our overall model essentially examines the time from age 25 until first arrest of any kind before age 32. The exogenous variables were determined at the age 25 interview, so we are able to explore how variations in adult social bonds explain survival rates from that point forward.

The crime-specific measurement scheme entails a new time clock if a person had previously been incarcerated for an offense of a different type—a fairly typical scenario. Suppose a person was arrested for a property crime at age 26, served three years in prison, and was then arrested for a violent crime at age 30. In this case the hazard of a violent arrest is calculated beginning at the time of release associated with the previous nonviolent incarceration (age 29), and hence the survival time to first violent arrest (age 30) would be 365 days. It would not make theoretical sense to consider age 25 as the starting point in light of the three-year prison term in the middle. Because there is variation among individuals in release dates—especially for the crime-specific analysis—age (in days) at release was controlled in all models. Persons not arrested by the end of each follow-up were treated as censored.

The main analytic procedure employed is Cox proportional hazards models (see Cox, 1972; Allison, 1984: 33–42; Chung et al., 1991). In general, a hazard rate may be conceptualized as the probability that an individual will fail (that is, will be arrested) in an interval of time given that he or she has survived prior to that point (Chung et al., 1991: 62). For continuous-time data, it is more accurate to think of the hazard rate as the unobserved rate at which events occur among those in the risk pool (Allison, 1984: 23). The proportional hazards model estimates the effect of exogenous characteristics on hazard rates without assuming a specific form of the distribution of time until failure (Chung et al., 1991: 77). For an individual with measured characteristics represented by vector x, the proportional hazards model assumes a hazard rate: $h(t|x) = h_0(t) \exp^{x'B}$, where $h_0(t)$ is an arbitrary (unspecified) baseline hazard function. Although no assumptions guide the distribution of the baseline hazard, the model does assume that the ratio of actual hazards to the baseline differs only as a function of x and not of time. In other words, the hazard functions of individuals differ by a factor of proportionality—they follow the exact same pattern over time (for example, individual A's hazard is always 10 times higher than individual B's over time). This assumption is consistent with our theory, for we have no reason to believe that the effects of explanatory factors differ with time. Moreover, Allison (1984: 38–39) notes that the proportional hazards model is extraordinarily general and nonrestrictive, and is quite robust to violations. As he argues, in most cases (including ours), "the main concern is with the effects of explanatory variables, and the dependence on time is of little interest" (Allison, 1984: 35).[27]

The multivariate Cox proportional hazards models for the four crime types are displayed in Table 7.11. As noted, to avoid reciprocity problems we examine the time-ordered effect of our exogenous factors measured at ages 17–25 on the logged hazard rate at ages 25–32. The Cox model may be interpreted in a manner analogous to OLS multiple regression, where the coefficients represent the change in the logged hazard rate associated with a change in the exogenous variables, net of other factors [that is, $\log h(t) = a(t) + b_1x_1 + b_2x_2 \ldots$, where $h(t)$ is the unspecified baseline hazard]. More intuitively, the percentage change from the baseline hazard associated with a unit change in the exogenous variable is equal to $100 * (e^b - 1)$.

The coefficients and standard errors in Table 7.11 for the hazards of first arrest in the transition to middle adulthood are remarkably consistent with previous substantive results. In model 1 we see that juvenile crime and sample exclusion risk significantly increase the hazard rate, while job stability has large negative effects on the hazard of first arrest after age 25 (t-ratio = –4.09). In model 2, job stability is reduced in magnitude but marital attachment emerges as a significant predictor—men with high marital attachment have a 58 percent lower hazard rate than those with low attachment, controlling for other factors [$(e^{-.88} - 1) * 100$].

The estimated models for property crime, violent crime, and even drunkenness arrests are also generally consistent. For all crime types, job stability has a significant negative effect on the hazard rate in model 1. Exclusion risk and/or prior criminal behavior increase the hazard risk, as expected, and the effects of marital status, commitment, and wages are insignificant as usual. For the most part the effect of release age is insignificant too, but this is not surprising given the relatively little variation in this factor. In point of fact, for the first arrest of any crime type, the age at which the clock starts is virtually a constant—25—for almost all men.

In model 2, marital attachment has a large effect on the hazard rate of property arrest—men with close ties to their spouses have a 70 percent lower hazard of arrest for property crime than men with discordant relations, all else being equal. The effect of marital attachment is also significantly negative ($p < .10$) for drunkenness, while job stability emerges with significant negative effects on the hazard rates of all three crime types. And again, with the exception of exclusion risk and prior crime, no other factors explain the dynamics of arrests for property crime, violent crime, and drunkenness at ages 25–32.

Table 7.11   Event History Analyses Predicting the Hazard Rate of First Post-Incarceration Arrest at Ages 25–32 by Juvenile Delinquency (< 17), Young Adult Social Bonds (17–25), and Age at Release: Cox Proportional Hazards Models for Delinquent Group, by Type of Crime

Predictor Variables	Any Crime		Property Crime		Violent Crime		Drunkenness	
	Coefficient	t-ratio	Coefficient	t-ratio	Coefficient	t-ratio	Coefficient	t-ratio
Model 1 (All men, N = 262)								
Juvenile (age < 17)								
Arrests per year free	.78	2.99*	.76	1.76	1.40	2.69*	1.06	2.39*
Unofficial delinquency	.03	1.41	.05	1.38	-.00	-.09	.10	3.56*
Adult								
Exclusion risk (17–25)	1.23	2.54*	3.68	5.25*	2.88	3.06*	1.23	1.63
Age at release (25–32)	.00	.03	.00	2.75*	.00	.26	-.00	-.83
Income (17–25)	-.04	-.69	-.16	-1.49	.08	.60	-.03	-.33
Marriage (17–25)	-.14	-.83	.60	1.95	.28	.75	-.15	-.62
Commitment (17–25)	-.03	-.97	-.06	-1.05	-.05	-.63	-.00	-.10
Job stability (17–25)	-.14	-4.09*	-.24	-4.36*	-.24	-3.32*	-.13	-2.61*
Global chi-square (8 d.f.)	67.9		102.1		42.0		37.8	
Percent censored	30.9		74.8		85.4		68.2	

Model 2 (Ever-married men, N = 162)

Juvenile (age < 17)								
Arrests per year free	.64	1.74	.05	.07	1.09	1.52	1.37	2.20*
Unofficial delinquency	.01	.53	.05	.98	-.03	-.58	.07	1.94
Adult								
Exclusion risk (17–25)	.44	.66	2.89	2.41*	4.21	3.02*	-.03	-.03
Age at release (25–32)	.01	1.15	.00	1.74	-.00	-.06	-.00	-1.43
Income (17–25)	-.11	-1.38	-.05	-.37	.01	.06	.14	1.16
Commitment (17–25)	.01	.17	.06	.76	.10	.83	.05	.66
Job stability (17–25)	-.07	-1.27	-.21	-2.38*	-.27	-2.32*	-.17	-2.03*
Marital attachment (17–25)	-.88	-3.38*	-1.21	-2.24*	-.65	-1.09	-.65	-1.70
Global chi-square (8 d.f.)	54.8		45.0		33.3		24.2	
Percent censored	37.0		81.5		86.9		73.3	

*p < .05.

Table 7.12 Event History Analyses Predicting Survival Time to First Post-Incarceration Arrest at Ages 25–32 by Juvenile Delinquency (< 17), Young Adult Social Bonds (17–25), and Age at Release: Parametric Weibull Models for Delinquent Group, by Type of Crime

Predictor Variables	Any Crime		Property Crime		Violent Crime		Drunkenness	
	Coefficient	t-ratio	Coefficient	t-ratio	Coefficient	t-ratio	Coefficient	t-ratio
Model 1 (All men, N = 262)								
Juvenile (age < 17)								
Arrests per year free	-1.17	-3.09*	-1.16	-1.78	-1.98	-2.65*	-1.93	-2.45*
Unofficial delinquency	-.03	-1.42	-.08	-1.53	.00	.09	-.18	-3.41*
Adult								
Exclusion risk (17–25)	-1.84	-2.59*	-5.63	-5.00*	-3.89	-2.82*	-2.14	-1.61
Age at release (25–32)	-.00	-.10	-.00	-3.26*	-.00	-.50	.00	.08
Income (17–25)	-.06	-.66	.24	1.46	-.12	-.63	.04	.28
Marriage (17–25)	.25	.87	-.91	-1.99*	-.42	-.82	.28	.63
Commitment (17–25)	.04	.95	.08	-1.02	.07	.67	.01	.07
Job stability (17–25)	.22	4.24*	.35	4.10*	.33	3.05*	.23	2.62*
Weibull log likelihood	-441.5		-213.5		-145.3		-282.5	
Percent censored	30.9		74.8		85.4		68.2	

Model 2 (Ever-married men, N = 162)

Juvenile (age < 17)								
Arrests per year free	-.96	-1.77	-.12	-.10	-1.38	-1.61	-2.32	-2.27*
Unofficial delinquency	-.02	-.58	-.08	-1.03	.03	.53	-.12	-1.92
Adult								
Exclusion risk (17–25)	-.77	-.77	4.22	2.34*	-4.89	-2.72*	.08	.05
Age at release (25–32)	-.01	-1.29	-.00	-1.94	.00	.04	.00	.35
Income (17–25)	.16	1.40	.08	.39	-.04	-.18	-.24	-1.27
Commitment (17–25)	-.01	-.20	-.09	-.76	-.10	-.77	-.07	-.60
Job stability (17–25)	.10	1.27	.30	2.29*	.32	2.23*	.28	2.16*
Marital attachment (17–25)	1.31	3.40*	1.74	2.12*	.65	1.07	1.04	1.66
Weibull log likelihood	-255.9		-103.4		-74.4		-149.2	
Percent censored	37.0		81.5		86.9		73.3	

*$p < .05$.

To shed further light on the adequacy of our assumption regarding the proportionality of the hazards function, we estimated a model that assumes a parametric distribution of failure times. Specifically, assuming that the hazard rate may increase or decrease monotonically over time, we examined a survival model of time to failure from the Weibull family (see Chung et al., 1991; Schmidt and Witte, 1988). The assumption of a monotonically decreasing hazard rate over time seems reasonable for crime after age 25.

The results of the Weibull model are presented in Table 7.12. Note that the coefficients in this case represent the effects of exogenous variables on survival time, and hence should be opposite in sign to a proportional hazards model. This is exactly the pattern—the Weibull parametric model is virtually indistinguishable from the proportional hazards model in substantive meaning. Job stability and marital attachment increase the time until failure, and juvenile propensity shortens it. This is the same message as before, yet this time from a model that assumes a parametric distribution of the underlying hazard. Apparently, the data are robust to the specific form of the distribution used to estimate the effects of explanatory variables on the dynamic nature of criminal offending.

CONCLUSIONS

Using multiple data-analytic techniques, we have analyzed participation in crime and deviance, arrest counts, the frequency of crimes per unit of time free in the community, and the timing of arrest events. In addition to using different methodologies (for example, cross-tabular analysis, logistic and OLS regression, event history analysis, Poisson and negative binomial regression models, simultaneous structural equations) and dependent variables, we estimated a variety of model specifications, and we have analyzed adult offending at three different age periods—17–25, 25–32, and 32–45. Despite these varying procedures and specifications, virtually every model produced a fairly straightforward and compelling picture: namely, childhood delinquency and adult social bonds in the form of job stability and marital attachment independently explain significant variations in adult crime. This general empirical finding supports our dual concern with continuity and change, or, alternatively, our focus on both childhood and adult social bonds.

COMPARATIVE
MODELS
OF CRIME
AND DEVIANCE

8

In this chapter we examine the effects of adult social bonds on the adult crime and deviance of the 500 control-group subjects, and then directly compare key models with the delinquent group. Because the control group as a whole was not officially delinquent in early adolescence, we are in essence looking at the sources of "late onset." The nondelinquents thus serve as an ideal comparison group in which to assess the generalizability and explanatory power of our theoretical framework on social capital and informal social control in adulthood. Where the results are similar despite dramatic differences in childhood misbehavior, we will have further evidence for the importance of adult social control in understanding adult crime.

We begin in Table 8.1 with a simple overview of the concurrent and predictive relationships of job stability, commitment, and attachment to spouse with participation in deviant and troublesome behaviors over the life span. As expected from Chapter 6, the overall level of adult crime/deviance is lower among the controls than in the delinquent sample (cf. Table 7.1). Despite this fact, job stability is strongly related to later crime and deviance. For example, those control subjects with low job stability at ages 17–25 were four times more likely to be arrested, eight times more likely to be unofficially deviant, and over six times more likely to use alcohol excessively at ages 25–32 than those with high job stability. Because of the nature of the research design, these relationships clearly undermine a simple "self-selection" argument.

A similar pattern obtains regarding marital attachment and adult commitment to educational/occupational goals. Subjects with high aspirations and efforts to advance educationally and occupationally were much less likely to engage in deviant behavior, to use alcohol excessively, or to be arrested at ages 17–25 and 25–32. Among those married, all predictive relationships are in the expected direction, significant,

Table 8.1 Concurrent and Predictive Relationships between Adult Social Bonds and Adult Crime and Deviance within Control Group Sample

Adult Crime and Deviance	Job Stability, Ages 17–25			Commitment, Ages 17–25		Marital Attachment, Ages 17–25	
	Low	Medium	High	Weak	Strong	Weak	Strong
% Excessive alcohol (17–25)	32	8	5*	21	5*	46	4*
% Excessive alcohol (25–32)	27	6	4*	15	4*	32	6*
% General deviance (17–25)	12	4	3*	10	3*	12	4*
% General deviance (25–32)	17	7	2*	8	5*	36	7*
% Arrested (17–25)	36	17	17*	34	12*	61	15*
% Arrested (25–32)	36	11	9*	22	10*	39	12*

Adult Crime and Deviance	Job Stability, Ages 25–32			Commitment, Ages 25–32		Marital Attachment, Ages 25–32	
	Low	Medium	High	Weak	Strong	Weak	Strong
% Excessive alcohol (25–32)	31	7	2*	16	4*	29	3*
% General deviance (25–32)	24	4	1*	10	4*	29	1*
% Arrested (25–32)	45	13	6*	22	10*	35	7*
% Arrested (32–45)	31	19	9*	20	13	36	11*

*$p < .05$.

and substantively large. In particular, those in discordant marital relationships at ages 17–25 were at least three times more likely to engage
in a later criminal or deviant event.

The second panel of Table 8.1 replicates the relationship between
social bonds at ages 25–32 and criminal/deviant behavior at ages 25–32
and 32–45. Except for commitment and arrest at ages 32–45, all relationships are again in the predicted direction, significant, and substantively important. The effects of job stability and marital attachment on
excessive alcohol use and deviance are especially large, and, as with
the delinquent group, the predictive power of these factors is evident
up to age 45. For example, more than 30 percent of those with low job
stability at ages 25–32 were later arrested in the age 32–45 period,
compared to only 9 percent of those with high job stability. Marital
attachment in middle adulthood shows a similar negative relationship
with later crime and deviance.

The evidence suggests that informal social controls in young adulthood are significantly and substantially related to adult antisocial behavior, but this time within a sample of formerly nondelinquent youth.
As we saw in Chapter 7, then, the "ontogenetic" model's emphasis on
stability appears insufficient as an explanatory model for crime in the
adult life course. In order to explore further the sources of adult crime,
we thus turn to a multivariate model of social bonds to the adult
institutions of work, education, and the family.

MULTIVARIATE ASSESSMENT OF ADULT CRIME
AMONG CONTROL SUBJECTS

Proceeding in a fashion analogous to that in Chapter 7, our multivariate
analysis of the control group begins in Table 8.2 with the twofold model
of crime and deviance at ages 25–32. Because of the extremely skewed
distribution of arrests among the controls (for example, over 80 percent had zero arrests at ages 25–32), we focus first on the maximum-
likelihood logistic estimates of participation in crime. The results (model
1) indicate that variations in unofficial childhood delinquency predict
excessive drinking and arrest at these later ages. Obviously some of the
officially nondelinquent boys committed delinquencies, even though
these unofficial acts were generally minor (for instance, truancy, smoking).[1] Independent of these prior differences in juvenile misbehavior,
however, job stability has a significant negative effect on later deviance,

Table 8.2   ML Logistic Coefficients and T-ratios Predicting Participation in Crime and Deviance at Ages 25–32 by Juvenile Delinquency and Social Bonds at Ages 17–25: Control Group

	Crime and Deviance, Ages 25–32					
Independent Variables	General Deviance		Excessive Drinking		Arrest	
Model 1 (All men, N = 378)						
Juvenile (age < 17)						
Post-interview arrests	−.27	(−.55)	.52	(1.66)	−.21	(−.64)
Unofficial delinquency	.09	(1.01)	.20	(2.80)*	.25	(4.24)*
Young adult (ages 17–25)						
Exclusion risk	.91	(.35)	−3.37	(−1.33)	1.74	(.96)
Income	.00	(.01)	−.03	(−.21)	.07	(.62)
Marriage	.70	(1.46)	.22	(.51)	−.02	(−.05)
Commitment	−.04	(.32)	−.13	(−1.25)	−.04	(−.44)
Job stability	−.40	(−3.38)*	−.36	(−3.33)*	−.38	(−4.14)*
Model χ^2, 7 d.f.	16.7		35.9		42.6	
Model 2 (Ever-married men, N = 204)						
Juvenile (age < 17)						
Post-interview arrests	−.04	(−.06)	.70	(1.36)	.24	(.52)
Unofficial delinquency	.08	(.39)	−.20	(−.92)	−.01	(−.07)
Young adult (ages 17–25)						
Exclusion risk	2.84	(.37)	−11.39	(−1.40)	−3.49	(−.56)
Income	−.06	(−.31)	−.04	(−.19)	−.04	(−.28)
Commitment	.08	(.51)	−.05	(−.32)	−.01	(−.10)
Job stability	−.36	(−2.38)*	−.39	(−2.49)*	−.44	(−3.16)*
Attachment to spouse	−1.69	(−2.84)*	−1.45	(−2.32)*	−.89	(−1.65)
Model χ^2, 7 d.f.	24.6		23.4		24.9	

*$p < .05$.

excessive drinking, and arrest (t-ratios = −3.38, −3.33, and −4.14, respectively). The pattern for commitment to conventional goals is also clear: high commitment in young adulthood has no inhibitory effect on later antisocial behaviors. As in the delinquent sample, the effects of income and marriage are not significant. In contrast to the delinquent sample, exclusion risk has no relationship to later crime and deviance.[2]

In model 2, attachment to a spouse in the transition to young adulthood has large independent effects on excessive drinking and deviance at ages 25–32. Evaluated at the mean, the logistic coefficients tell us that deviance and excessive drinking are approximately 75 percent lower among those with high marital attachment than among those with low attachment. The effect of marital attachment on arrest is weaker, although it is still significant at $p < .10$. As in model 1, job stability continues to have significant negative effects (and commitment has insignificant effects) on all three measures.

The general pattern to this point is very similar to that in the delinquent group—job instability and weak marital attachment are directly related to later adult crime and deviance. These results are replicated in concurrent models for crime participation at ages 17–25. For example, job stability at ages 17–25 has significant negative effects on deviance and drinking at ages 17–25 (ML t-ratios are –2.74 and –3.92, respectively, for model 1). Marital attachment at ages 17–25 also has significant negative effects on crime participation at ages 17–25. Apparently, then, social bonds in the transition to young adulthood must be considered alongside early delinquent tendencies to explain adult crime by the controls as well as delinquents.

We now turn to control-group models of the effects of adult social bonds on variations in the *frequency* of arrest events at ages 25–32 and 32–45. Our initial analysis was conducted using the natural logarithm (+1) of the number of arrests. These results revealed significant negative effects of both job stability and marital attachment on later arrest frequencies (data not shown). However, as detailed in Chapter 7, OLS models are biased and inefficient in the face of skewed event counts such as arrests in the control group. To address this problem, maximum-likelihood (ML) Poisson and negative binomial regression models were estimated for raw arrest counts at ages 25–32 and 32–45. The results indicated significant overdispersion of events (all t-ratios for alpha were $p < .05$); hence the simple Poisson assumption of equal means and variances is untenable.

Table 8.3 therefore presents negative binomial (NB) models for frequency counts of arrest at ages 25–32 and 32–45 as predicted by lagged adult social bonds and control variables. The NB estimates for ages 25–32 indicate that, as in Table 8.2, job stability significantly inhibits later crime. For ages 32–45 the data suggest that job stability is the *only* significant predictor of arrest counts, with a t-ratio greater than 3. For both adult developmental periods, then, job stability reduces the

Table 8.3   ML Negative Binomial Regression Coefficients and T-ratios Predicting Frequency Counts of Arrest at Ages 25–32 and 32–45 by Juvenile Delinquency and Social Bonds at Ages 17–25/25–32: Control Group

Independent Variables	Arrest Frequency, Ages 25–32		Arrest Frequency, Ages 32–45	
	Coefficient	Coefficient/S.E.	Coefficient	Coefficient/S.E.
Model 1 (All men)				
Juvenile (age < 17)				
Post-interview arrests	.36	.94	.20	.57
Unofficial delinquency	.20	2.57*	.06	.67
Adult (ages 17–25/25–32)[a]				
Exclusion risk	−2.16	−1.01	.62	.22
Income	−.03	−.20	.02	.15
Marriage	.35	1.11	.03	.08
Commitment	.22	.99	.05	.20
Job stability	−.43	−4.04*	−.36	−3.69*
Log-likelihood	−257.4		−266.9	
T-ratio for alpha	4.16*		4.21*	
Number of cases	383		418	
Model 2 (Ever-married men)				
Juvenile (age < 17)				
Post-interview arrests	.62	1.16	.01	.04
Unofficial delinquency	.01	.05	.02	.18
Adult (ages 17–25/25–32)[a]				
Exclusion risk	−6.34	−.74	−3.74	−.80
Income	−.11	−.66	−.00	−.02
Commitment	.60	1.18	.17	.60
Job stability	−.41	−2.28*	−.35	−2.86*
Attachment to spouse	−1.14	−1.71	−.17	−1.08
Log-likelihood	−144.8		−211.1	
T-ratio for alpha	3.07*		3.73*	
Number of cases	206		339	

a. In explaining arrest frequency at ages 25–32, the exogenous variables pertain to the transition to young adulthood (ages 17–25). For ages 32–45 arrest frequency, the exogenous variables pertain to ages 25–32.

*p < .05.

number of later crimes. In fact, no other variable comes close in predictive power, and the effects of marriage, wages, and commitment are weak and insignificant.

Model 2 reveals a continued significant effect of job stability among married men. On the other hand, marital attachment has a somewhat weaker role in the explanation of arrest frequencies: its effect is significant at the .10 level for crime at ages 25–32, but it is insignificant at ages 32–45. Further analysis suggested such a skewed distribution of crime at this later period that it resembles a simple dichotomy—fewer than 8 percent of the subjects had more than one arrest. We thus estimated a ML logistic regression and found that marital attachment significantly explains participation in crime (1 = arrest, 0 = no arrest) at ages 32–45 for model 2 of Table 8.3 (t-ratio = −2.53, data not shown). The fact that marital attachment explains participation better than the actual number of events is taken into account in later models.

To assess the validity of these results, we then introduced a series of alternative measures and model specifications. First, as in Chapter 7, we re-estimated all models using both Heckman's (1979) probit-based measure of sample selection bias and the exclusion-risk hazard for the married subsample formed by job stability and income in addition to military service and prior crime. As with delinquents, the key findings were the same.

Second, as for the delinquents, we estimated the independent effects of job stability at ages 17–25 and 25–32 on crime at ages 25–32, controlling for prior adult crime. The results are sturdy—increases in job stability are directly associated with concurrent decreases in crime. For example, the negative binomial effect of job stability at ages 25–32, controlling for job stability at ages 17–25, on change in arrest counts at ages 25–32 was highly significant (t-ratio = −5.06). This was the largest t-ratio in explaining adult crime, including the effect of prior crime at ages 17–25 (t-ratio = 3.86). These results reinforce the salience of changes in social ties in explaining change in adult crime.

Third, we estimated Poisson and negative binomial regression models of crime-specific arrest counts. In the maximum-likelihood models that were estimable (some failed to converge, apparently because of extreme skew), the results mirrored those for total arrest counts. For example, job stability in the transition to young adulthood had significant negative effects on later arrests for property crime, violent crime, and drunkenness (t-ratios = −5.48, −3.26, and −2.07, respectively).

In short, the results for the control group parallel those for the delinquent group in Chapter 7 and support the idea that informal social bonds in adulthood predict adult crime. In light of these initial convergent results, we turn to a direct comparison of the effects of adult social bonds on adult deviance in the delinquent and control groups.

COMPARATIVE MODELS OF ADULT CRIME AND DEVIANCE

To facilitate cross-group comparison, we constructed a global scale by summing the indicators of excessive drinking, general deviance, and arrest over the 25–32 age span. This scale ranges from 0 to 3, and reflects an individual's breadth of participation in crime and deviance during young adulthood. By combining unofficial and official indicators, we offset the differing limitations associated with each data source. Moreover, the crime and deviance scale is much less skewed than the frequency of official arrests alone—especially for the control group.[3] In explaining variation in crime and deviance at ages 25–32, the social control variables are determined from the age 25 interview to eliminate the possibility of reciprocal effects.

For purposes of cross-group comparison, unstandardized OLS coefficients in addition to beta weights and the ratios of coefficients to standard errors are displayed in Table 8.4. The results for all men (model 1) are consistent across samples: independent of juvenile delinquency,[4] the largest significant influence on crime and deviance is job stability. Namely, the standardized effect of job stability in young adulthood on later adult crime is −.34 ($b = -.15$) for delinquents and −.29 ($b = -.12$) for nondelinquents. Also consistent with previous results, marriage, income, and commitment are unimportant in the presence of job stability, while juvenile delinquency continues to have important effects on adult crime.

Model 2, based on ever-married men, confirms that job stability has significant and very similar negative effects on adult crime. For example, the unstandardized coefficients are −.10 and −.16 for delinquents and nondelinquents, respectively. Furthermore, for both groups, men with close ties to their spouses in young adulthood were much less likely to engage in adult crime and deviance than men with weak ties, net of other factors. As with job stability, the unstandardized coefficients for marital attachment are similar across groups and the beta weights are large.[5]

In Table 8.5 we examine comparison models for social bonds at ages

Table 8.4 Comparative OLS Models Predicting Crime and Deviance at Ages 25–32 by Juvenile Delinquency and Social Bonds in Young Adulthood (Ages 17–25)

| | Crime and Deviance, Ages 25–32 | | | | | |
| | Delinquent Group | | | Control Group | | |
Independent Variables	b	β	t-ratio	b	β	t-ratio
Model 1 (All men)						
Juvenile (age < 17)						
Arrest frequency	.90	.21	3.74*	.02	.01	.28
Unofficial delinquency	.03	.11	1.96	.06	.21	4.30*
Young adult (ages 17–25)						
Exclusion risk	.58	.09	1.47	-.04	-.01	-.11
Income	-.06	-.08	-1.28	.00	.01	.11
Marriage	-.00	-.00	-.01	.03	.02	.42
Commitment	-.02	-.05	-.76	-.03	-.06	-1.27
Job stability	-.15	-.34	-5.10*	-.12	-.29	-5.71*
R^2		.26			.16	
Number of cases		246			376	
Model 2 (Ever-married men)						
Juvenile (age < 17)						
Arrest frequency	.67	.15	2.17*	.09	.06	.81
Unofficial delinquency	.02	.06	.87	-.02	-.05	-.48
Young adult (ages 17–25)						
Exclusion risk	.85	.12	1.73	-1.34	-.11	-.98
Income	-.02	-.02	-.30	-.01	-.02	-.34
Commitment	.01	.03	.36	-.00	-.01	-.13
Job stability	-.10	-.20	-2.20*	-.16	-.32	-4.65*
Attachment to spouse	-.80	-.37	-4.19*	-.60	-.27	-3.85*
R^2		.34			.24	
Number of cases		150			204	

*$p < .05$.

25–32. For a strict test of time-ordered effects, we restrict attention to crime outcomes in the later adult (age 32–45) period.[6] The results in Table 8.5 continue previous trends in that job stability has larger effects on age 32–45 crime in the control group than the delinquent group. In fact, the raw coefficients are larger for the controls by a factor of two. In model 2, marital attachment has significant negative effects on crime in later adulthood regardless of job stability, prior crime, and hazard risk. Moreover, the magnitude of the marital attachment effect is not significantly different across groups (-.28 and -.26). This finding con-

Table 8.5   Comparative ML Logistic Regression Predicting Participation in Crime at Ages 32–45 by Juvenile Delinquency and Social Bonds at Ages 25–32

| | Crime Participation, Ages 32–45 | | | |
| | Delinquent Group | | Control Group | |
Independent Variables	Coefficient	Coefficient/S.E.	Coefficient	Coefficient/S.E.
Model 1 (All men)				
Juvenile (age < 17)				
Arrest frequency	.18	.35	.29	1.17
Unofficial delinquency	.09	3.20*	.08	1.29
Adult (ages 25–32)				
Exclusion risk	.75	1.29	.30	.14
Income	−.01	−.19	.06	.51
Marriage	−.13	−.51	.03	.10
Commitment	−.20	−1.03	−.09	−.45
Job stability	−.13	−2.06*	−.27	−3.66*
Model χ^2, 7 d.f.		36.7		26.5
Number of cases		332		418
Model 2 (Ever-married men)				
Juvenile (age < 17)				
Arrest frequency	.64	1.04	−.04	−.10
Unofficial delinquency	.13	3.80*	.07	.94
Adult (ages 25–32)				
Exclusion risk	1.21	1.51	−1.77	−.48
Income	.04	.40	−.03	−.19
Commitment	−.11	−.49	.12	.49
Job stability	−.01	−.16	−.20	−2.22*
Attachment to spouse	−.28	−3.04*	−.26	−2.53*
Model χ^2, 7 d.f.		44.6		32.3
Number of cases		258		339

*$p < .05$.

firms the salience of adult marital attachment regardless of childhood antisocial tendencies. Furthermore, job stability in the control group has significant negative effects on adult crime at ages 32–45, underscoring the importance of both elements of the social bond in the later period of adulthood for these men.

Change in Social Bonds and Crime

To gain further insight on cross-group comparisons of change, we estimated a model that distinguished persistent offenders from those who
desisted completely (see Blumstein et al., 1985). We assigned a 1 to
those who were arrested at ages 17–25 and 25–32, and a 0 to those with
no adult arrests. There were 117 delinquent and 170 nondelinquent
"occasional" offenders, that is, men who had an arrest in one but not
both periods. They were eliminated from the analysis to maximize the
contrast. Because of the reduced sample size and the insignificant effects
of income, marriage, commitment, and exclusion risk in Tables 8.4
and 8.5, we estimated reduced models including only the measures of
juvenile delinquency (both official and unofficial), marital attachment,
and job stability. The maximum-likelihood logistic coefficient for the
independent effect of job stability on persistent deviance as an adult
was –.41 for the delinquent group and –.54 for the nondelinquent
group (t-ratio = –2.01 and –2.85, respectively). The coefficients for
marital attachment were –2.28 for delinquents and –2.52 for nondelinquents (t-ratio = –3.18 and –3.64, respectively). Clearly, marital attachment and job stability substantially reduce the log-odds of persistence
in crime among young adult men with vastly different delinquent
backgrounds.

We also estimated a model that permits direct examination of how
change in social bonds affected change in crime. For both the delinquent
and control groups, we created a variable that taps the direction of
change in job stability from ages 17–25 to ages 25–32. After cross-
tabulating trichotomized measures of job stability at these two time
periods, we assigned a 1 to those who increased at least one category
in level of job stability, whereas those whose job stability decreased
over time were assigned a 0. Those on the diagonal who did not change
at all—hence providing no information on change—were eliminated
from the analysis. In all, 130 men in the delinquent group and 235 men
in the control group experienced a change in job stability. Because
marital attachment was both more stable over time and extremely
skewed in direction (for example, only 4 controls experienced decreasing attachment compared to 195 who increased), we focus our attention
on change in job stability.

The results indicated that increases in job stability were significantly
and negatively related to change in adult crime. More specifically, after

controlling for juvenile delinquency (official and unofficial) and the hazard risk of exclusion, increasing job stability had a standardized effect of –.24 on crime and deviance among the delinquent group members ($p < .05$). No other variable had a larger effect. The corresponding coefficient for the controls was –.12, smaller but still significant and notable given that the largest effect overall was .16 for unofficial delinquency (data not shown).

These models suggest not only the importance of the strength of social ties that bind adults to society, but the relative nature of change in those social ties. Those men who experienced an increase in social capital tied to the labor force were more likely to desist from crime than were same-age counterparts whose linkages to work were attenuated. Change in social bonding thus appears to be salient in understanding change in adult crime.

Marital Attachment and Deviance of Spouse

We performed two additional sets of analyses to assess the validity and robustness of the comparison models described above. The first involved the criminal and deviant behavior of the subject's spouse. It is quite possible that men in noncohesive marriages were exposed to deviant role models. For example, according to the logic of differential association theory, it is not attachment or social control that explains crime but rather the exposure and intensity of contact with criminal and deviant values. If low marital attachment is associated with deviance of wives, our interpretation of the marital attachment effect may thus be erroneous. On the other hand, social control theory predicts that attachment to significant others should reduce crime, regardless of their deviance. This argument is analogous to the case for delinquent peers and attachment to friends, where control theory predicts that attachment should reduce crime even if one's friends are deviant.

To explore this issue we analyzed a three-category variable that taps the crime and deviance of the men's wives for the age 17–25 period.[7] Consistent with the principle of marital homogamy (Caspi and Herbener, 1990; Knight et al., 1977: 352; Osborn and West, 1979), the delinquency of men was closely intertwined with the deviance of their wives—only 19 percent of the control-group wives had a prior criminal or deviant history compared to fully 50 percent of wives in the delinquent group. Moreover, the correlation between deviance of wife and marital attachment among controls at ages 17–25 was –.68 ($p < .05$),

Table 8.6   Trimmed Replication of Comparative OLS Models Predicting Crime and Deviance at Ages 25–32 by Juvenile Delinquency, Social Bonds in Young Adulthood, and Deviance of Spouse among Married Men

Independent Variables	Crime and Deviance, Ages 25–32					
	Delinquent Group			Control Group		
	b	β	t-ratio	b	β	t-ratio
Juvenile (age < 17)						
Arrest frequency	.74	.16	2.55*	.28	.12	1.94
Unofficial delinquency	.01	.05	.78	−.00	−.00	−.05
Young adult (ages 17–25)						
Exclusion risk	.75	.11	1.74	−.95	−.08	−.72
Job stability	−.06	−.12	−1.51	−.17	−.33	−5.18*
Deviance of spouse	−.03	−.02	−.24	−.08	−.05	−.59
Attachment to spouse	−.94	−.43	−5.12*	−.47	−.21	−2.52*
R^2		.34			.26	
Number of cases		177			216	

*$p < .05$.

raising the possibility of spurious results in prior models. For the delinquent group, the correlation between marital attachment and criminality of wife was −.46 ($p < .05$). These correlations motivate a consideration of the simultaneous effects of attachment and criminal exposure.

Table 8.6 displays the comparative results for the control and delinquent groups of the effects of marital attachment on the breadth of crime and deviance at ages 25–32, controlling for deviance of wife. To achieve parsimony we estimated a "trimmed" model that eliminated insignificant predictors from Tables 8.4 and 8.5. Despite the overlap between the wife's criminal background and the noncohesive nature of marriage, the results are consistent and clear in their support of previous patterns. For both groups, marital attachment continues to have a large negative effect on crime, whereas the effect of a deviant spouse is insignificant and close to zero. For example, the β's for marital attachment are −.43 and −.21 for delinquents and controls, respectively, for the prediction of crime and deviance at ages 25–32. The corresponding β's for spouse's deviance are −.02 and −.05 (n.s.).[8]

Overall, the replication demonstrates that attachment to spouse inhibits crime and deviance regardless of that spouse's criminal and deviant activity. These findings support the general thrust of the theory of

informal social control developed throughout this book—that is, bonds
of attachment and networks of obligation appear central to understanding crime in the life course.

Drinking and Social Bonds

Our second test involved examination of the role of drinking in adult
crime. As shown in Chapter 7, drinking was negatively related to job
stability, which raises the possibility that the latter's effects are misleading. Moreover, the qualitative analysis to be presented in Chapter
9 reveals a pivotal role for drinking in understanding job instability and
also marital discord. To explore this area empirically, we created a
variable that pinpoints the onset of excessive drinking. Specifically, we
created a dichotomous variable by assigning a 1 to men who began
serious or excessive drinking in adolescence (that is, age 19 or younger)
as documented in the social investigation based on official arrests for
drunkenness, self-reports, parental reports, and social agency records.
Recall that job stability was assessed for the age period 20 to 25 (see
Chapter 7), and marital attachment was assessed mainly from information pertaining to the years immediately before the age 25 interview.
We are thus assured that the onset of heavy drinking for men assigned
a 1 on this variable preceded the measurement of job stability and
marital attachment.

In addition to time ordering, the indicator of excessive drinking before
age 20 is validated by external criteria. First, the teen drinking measure
is related to delinquency status in the expected direction: 14 percent of
the control group members were excessive teen drinkers compared to
54 percent of the delinquent group members ($p < .05$). Second, teen
drinking predicts excessive drinking in later adulthood: within the control group 37 percent of heavy teen drinkers were also heavy drinkers
at ages 25 to 32 compared to only 4 percent of non-drinkers ($p < .05$).
The corresponding figures for the delinquent group are 56 and 11
percent ($p < .05$). Third, as shown below, excessive teen drinking predicts later crime and deviance within both the delinquent and control
groups even after accounting for the effects of juvenile delinquency,
which suggests that the drinking measure taps additional between-
individual differences in low self-control (cf. Gottfredson and Hirschi,
1990).

We now address the key remaining question: do the effects of marital
attachment and job stability remain when problem drinking is con-

Table 8.7 Trimmed Replication of Comparative OLS Models Predicting Crime and Deviance at Ages 25–32 by Juvenile Delinquency, Social Bonds in Young Adulthood, and Excessive Drinking before Age 20

| | Crime and Deviance, Ages 25–32 | | | | | |
| | Delinquent Group | | | Control Group | | |
Independent Variables	b	β	t-ratio	b	β	t-ratio
Model 1 (All men)						
Juvenile (age < 17)						
Arrest frequency	.80	.17	3.60*	.02	.01	.30
Unofficial delinquency	.01	.06	1.14	.05	.17	3.70*
Late adolescence						
Drinking before age 20	.50	.23	4.72*	.62	.32	6.92*
Young adult (ages 17–25)						
Exclusion risk	.80	.12	2.39*	−.10	−.01	−.29
Job stability	−.16	−.38	−7.69*	−.10	−.24	−5.36*
R^2		.32			.26	
Number of cases		301			401	
Model 2 (Ever-married men)						
Juvenile (age < 17)						
Arrest frequency	.59	.12	1.89	.05	.03	.51
Unofficial delinquency	.00	.01	.22	−.00	−.02	−.15
Late adolescence						
Drinking before age 20	.36	.16	2.58*	.54	.26	3.84*
Young adult (ages 17–25)						
Exclusion risk	.83	.12	1.92	−.75	−.06	−.58
Job stability	−.07	−.16	−2.00*	−.13	−.27	−4.10*
Attachment to spouse	−.88	−.40	−5.20*	−.41	−.18	−2.69*
R^2		.37			.29	
Number of cases		176			212	

*$p < .05$.

trolled? The answer, shown in Table 8.7 for crime and deviance at ages 25–32, is yes. Within the delinquent group job stability has the largest effect on the breadth of later crime/deviance in model 1 ($\beta = -.38$).[9] In model 2 marital attachment continues to have a very strong negative effect ($\beta = -.40$), while the effect of job stability is reduced as in previous analyses. Within the control group job stability has a rather large negative effect on crime/deviance at ages 25–32, and both job stability and marital attachment inhibit crime and deviance in model 2. While the effect of teen drinking is significant in all four models, this is hardly surprising since excessive drinking is in fact one component of the adult crime and deviance measure. In other words, the effect of drinking reflects yet another form of continuity in deviant behavior.[10]

The data in Table 8.7, coupled with the additional analyses reported above, underscore the continued salience of job stability and marital attachment in explaining adult crime. Drinking *is* related to disrupted marriages and job instability—perhaps even reciprocally—but this relationship does not appear to explain the latter's role in fostering crime. The potential reciprocal and mutually reinforcing effects of drinking and attenuated social bonds on crime are explored in more detail in Chapter 9, where we present a qualitative analysis of individual life histories.

INDIVIDUAL DIFFERENCES AND UNOBSERVED HETEROGENEITY

Throughout this book we have tried to control for early differences in the tendency to commit crimes and other antisocial behaviors. Despite our efforts to control for previous crime and hazard risks in numerous different ways, it is still possible that between-individual differences are confounding the results. For example, although boys in the two samples were matched, within each sample individuals varied on potentially important characteristics. Perhaps the most important of these, as suggested by proponents of individual differences, is IQ (see especially Wilson and Herrnstein, 1985). Other dimensions include difficult temperament, antisocial personality, early onset of conduct disorder, and related manifestations of low self-control (Gottfredson and Hirschi, 1990).

To assess these factors we estimated a model that takes into account the effects of IQ as measured by the Wechsler-Bellevue Test. Three individual-difference constructs already validated by their predictive power (see Chapters 4 and 5) are also examined—difficult child, early onset of misbehavior, and tantrums. As argued previously, these measures were constructed to reflect poor temperament and lack of self-control at a young age.[11] In particular, unofficial delinquency, tantrums, and early onset respond directly to Gottfredson and Hirschi's (1990: 220) call for measures of early criminality (low self-control) assessed before crime is a legal possibility and constructed from information in the preadolescent years that is validated by its ability to predict subsequent behavior.

Furthermore, the Gluecks' data include a personality measure of low self-control as determined by the Rorschach (ROR) ink-blot test administered at the age 14 interview (see Glueck and Glueck, 1950: 57–60 for details). The ROR protocols were scored blindly by independent experts hired by the Gluecks (1950: 58). Although the Rorschach method has been criticized (see Gittelman, 1980), we include the self-control measure out of theoretical interest and also because it shows signs of both concurrent and predictive validity. For example, 33 percent of those characterized by high self-control were delinquent in adolescence, compared to 65 percent of those classified as having low self-control ($p < .05$). The relationship between self-control and deviance maintained for both follow-up periods as well, and even extended to crime at ages 32–45. In particular, some 27 percent of those measured as having high self-control were arrested at ages 32–45 compared with 42 percent of those defined as having low self-control ($p < .05$). Combined with the within-group nature of our research design, which counteracts any residual influence of bias on the part of the Rorschach administration (that is, knowledge that the boy was or was not officially delinquent), the self-control measure is included as an additional control variable in assessing the effects of adult social bonds.

Table 8.8 presents the comparative results of crime and deviance at ages 25–32. To provide as strict a test as possible of the effects of adult social bonds, we examine the simultaneous predictive effects of all five individual characteristics plus juvenile delinquency on later adult crime (with the delinquent group rates adjusted for time served). The effects of these child/juvenile characteristics on adult crime are for the most part limited to actual misbehavior (for example, unofficial delinquency as a juvenile has direct effects on adult crime for both delinquents and controls in model 1). The exception is a significant negative effect of IQ on crime/deviance in model 1 for the controls, and a positive effect ($p < .10$) of tantrums on crime frequency among delinquents in model 2. However, these individual-difference effects are not consistent, and other child factors are clearly insignificant (for example, early onset, difficult child). The long-term effects of the ROR self-control measure are also insignificant once delinquency is taken into account. Conceptually, then, the results imply that adolescent misbehavior absorbs the effect of early individual factors on later adult crime.

Table 8.8   Comparative OLS Models Predicting Crime and Deviance at Ages 25–32[a] by Juvenile Delinquency, Child Characteristics, and Social Bonds in Young Adulthood

Independent Variables	Delinquent Group		Control Group	
	β	t-ratio	β	t-ratio
Model 1 (All men)				
Juvenile/child (age < 17)				
Arrest frequency	.21	3.51*	.02	.32
Unofficial delinquency	.12	2.01*	.23	4.08*
IQ	.10	1.74	−.11	−2.07*
Difficult child	.00	.03	−.04	−.85
Early onset	.07	1.15	−.06	−1.10
Tantrums	.06	1.06	−.03	−.60
Self-control	−.10	−1.63	.01	.21
Young adult (ages 17–25)				
Exclusion risk	.27	4.35*	−.00	−.02
Income	.03	.41	.02	.33
Marriage	.09	1.38	.03	.56
Commitment	−.07	−1.05	−.04	−.79
Job stability	−.38	−5.29*	−.28	−5.06*
R^2	.35		.18	
Number of cases	211		317	
Model 2 (Ever-married men)				
Juvenile/child (age < 17)				
Arrest frequency	.23	3.02*	.09	1.16
Unofficial delinquency	.05	.67	−.09	−.69
IQ	.03	.38	−.08	−1.04
Difficult child	.11	1.40	.03	.43
Early onset	−.03	−.34	b	b
Tantrums	.16	1.96	−.04	−.52
Self-control	−.10	−1.26	.03	.38
Young adult (ages 17–25)				
Exclusion risk	.07	.84	−.14	−1.07
Income	.04	.46	−.05	−.63
Commitment	.02	.18	−.04	−.63
Job stability	−.24	−2.34*	−.29	−3.64*
Attachment to spouse	−.30	−2.96*	−.28	−3.59*
R^2	.38		.27	
Number of cases	127		165	

a. The dependent variables are the frequency of arrests per year free and the four-category crime and deviance scale, respectively, for the delinquent and control groups at ages 25–32.

b. Early onset is a constant in the control group for model 2.

*$p < .05$.

The other main result in Table 8.8 is that adult social bonds are impervious to controls for early individual differences. In fact, the effect of job stability at ages 17–25 on crime at ages 25–32 represents the largest standardized coefficient for both the control and delinquent groups. Job stability therefore has a large effect on deflecting crime for men with *opposite* criminal backgrounds—regardless of their IQ or early propensities for antisocial behavior. The pattern of effects for job stability and marital attachment is also similar in model 2 across the groups.

The results for crime participation at ages 32–45 (see Table 8.5) maintain when we consider the individual difference constructs in Table 8.8. In particular, the ML *t*-ratios reflecting the effect of marital attachment at ages 25–32 on crime at ages 32–45 are –2.75 and –3.03 for delinquents and controls, respectively ($p < .05$). Tantrums, early onset of misbehavior, child temperament, and IQ are thus unable to reduce the salience of social bonds in later adulthood. Recall also from Chapter 6 that family social control factors had no impact on adult crime once juvenile delinquency was controlled in each sample. Not surprisingly, then, controlling for family social controls in Tables 8.4 to 8.6 does not materially alter the results.[12]

Unobserved Heterogeneity

Of course, one can always argue that a particular variable was left out of the above equations, resulting in misspecification bias. Although we have tried to counteract the major possibilities, there is one issue that remains in the consideration of individual effects. Namely, it is possible that our control variables inadequately account for *persistent unobserved heterogeneity* among individuals in criminal propensity. Nagin and Paternoster (1991) have recently argued that panel models of crime need to account for such individual-specific components in the prediction of crime. We think their argument is important, and we thus explore it in some detail.

In a "random effects" panel model (for details see Nagin and Paternoster, 1991; Nagin, 1991; Greene, 1989), errors in predicting an outcome variable are assumed to have two components—an individual-specific component that is invariant over time (denoted here as u_i), and a random component that varies over time (denoted as e_{it}). The individual-specific component captures the influence of any enduring, but unmeasured, individual characteristics affecting the propensity to offend (Nagin and Paternoster, 1991: 171). The random component captures variations across time *(t)* and persons *(i)* in factors that affect crime but that are not part of the substantive equation (for example, criminal opportunities).[13]

The key to the random-effects model with panel data is that we can estimate the proportion of the joint variation in error terms that is attributable to population heterogeneity (that is, the magnitude of persistent heterogeneity is found in the correlation of the combined two-component error terms across time). To the extent that individual-specific heterogeneity increasingly dominates variation in the combined error term, the correlation will approach one (Nagin and Paternoster, 1991: 171). Moreover, controlling for the joint correlation of random errors and individual-specific errors over time bears on the parameter estimates of explanatory factors. The reason is that the presence of persistent but uncontrolled heterogeneity may bias the coefficients for variables other than prior criminal behavior.[14] As Nagin correctly argues (1991: 10), "The problem is that the association between the response variable and some specific covariate at the level of the individual is confounded with variation in the persistent unobserved heterogeneity across the population."

We therefore replicated our key results using a variation on Nagin and Paternoster's (1991) maximum-likelihood probit model. Specifically, we employ a generalized least squares (GLS) random-effects model of the frequency of crime at ages 25–32 and ages 32–45. In essence this is a pooled cross-section time-series design that assumes a parallel variable structure across time.[15] This model is of the general form: $y_{it} = a + bx_{it} + e_{it} + u_i$, where x represents a vector of exogenous characteristics at waves 2 and 3. Our model provides a strict test for the effect of adult social bonds, since we control not only for observed levels of childhood delinquency, exclusion risk, and prior adult crime, but for persistent unobserved heterogeneity as well.

The GLS random-effects results are presented in Table 8.9. The coefficients and standard errors for model 1 are quite revealing. First, note that job stability has significant negative effects on crime frequency for both the delinquents and the controls, independent of prior arrest frequency, hazard risk, and unofficial juvenile propensity. In fact, the largest t-ratios in both groups belong to job stability. Second, it is interesting that juvenile delinquency—both official and unofficial—continues to have significant positive effects on later criminal activity, controlling for unobserved heterogeneity. Taken together, these findings support the idea that state dependence underlies the effects of

Table 8.9 GLS Coefficients and T-ratios from Pooled Random-Effects Panel Model Predicting Crime Frequency at Ages 25–32 and Ages 32–45 by Unofficial Juvenile Delinquency, Prior Arrest Frequency, Hazard Risk, and Adult Social Bonds: Delinquent and Control Groups, Controlling for Persistent Unobserved Heterogeneity

| | Crime Frequency, Ages 25–32, 32–45 | | | |
| | Delinquent Group | | Control Group | |
Independent Variables	Coefficient	t-ratio	Coefficient	t-ratio
Model 1 (All men)				
Prior arrest frequency	.34	3.32*	.11	3.04*
Unofficial delinquency	.02	2.99*	.02	2.89*
Exclusion risk	1.21	6.04*	−.05	−.28
Job stability	−.09	−6.38*	−.05	−6.35*
R^2	.23		.12	
Number of observations	578		802	
Correlation ($e_{it} + u_i$)	.22		.29	
Model 2 (Ever-married men)				
Prior arrest frequency	.52	3.46*	.06	1.25
Unofficial delinquency	.02	2.10*	.01	1.01
Exclusion risk	.92	4.07*	.08	.51
Job stability	−.00	−.18	−.04	−2.94*
Marital attachment	−.57	−5.11*	−.21	−3.35*
R^2	.27		.14	
Number of observations	322		415	
Correlation ($e_{it} + u_i$)	.18		.34	

*$p < .05$.

both prior crime and weak social bonds on later crime (see Nagin and Paternoster, 1991).

Model 2 yields further support for a theory of informal social control in much the same manner as previous OLS and ML models. For both delinquents and controls, marital attachment has significant and large negative effects on crime frequency, exclusive of other factors. As in previous analyses of crime at ages 32–45, the effect of job stability is reduced among married men in the delinquent group. However, the effect of job stability continues to exert a negative effect among the control-group members. In point of fact, the only two significant predictors of adult crime among married men in this group are job stability and marital attachment.

The main reason the substantive results look so similar to previous models is the generally modest correlations of the error terms over time. As Nagin and Paternoster (1991) argue, as the magnitude of the unobserved heterogeneity component approaches zero, the random-effects model reduces to a standard fixed-effects model with no accompanying bias. In Table 8.9 the correlations for the delinquent group are especially noteworthy for their magnitude—the largest estimate is only .22, meaning that less than 25 percent of the error covariance over time is due to individual-specific heterogeneity. The correlations for the control group are somewhat larger, but even here less than a third of the error covariance can be attributed to unobserved heterogeneity, on average.

More crucially, accounting for persistent heterogeneity does not alter materially the effects of exogenous characteristics on crime. For example, a simple OLS panel model for the same specification in model 1 of Table 8.9 produces a coefficient of –.099 for the effect of job stability in the delinquent group compared to the random-effects GLS estimate of –.094. The corresponding OLS and GLS coefficients for job stability among the controls are –.059 and –.052, respectively.

Clearly, then, accounting for individual-specific persistent heterogeneity in the disturbance terms changes the parameter estimates of exogenous characteristics very little, if at all. One way of interpreting these results is that our controls for unofficial delinquency and prior arrest frequency adequately account for between-individual differences in crime propensity, especially among delinquents. This is the argument we have made all along, and hence it seems fair to conclude that introducing methods for unobserved heterogeneity does little to improve upon the combination of our within-group research design and models that employ explicit controls for observed levels of prior delinquent and criminal activity.[16]

SUMMARY MODELS OF SOCIAL BONDS AND CRIME

A central thesis of our book has been that early tendencies to juvenile delinquency—in conjunction with weak adult social bonds—explain variations in adult crime. Building on the empirical results obtained thus far, we provide a final overall assessment of this theoretical scenario by estimating models wherein the key indicators of social bonding are combined into a summary scale. For those men who were married, we summed standardized scales of job stability and marital attachment.

Men who were unmarried and hence had no marital bonds were assigned their value on job stability for the measure of social bonds. This twofold procedure retains the sample of nonmarried men, and hence increases the degrees of freedom. It also is consistent with our theory because it weights social bonds according to the nature of institutional connections. That is, single men are characterized by their work attachment alone, whereas for men who are married we take into account strength of marital bonds in addition to their work bonds. The creation of a summary adult "social bonds" scale is supported by the significant covariation of attachment and job stability among those married.

The model in Panel A of Table 8.10 estimates the effects of both prior social bonds and *change* in social bonds on adult crime and deviance at ages 25–32, controlling not only for juvenile delinquency but for prior adult crime as well. This model provides a strict test of the overall effects of change in age-varying social bonds on change in adult crime.[17] The results are quite clear: social bonds in the transition to young adulthood (ages 17–25) and changes in social bonds at ages 25–32 predict variations in crime at ages 25–32 unexplained by prior criminal propensities—whether juvenile or adult. Interestingly, the largest predictor of decreases in crime and deviance at ages 25–32 for both the delinquent and control groups is prior social bonds at ages 17–25 (β = −.63 and −.44, respectively). It is important, however, that increases in levels of young-adult social bonding continue to inhibit crime and deviance in both groups. The effects of change in social bonding on crime are even larger than the effects of prior adult crime for both groups.

Panel B presents the ML negative binomial estimates of the effects of social bonds at ages 17–25 and change in social bonds at ages 25–32 on later crime frequency at ages 32–45, controlling for prior crime in adolescence and adulthood. Again the results are consistent across the two groups: changes in social bonds at ages 25–32 explain reductions in crime at ages 32–45 that are unaccounted for by prior crime. Social bonding at ages 17–25 is also significant—apparently, bonds formed in the transition to young adulthood have a lasting impact on crime and deviance. These results are fully replicated using ML logistic models of crime participation at ages 32–45 (for example, the *t*-ratios reflecting the effects of change in social bonds at ages 25–32 on change in later crime at ages 32–45 are −2.92 and −3.44 for the delinquent and control groups, respectively). Therefore, the overall patterns in Table 8.10 confirm earlier results that social bonds—both prior levels and concurrent

Table 8.10   Comparative OLS and ML Negative Binomial Models Predicting Crime and Deviance at Ages 25–32 and 32–45 by Juvenile Delinquency, Adult Crime, and Adult Social Bonds (Ages 17–25 and Ages 25–32)

| A. OLS Model | Crime and Deviance, Ages 25–32 | | | | | |
| | Delinquent Group | | | Control Group | | |
Independent Variables	b	β	t-ratio	b	β	t-ratio
Juvenile (age < 17)						
Arrest frequency	.55	.12	2.88*	.01	.01	.21
Unofficial delinquency	.00	.02	.48	.02	.09	2.13*
Adult (ages 17–32)						
Exclusion risk (17–25)	−.22	−.03	−.69	.20	.03	.69
Arrest frequency (17–25)	.17	.20	3.90*	.13	.30	6.66*
Social bonds (17–25)	−.49	−.63	−12.93*	−.24	−.44	−9.02*
Change in social bonds (25–32)	−.40	−.49	−10.59*	−.17	−.33	−7.09*
R^2		.54			.39	
Number of cases		283			400	

| B. ML Negative Binomial Model | Crime Frequency, Ages 32–45 | | | |
| | Delinquent Group | | Control Group | |
Independent Variables	Coefficient	t-ratio	Coefficient	t-ratio
Juvenile (age < 17)				
Arrest frequency	−.53	−1.27	−.12	−.18
Unofficial delinquency	.04	3.06*	−.09	−1.63
Adult (ages 17–32)				
Arrest frequency (17–25)	.26	2.60*	.06	.33
Exclusion risk (25–32)	1.26	2.24*	−6.80	−5.48*
Social bonds (17–25)	−.37	−4.65*	−.59	−3.11*
Change in social bonds (25–32)	−.26	−2.86*	−.52	−3.14*
Log-likelihood	−540.9		−256.1	
T-ratio for alpha	8.56*		4.41*	
Number of cases	288		401	

*$p < .05$.

change—inhibit crime and deviance throughout a major period of adult development.

We also estimated a series of random-effects models that controlled for persistent unobserved heterogeneity. Consistent with Table 8.10, however, we found that individual-specific error components did not confound the explanatory power of our summary scale of social bonds in predicting crime. In fact, the GLS random-effects t-ratios reflecting the effects of social bonds on later crime were -6.26 and -7.27 for the delinquents and controls, respectively ($p < .05$). These were by far the largest t-ratios after controlling for prior crime (both juvenile and adult) and hazard exclusion risk, which underscores once again the salience of social bonds in explaining crime and deviance.[18]

CONCLUSIONS

The results in this chapter support empirically the major contention of our theoretical model—that job stability and marital attachment in adulthood have significant negative effects on later crime. These effects are significant, large, and of similar magnitude across the delinquent and nondelinquent groups. Despite vast differences in early childhood experiences, therefore, adult social bonds have similar consequences for the adult life histories of these men. Perhaps more intriguing is the finding that the predictive power of early individual difference constructs is virtually nonexistent within each sample, and neither the addition of prior drinking, wife's deviance, IQ, childhood difficulty, tantrums, early onset of misbehavior, and self-control as exogenous variables nor the introduction of error terms for persistent unobserved heterogeneity changed our major conclusion.

EXPLORING LIFE HISTORIES

9

Our research strategy in this book has two distinct components. The first involves quantitative analysis of the longitudinal data from the Gluecks' study. The second entails an intensive qualitative analysis of the life history records for a subset of cases from the Gluecks' study.[1] These records represent rich and varied life history data for nearly 880 subjects spanning a significant portion of adult development (up to age 32).

There is a strong tradition in criminology of using life histories of offenders as a data source about crime and criminality (see Bennett, 1981 for a historical overview). Contemporary students of criminology are familiar with works such as Clifford Shaw's *The Jack-Roller: A Delinquent Boy's Own Story* (1930) and Edwin Sutherland's *The Professional Thief* (1937). These classics in criminology illustrate the power of life history data to illuminate the complex processes of criminal offending (see also Katz, 1988). Our analysis of the life histories of the Glueck men seeks the same goal. A major difference from these earlier works, however, is that we merge quantitative and qualitative analysis in order to provide a more complete portrait of offending over the life course.

Our focus in this chapter shifts from a "variable orientation" to a "person orientation" wherein we analyze individual life histories or persons as the main unit of analysis (Magnusson and Bergman, 1990: 101). More precisely, we develop and examine several profiles of individuals derived from a combination of key variables used in our earlier analyses. This strategy allows us to explore "patterns or configurations of relevant person characteristics in a developmental perspective" (Magnusson and Bergman, 1990: 101). This "person orientation" offers a more comprehensive view of person-environment interactions, developmental change, and individual transformations over time (Magnusson and Bergman, 1988: 47). Overall, our plan to combine data on variables and persons follows Cook's call for "multiplism" in social science research. According to Cook, multiplism aims to foster consensus on empirical findings "by establishing correspondences across many different, but conceptually related, ways of posing a question" (1985: 46).

Our methodological strategy for merging quantitative and qualitative data is as follows. For each subject in the Gluecks' study, qualitative data can be found in the detailed handwritten interviews conducted by the Gluecks' research team, in the interviewer narratives that were produced for each subject at each interview, and in the volumes of miscellaneous notes and correspondence relating to family and school experiences, employment histories, military service, and the like. Through a preliminary analysis of case records for a small group of the delinquent subjects,[2] several dimensions were identified as worthy of intensive qualitative analysis for purposes of our investigation.

The first dimension targeted for analysis is *marital relationships.* Here attention is placed on the nature of the attachment or bond between the subject and his spouse—that is, the conjugal relationship. Also of importance is the extent of material and emotional support provided by the subject. One should keep in mind that, because of the historical period when these follow-up data were collected (1948–1965), the available information often casts the wife in a role that is subordinate to her husband. Thus, narrative information is present in the case files that allows an assessment of the degree of emotional support offered by the spouse to assist the subject in achieving his ambitions.

The second dimension centers on *employment histories,* especially with regard to job stability in adulthood. Extensive qualitative information is available concerning the nature of full- and part-time work by the subjects, including a summary assessment of work habits. In addition, detailed information on the reasons for unemployment, especially as the result of termination by the employer, can be captured through a careful reading of the original case records. One area of particular importance that the Glueck data can shed light on is the role of crime, alcohol, or other drug use by the subject in the process of finding and securing long-term employment.

The third area concerns the nature of *criminal offending* in adulthood. Although all subjects in the delinquent group had rather extensive records as adolescents, there is marked variation in offending in adulthood, as described earlier in Chapter 7. Therefore, we investigate in more detail the life histories of *persistent* offenders (for example, those with arrests, primarily for serious crimes, as an adult during waves 2 and 3) and *desisters* (for example, those with no arrests as an adult).

Given the large size of the Glueck sample, our plan entailed identification of a subset of cases for intensive qualitative analysis along the dimensions outlined above. Consistent with the goal of merging quantitative and qualitative methods, we used the results from our quantitative chapters as a means of identifying cases for in-depth qualitative analysis. To illustrate, in our quantitative analysis we presented evidence suggesting that job stability was an important mechanism in fostering desistance from crime. On the basis of this finding, we used the frequency distribution for job stability to select cases that displayed *high* job stability (the upper 10 to 15 percent of the distribution) in combination with no arrest experiences as an adult. Similarly, we selected cases exhibiting *low* job stability (the bottom quartile of the distribution) that had experienced arrests as an adult. We followed the same procedures for the marital attachment variable.

We also targeted cases that were clearly inconsistent with our quantitative findings. For example, using the frequency distribution on job stability plus information from the criminal histories of the Glueck men, we selected those who had low job stability yet desisted from crime. At the other end of the spectrum, we selected cases where job stability was high yet recurring criminal activity as an adult was evident. Again, we followed a similar strategy for marital attachment in selecting "off-diagonal" cases.

We were able to analyze qualitative data for at least eight unique cases within each cell of interest. When there was a sufficient number of cases in a cell (usually on the diagonal), they were randomly selected for in-depth analysis (for example, strong marital attachment and no offending in adulthood). In other instances, we were forced to use all available cases for our qualitative analysis (for example, strong job stability and persistent offending as an adult). In total, we reconstructed and then examined in detail 70 life histories from the Gluecks' delinquent sample.

Such a strategy has two distinct benefits. First, the quantitative findings are enhanced by the analysis of qualitative data, resulting in greater illumination of the complex processes underlying persistence in and desistance from crime (see Jick, 1979; Kidder and Fine, 1987; Cairns, 1986; Magnusson and Bergman, 1990; Werner and Smith, 1982). Following Kidder and Fine's usage, we are seeking *triangulation* that involves agreement about research conclusions across methods within the same study (1987: 63; see also Cook, 1985). Second, by examining residual cases that do not fit with empirical results, we expand and enrich our analytical model in order to account for previously unidentified pathways out of crime (see Giordano, 1989). This strategy is often referred to as *negative case analysis* (Giordano, 1989: 261).[3] As Jick argues: "In fact, divergence can often turn out to be an opportunity for enriching the explanation" (1979: 607).

The overall goal in this chapter is therefore to systematically integrate analyses of both the quantitative and the qualitative data found in the Gluecks' longitudinal study. Our approach is to first provide a detailed case history of one subject for each of eight dimensions of social bonds and criminal behavior that we are investigating. Second, we discuss various aspects of several other cases for each of the major dimensions of interest, highlighting significant patterns and themes. Third, we assess the viability of our theory of informal social control over the life course in light of the qualitative data presented. We believe that this approach represents an innovative strategy for integrating quantitative and qualitative data and provides an important assessment of our theoretical model.

We turn first to a presentation of cases that are consistent with our theory of crime and informal social control over the life course. For all of the life histories we describe, identifying dates (for example, birthdays, marriage dates) along with any other potentially revealing information have been altered slightly in order to protect the confidentiality of the subjects. The names for the eight subjects whose lives we explore in detail are fictitious, as are all case numbers.

WEAK MARITAL ATTACHMENT AND PERSISTENT OFFENDING

Arnold "Chick" Candil (born 8/28/26) had an extensive record of arrests including serious (index) offenses during the age periods 17 to 25 and 25 to 32. At the wave 2 interview, the subject was living with his wife and child in the Boston area. He was married in September 1950, and, according to interviewer notes, the marriage was "forced" in that their child was born three months after the date of marriage. At the time of his marriage, the subject was 24 years old and his wife was 25. During their first year of marriage there were domestic difficulties, and their conjugal relationship was characterized as poor. The subject's wife left him on and off during the year. During these periods of separation the subject's wife apparently visited her mother often, staying for several weeks at a time. With regard to financial responsibilities, Candil bought groceries and paid the rent, but only after much quarreling. However, he provided no money for clothes for his wife or child. Despite these financial difficulties and temporary breakups, the couple were living together at the subject's age 25 interview.

According to narrative data recorded in the interview schedule, there were also indications of domestic violence. It appeared that on one occasion Candil grabbed his wife by the throat. Moreover, he had repeatedly threatened her with violence. His wife stated that she was afraid of him, and the subject was later arrested for assault and battery on his wife as well as child neglect. The case was eventually dismissed in court because his wife was reluctant to move forward on the charges.

The source of trouble appeared to be that the subject drank excessively, which led to much arguing in the home. In fact, according to interviewer notes, Candil appeared to be drunk during the interview. He accused his wife of being a "tramp" when he married her—a "divorcee" who was already six months pregnant before the marriage took place. According to interview data, the subject stayed out until 2:00 A.M. each night to spite his wife. Overall, the marital relationship involved a fair share of bickering and arguing and was marked by temporary separations, neglect, and assault.

The problems with regard to alcohol appeared prior to Candil's marriage. While on parole, the subject enlisted in the Navy where he spent 28 months before turning 20. He eventually received a "Bad Conduct Discharge"—the result of a General Court Martial for being AWOL. According to narrative data in the case files, Candil did not get along with some officers in the service. He also overstayed his leave several times while on liberty—"running around with wild sailors, wild women, and wild drinking bouts." Thus, the main sources of difficulty in the service continued into his civilian life in the family setting.

The subject had similar problems when he began working at age 16. The Gluecks classified his work experiences as "unskilled laborer." At the wave 2 interview, Candil had been employed as a steel worker for the three months prior to the interview. He made no effort to improve his occupational status and appeared content just to drift from job to job. The subject's generally poor work habits appeared directly linked to his drinking.

This portrait did not change very much at the wave 3 interview. At age 32, Candil was being sought as a fugitive from justice. He had been living with his sister, her husband, and their two children. The subject was formally divorced in 1953, but he lived with his wife after that and they had a second child in 1955. The reason for the divorce was cruel and abusive treatment, reflecting the subject's neglect of his children and his bouts with drinking. During the age 25–32 period, Candil was also arrested for destroying property (a door) at his mother-in-law's house. In addition, the subject threatened his wife on the street and at the secretarial school she attended, forcing her eventually to leave the school. The Gluecks' interviewer characterized the subject as a "chronic alcoholic and wife beater."

Candil worked as a structural iron worker throughout the age 25–32 period. The work was seasonal, and there were periods of unemployment. Some of these jobs took him out of state. According to narrative data, the subject deliberately chose this line of work because of the high wages ($50.00 a day) plus the fact that it took him away from his family. It also appeared from the narrative data that the subject purposely loafed to avoid paying financial support to his wife and child. Apparently, heavy drinking among iron workers was quite common, and the subject "went along with the best in the lot," according to his sister.

In sum, according to notes drawn from various interviews, "Chick" Candil's favorite recreation was getting drunk at local bars, making scenes outside of his ex-wife's house, and trying to pick a fight with his ex-wife's boyfriend, who was, as of the date of the wave 3 interview, her husband.

WEAK JOB STABILITY AND PERSISTENT OFFENDING

Eddie Bicotte (born 7/14/26) was arrested frequently during the two follow-up periods and had spent 21 months in jail or prison during the age 17–25 period and six months in jail during the age 25–32 period. During the latter period, the subject also spent 23 months in mental hospitals. As an adult, he drifted aimlessly around the United States and was in and out of jails and mental institutions. According to narrative data in the case file, Bicotte was a vagrant for a full three years— from ages 27 to 30. Although the Gluecks' second follow-up interview took place at age 32, there was additional information in the file indicating that he was a vagrant again after his 32nd birthday.

At the time of the wave 2 interview, the subject was living with his sister. Bicotte's father had recently died and left a house to him and his sister, in which they were both living. The subject admired his father a great deal. His mother had died when he was $16^1/2$ years old. According to the narrative data in the interview schedule, the subject was very attached to his sister, who supervised him closely. The subject remained single during the age 17–25 period.

Bicotte's work life involved a succession of busboy jobs in various restaurants. His work habits were described by the Gluecks' interviewer as "irregular." It appeared that the subject had loafed for about 12 months during the period, and he had not held a single job for more than six months. The typical pattern was that he usually held a job for two to three weeks; then he proceeded to do something like oversleeping, and he would get fired. At the time of the age 25 interview, the subject was unemployed. Bicotte disliked the jobs he had had because he was not earning enough money, although he claimed, "I can work steady if I want to."

Bicotte also had some military experience, serving seven months in both the Army and the Navy. He first enlisted in the U.S. Naval Reserve in September 1943 and was discharged a month later. The subject received a "Special Order Discharge" because it was determined by the Aptitude Board that he had an "inadequate personality." More than five years later, Bicotte enlisted in the Army. However, he was discharged about six months after his enlistment for fraudulent concealment of both his court record and his prior Navy experience. He received an "Undesirable Discharge" from the Army. In fact, the subject was in a hospital for four months prior to his discharge because he was "mentally sick" as a result of his extreme dislike of the Army.

At the time of the wave 3 interview, Bicotte was living in a rooming house that his siblings ran. The subject's brother claimed that he was a vagrant who had few, if any, goals in life. He described his brother as "emotionally unstable, alcoholic, immature, and poorly adjusted." During the age 25–32 period, the subject did not marry. He continued sporadic employment as an unskilled laborer (for example, a porter, a kitchen worker, a general handyman, and a worker in a box factory). It seemed that the subject was unable to hold a job for more than three or four days at a time. According to narrative data, once the subject made enough money to get by, he would quit working. The reasons offered for his lack of employment were aimless drifting, excessive drinking, and institutionalization. It appeared that Bicotte made no effort to keep working on a continuous basis.

FURTHER EVIDENCE OF WEAK SOCIAL BONDS AND PERSISTENT OFFENDING

We examined 20 additional cases involving weak marital attachment or weak job stability and continued involvement in persistent offending. In general, we discovered life histories consistent with our theoretical model. Several distinct patterns emerged from the narrative data, and each of these is discussed in some depth.

Family Life

By definition, marital relationships for these men were characterized by frequent separations and, in some instances, divorce. Emotional bonds were tenuous, communication was poor, and communal goals were nonexistent. In addition, incidents of adultery, desertion, nonsupport, and neglect, especially of children, were customary. Indeed, many of the subjects whose case histories we examined had arrests for nonsupport. There is also evidence that some subjects purposely did not work to avoid child support and alimony payments. These men clearly did not take their emotional or financial responsibilities in the marriage very seriously.

A segment of a case history is presented here that aptly illustrates these themes of family discord. The subject (Case #390) married at the age of 20, while his wife was only 16—a third-year high school student. They were temporarily separated three years later. The couple had two children, the first born seven months after the marriage. After their breakup, the subject was arrested and subsequently pleaded guilty to child neglect. However, he later defaulted on child support payments. The subject blamed his wife for impossible bills, and he stated that he was reluctant to support his children if he was not living with his wife. The subject was formally divorced at age 27. At the age 32 interview, this subject was confined in the Massachusetts Reformatory. In total, he spent 37 months in penal institutions during the third follow-up period for several crimes including armed robbery and kidnapping.

There is also evidence of deception and betrayal in the marriages of some of the Glueck men. The best example is Case #412. This subject stopped working in the merchant service and informed his wife that he was "in bad" with the union and couldn't get any more of that kind of work. He told her that he wanted to go into business for himself—to set up a small luncheonette. His wife borrowed $500 in order to set him up in that business. Two weeks later he sold the business and went to New York with the proceeds. He later returned and gave his wife $100, and then he disappeared again. His probation officer straightened out the union problem, and he was supposed to leave on a merchant ship and send money home to his wife. The subject never showed up for the job. This subject had an extensive criminal history including arrests for burglary, receiving stolen goods, and forgery.

Similarly, Case #573 enlisted in the military as a single person to avoid his family responsibilities. He allotted money to his mother and siblings, but none to his wife. This subject left two weeks before his first child was born. Furthermore, he refused to work after marriage to avoid family responsibilities. In addition to these domestic disputes, this subject was arrested twice for burglary (in waves 2 and 3) and three times for drunk driving.

There is also considerable evidence of domestic violence in the lives of the Glueck men and their families. Some of these incidents were reported to the police, but many were not. For instance, Case #912 gave his father a severe beating—two black eyes and a sprained neck. It should be noted that the subject's father was described in the narrative data as being a drunkard and very abusive. When the subject drank, he became quite violent. In addition, there is evidence that while intoxicated he beat up his sister (narrative data described black and blue marks all over her body). This subject also had an extensive criminal record for non-family-related offenses including burglary, auto theft, and arson.

Case #543 was physically abusive to his wife when he was drunk. In fact, according to interviewer notes, his wife had a swollen jaw at the time of the interview. Moreover, his wife would speak only when spoken to. This subject got drunk on average once a week. His uncle, who had served time in both juvenile and adult correctional institutions in Massachusetts and was an excessive drinker as well, lived with the subject and his wife. In addition to his arrests for domestic crimes (for example, assaulting his wife, adultery, and nonsupport), this subject was arrested for burglary, larceny, forgery, and conspiracy to commit robbery.

The behavior of another subject (Case #573) was recounted by his wife: "After he got out of the Army he would call up here at 3:00 or 4:00 A.M., drunk, and he would demand to see his daughter. But I knew what he wanted, so I refused to let him come up or see my daughter. One morning about 3:00 A.M. he began to knock on my bedroom window, but I called the police. Then he began to threaten to kill my mother, me, and my daughter. That was when I decided to swear out a nonsupport warrant in order to get him sent away so that he would not bother us any more."

Case #904 displayed domestic violence with respect to several victims. For example, his wife first left him after he beat her. A year later the subject was arrested for another assault and battery on his wife. There is also evidence in the case file that the subject "knocked out his girlfriend with a punch following an argument." As found in the narrative data, the activities of the subject at age 17 included drinking, loafing, running around with married women, mistreating his younger siblings, and stealing from his mother. At age 19, he was drinking excessively and was described as "industrially unstable" (for example, he held eight jobs, each for a short time period). At age 20, he drank heavily and was abusive to his wife and mother. At age 22, he drank to excess and neglected to support his wife and son. At age 29, the subject was arrested for assault and battery on his stepfather—he hit him with a bottle.

In these particular life histories there is a threat of tautology, in that it appears that part of the definition of weak marital bonds includes domestic violence and other domestic disputes. Recall that the Gluecks used independent sources of data in their original data collection scheme to measure the quality of marital relationships and criminal behavior. Information assessing the quality of the marital relationship was derived from the home investigation including interviews with the subject and his spouse, while information on criminal behavior was gathered mainly from records of criminal justice agencies. Of course, the interview data were supplemented and corroborated by agency and court records that may have contained material regarding officially recognized domestic disputes (for example, nonsupport). Nonetheless, it still appears from the qualitative data that weak marital attachment leads to increased crime and deviance, especially non-family offenses. Moreover, in our quantitative analyses in Chapters 7 and 8, we addressed directly the issue of reciprocality by estimating both lagged and simultaneous equation models. These models clearly demonstrated the strong effects of weak marital attachment on subsequent crime and deviance, controlling for prior crime as both a juvenile and an adult.

Employment

Many of the subjects we examined could be described as "floaters"—floating from job to job with frequent layoffs and/or terminations, sometimes for drinking. For example, Case #931 held various unskilled jobs (as laborer, junk collector, plumber's helper, general worker, and so on), including seven different jobs during the age 25–32 period. According to his mother, "he was fired from every one because of his excessive drinking" (this subject's drinking history is discussed further below). During the wave 3 follow-up period, this subject spent 14 months loafing and 14 months living off relief. The subject appeared content to live on unemployment compensation. Similarly, Case #410 liked to wander around, and, according to interviewer notes, was described as "a drifter and a transient." The subject worked on and off and made only enough money to get by occasionally. Likewise, Case #770 held only unskilled jobs, and he never worked longer than one month during the follow-up periods. According to interviewer notes, the subject "just didn't want to work." Case #640 also had problems with job stability, and had no steady work from ages 20 to 25. He worked as a laborer, mainly as a feeder for presses at his father's printing business. The subject claimed that he wouldn't work for low pay, so consequently he only worked on and off. He estimated that he had worked possibly six or seven weeks a year for the past four years. The Gluecks' interviewer speculated that this subject was a bookie and a bootlegger. According to the available narrative data, the subject did not make any effort to find or keep regular work because he preferred illegal activities. Finally, Case #361 simply quit two jobs because, as he stated, "I didn't want to get pushed around."

It is also of interest to note that some of the subjects mentioned the negative effects of criminal records on securing and maintaining employment. For example, Case #390 was fired from a hospital when it was learned that he had a criminal record and some hospital supplies were missing. Case #603 was unable to get a "hackney" license because of his record. Case #931, who held unskilled jobs such as a counterman and a factory hand, claimed that he was unable to get a good job because his "record is against him." Finally, although Case #110 referred to his wife and children as "a great stabilizing factor," he had difficulty finding stable work. In fact, this subject lost several jobs when his employers discovered his criminal record. There were also references in the narrative data to the police coming to his place of work and questioning him as a suspect for recent crimes under investigation.

Alcohol Abuse

The deleterious effects of alcohol in the work and family lives of the Glueck men were revealed in the narrative data. As one example, Case #931 had 25 arrests for drunkenness from ages 25 to 32. According to his mother, he had been drinking excessively since age 16, and his first official arrest for drunkenness was at age 18. In narrative data drawn from a personal interview, this subject insisted that the basis of most of his difficulties, both prior to and after marriage, was his compulsive drinking. He simply could not "stop for one beer." The subject became assaultive when drinking. He even showed the Gluecks' interviewer his missing teeth, the apparent result of fighting while drinking. The subject spent all of his pay on liquor, forcing his wife to go to welfare for food for her and their three children.

At age 32, this subject was in a correctional institution for abandonment and desertion of his wife and children. Overall, he spent 19 months in jail during this period for crimes such as auto theft, drunkenness, and assault. The subject was described as a drinker who went on "benders" that lasted two to three weeks at a time. He was married at age 28, and all of his subsequent separations were a result of his drinking—his wife threw him out of the house when he was drinking excessively.

Criminal Behavior

As a group, these men committed numerous offenses and served a considerable amount of time in jail and prison. Many were in prison or jail at the time of the interview. Others were fugitives from justice and were being sought for outstanding warrants or defaults from court. For example, Case #390 had committed more than 15 offenses since age 17, including armed robbery. He had also spent 10 months in jail since age 17. Similarly, Case #904 was in prison for 63 months from age 25 to age 31. He was incarcerated for arson, assault with intent to murder, and assault and battery with a dangerous weapon (he started a riot in jail). Overall, this subject was institutionalized for 18 of his 32 years.

There is further evidence of overlap between the criminal justice and mental health systems. For instance, Case #912 spent eight months in penal institutions and 23 months in nonpenal institutions from ages 17 to 25. The subject served in the military for seven months and received a medical discharge for "psychiatric reasons, attempted suicide." The subject worked at several unskilled jobs—apprentice sheet metal worker, hospital orderly, rubber factory worker, railroad laborer, farm laborer, and doughnut shop worker. The longest job he held was for three months. He was described as a good worker when employed; however, he was frequently absent because of hospitalizations. He was diagnosed as having epilepsy and "chronic brain syndrome," and was considered permanently disabled and unemployable. He spent time in various VA hospitals as well as mental hospitals and prisons. Specifically, he served 23 months in penal institutions and 34 months in mental hospitals during the wave 3 period. According to narrative data, the subject made several suicide attempts. His sister claimed, "I never knew him to work any job more than two weeks. He would be sick, go into hospital, escape, and once again start drifting around the country. When he got in trouble, he would tell the police that he was a mentally sick veteran and they would send him to a mental hospital. [The subject] never wanted to work—he just wanted to collect his VA check, drink, and then beat up the ones who tried to help him."

We also found evidence of the dual effects of weak marital attachment and poor job stability coupled with a negative attitude toward institutions. For example, at the wave 2 interview, Case #130 had been institutionalized in prison for 59 months since age 17 and was the youngest inmate in the Massachusetts adult correctional system at the time. The subject had left school in the ninth grade (at age 15) when he was institutionalized in the Lyman School for Boys, and had no interest in furthering his education. According to narrative data from the interview, the subject was bitter toward institutions and envisioned a life of confinement.

During the period from ages 25 to 32, this subject spent 68 months in penal institutions. The subject married at age $26^{1}/_{2}$; according to interview data and official record checks, his wife had had four arrests at the time of marriage and was described in the interview schedule as an "alcoholic." Despite the marriage, there was little evidence of strong attachment to his spouse. According to narrative data in the case file, while the subject was confined, his wife was out drinking in the company of sailors. Also, the subject's mother-in-law treated his wife for knife wounds inflicted by the subject, who carried a knife and used it more than once. As for employment, the subject was classified as an unskilled laborer and never worked at any one place for more than a few months. Therefore, along with weak marital attachment, this subject had experienced little job stability from ages 25 to 32.

STRONG MARITAL ATTACHMENT
AND DESISTANCE FROM CRIME

We now turn to the case of men with strong social bonds in adulthood who desisted from crime. We begin with Charles Wisberg (born 6/13/28), who had no official record of arrests during the wave 2 and 3 periods. This pattern in adulthood sharply contrasts with his criminal experiences in childhood and adolescence. The subject had 10 arrests as a juvenile, primarily for larcenies and burglaries. His first arrest occurred at the age of eight. Moreover, he was incarcerated three times (his first commitment took place when he was 11), and he spent a total of 30 months confined in reform schools.

At the time of the wave 2 interview, Wisberg was living with his wife in East Boston. They were married in May 1949. The subject was almost 21 at the time of marriage, and his wife was 19. According to interview data, the subject was devoted to his wife. They appeared especially united in their mutual desire to advance economically. According to data in the case files, they paid cash for all their furniture and for a new car. Their goal was to build their own home. The subject was appreciative of his wife's cooperation and her enduring help and desire to advance economically. When asked for reasons for his reformation, the subject offered, "I'm married, older, and settled down now."

At the age of 18, Wisberg had joined the U.S. Merchant Service. He remained with the same shipping line for two and a half years, working on the eastern seaboard from Canada to Cuba. Once every three months, the subject returned home. He gave virtually all of his earnings to his mother to bank for him. His parole officer speculated that the subject had joined the merchant service to remove himself from detrimental neighborhood influences that were leading him to delinquency and crime. During this same period (ages 18 to 20), the subject began a relationship with the woman who would eventually become his wife. Although classmates together in high school, they began "an active courtship via letters" while he was in the U.S.M.S., according to interviewer notes.

During the age 20–25 period the subject held other jobs, including defense worker, apprentice welder, and factory worker. From all accounts, Wisberg appeared to be a solid, industrious worker who came highly recommended. His job at the time of the age 25 interview was at a factory where he had worked for the past six months.

This portrait of Wisberg did not change very much at the wave 3 interview. At age 32, he was living with his wife and two children in a suburb close to Boston. He appeared happy with his wife and was devoted to their two children. In his spare time, he worked on home improvement. Throughout the age 25–32 period, the subject worked at one job and had recently been promoted to foreman. He had been a machine operator at the factory where he now acted as the foreman. According to interviewer notes, the subject was an industrious worker with no problems whatsoever on the job.

In sum, Wisberg claimed four factors as important in his reformation—his wife, his daughters, his house, and his job. The subject took extreme pride in his house and showed the interviewer from the Gluecks' research team both the inside and outside renovations that he had done. It should be noted that this subject also had strong job stability at waves 2 and 3.

STRONG JOB STABILITY AND DESISTANCE FROM CRIME

Although Fred Nullin (born 1/28/29) had no arrests as an adult, his earlier experiences were quite different. This subject experienced five arrests as a juvenile, mainly for burglaries and larcenies. He was incarcerated in reform school for a period of nine months for his crimes. At the age of 16, he left school to go to work in order to support his mother and five siblings. The subject served in the U.S. Merchant Service for about 18 months at ages 17–18, working on oil tankers along the east coast.

Throughout the age 17–25 period, the subject's marital status was single. He was living with his mother and siblings in Boston at the time of the wave 2 interview. The subject fully supported his mother and two siblings who were still in high school. According to narrative data in the case file, the subject had refrained from marriage until his younger siblings were out of high school. During the wave 2 period, Nullin

worked at unskilled jobs (for example, oil and coal truck helper, apprentice welder, factory worker). He had held his last job for six years, and
from all accounts he worked very hard to support his mother and
siblings. The subject stated that his "home responsibilities forced him
to be a stable and regular worker." He wanted to become an auto
mechanic and was taking courses on that subject at a local high school.

At the wave 3 interview, Nullin was living with his wife and son in
a city near Boston. The subject was married in June 1954 at age $25^1/2$.
From the narrative data, there is evidence that he got along well with
his wife. The couple had one son, and the available narrative data
indicate that they appeared to be united in their love for him.

Since marriage Nullin had worked steadily as a machine operator,
an "unskilled/semiskilled" position according to the Gluecks. He had
worked continuously at the same place since 1949 (note that the third
follow-up occurred in 1961) and was considered to be a good worker.
There is no evidence of drinking or any layoffs in this subject's work
history.

FURTHER EVIDENCE OF STRONG SOCIAL BONDS AND DESISTANCE

We examined 16 additional cases of strong marital attachment or strong
job stability and little or no offending in adulthood (ages 17–32). Overall
these life histories provided further support for our theory. The major
turning points in the life course for the men who refrained from crime
and deviance in adulthood were good marriages and stable employment. In addition, there is evidence from a few cases suggesting that
institutionalization at Lyman or Shirley (juvenile correctional facilities)
and/or military service had a *positive* effect on later adult development.
At present our framework does not emphasize either of these institutions as significant turning points in predicting positive adult outcomes.
We thus discuss these findings along with those for marriage and employment.

Marriage

Cases in which marriage and family were identified as important factors
in explaining desistance from crime in adulthood displayed a similar
set of patterns. Couples appeared devoted to each other and to their
children. Indeed, life seemed to be centered around the home, spouse,

and children. For example, Case #040 claimed that "marriage settled me down—a good wife and fine healthy sons." Communication patterns were good, especially concerning issues of money and future finances. In these cases the subjects were almost universally described as financially responsible not only to their spouses, but also to parents and even siblings if the need arose. For instance, Case #920 completely supported his mother and two siblings (who were still in high school) for six years. Similarly, Case #813 offered, "I married early and had a family. I worked steadily to support them and to take care of my responsibilities. I never had any time to get into trouble." Overall these subjects were characterized as "good family men" on the basis of the qualitative information that was gathered in interviews with them.

What seems particularly evident is the importance of social capital in adult relationships, especially between husbands and wives (Coleman, 1988). These subjects invested in marital relationships, and often their investment was reciprocated by their wives, both emotionally and financially. If the couple had children and displayed strong bonds to them, this usually added another dimension of social capital in the marital relationship. As a result of this establishment of social capital, these subjects were more likely to desist from crime and deviance.

Employment

Several common themes were revealed when we examined the work histories of the men who desisted from crime and deviance in adulthood. On the whole, these men had good work habits and were frequently described as "hard workers." They often worked for the same employer for long periods of time (for example, 7 to 12 years), denoting strong ties to work and investment in specific employers. As a group, they wanted to do better in life. They thought about the future and wanted to "get ahead" as well as maintain "job security." Some of the men worked at part-time jobs as well as full-time jobs to make ends meet, while others became involved in home repairs and remodeling. Some also took advantage of the G.I. Bill, taking special courses or enrolling in job training programs, while others did not. In our theoretical framework, taking courses or additional job training, thinking about future plans, and staying with a particular employer for an extended period are all indicators of social capital or social investment in work. As social capital increases, bonds to work grow stronger and desistance from crime and deviance is more likely. The following cases illustrate many of these themes in more detail.

At age 25, Case #230 was living with his mother and siblings in the Boston area. The subject's father died when the subject was almost 23 years old. The subject served 37 months in the U.S. Marine Corps during World War II. He fought in two battles, earned two medals, and, overall, had "pleasant memories of the service." Although the subject was single during the age 17–25 period, he exhibited strong attachment to his mother and siblings. For instance, he bought a house with a G.I. loan and turned it over to his mother, and he gave money to his mother as well. As for employment, he worked at several jobs, but he always seemed to be "in between work." In part, he lived off money derived from Veterans Readjustment Compensation. He was not interested in education or vocational training, only in "making money fast."

By the time the subject reached age 32, he was married and had two children. This marriage had taken place when the subject was 25 and his wife was almost 20. The subject lived in the same neighborhood in which he had grown up, and there is evidence of strong marital attachment. For instance, the subject was very responsible and was devoted to improving the lives of his two sons. The family seemed close knit and cohesive. In terms of employment, the subject was a licensed plumber and gas fitter and had held steady jobs for more than five years. Significantly, for two years the subject participated in a job training program that was conducted by the Veterans Administration and supported by the G.I. Bill. The subject decided to take advantage of the G.I. Bill shortly after he was married.

Another subject (Case #004) reported that he was "turning over a new leaf" because of the influence of his wife. At the wave 2 interview, this subject had been employed for one year as a maintenance man. He had also served in the U.S. Air Force for 31 months during the Korean War. Because of a charge of homosexuality while in the service, the subject received an "Undesirable Discharge." He also drank excessively in the military and was once reported to be AWOL. The subject was bitter about this type of discharge because it made him ineligible for G.I. benefits. Specifically, he believed that he was unable to get a job with the airlines because of the Air Force's charge of homosexuality. The subject stated in the interview that "I'll always have that undesirable discharge hanging around my neck for the rest of my life." This parallels our earlier discussion regarding the negative consequences of criminal records in securing and maintaining employment. During the age 25–32 follow-up, the subject lived with his wife and three sons. He was still employed with the same company and had worked there for approximately six years. The subject was not in any trouble in the age 25 to 32 period, and he credited his wife and family responsibilities for his "reformation."[4]

Military Service

Several cases we examined pointed to the military as a "settling influence" or turning point in the life course (see also Elder, 1986). Unfortunately, given the available information in the Gluecks' case files, it is hard to uncover exactly what it was about the military experience that facilitated a turning point. Moreover, this finding of a positive influence is somewhat surprising given our results on the continuity of antisocial behavior from adolescence into adult domains including misconduct in the military (see Chapter 6).[5] However, it is not inconsistent that the military can serve to turn some men's lives around, even as it disrupts other men's lives (Elder, 1986) or provides yet another setting for some men to continue their deviant behavior (cf. Chapter 6). Here we briefly present some representative cases where the military played a significant, positive role in men's lives.[6]

At both the wave 2 and 3 interviews, Case #280 was living with his wife and children. The subject married when he was almost 22. At the time, his wife was nearly 21. There was a strong marital attachment between the subject and his spouse that centered around their home and children. Although the subject's career was in the Navy, the family lived together during the military service. According to narrative data, the subject's wife "is considered to be a stable force in the subject's life; highly respected by the subject's family, who feel she is directly responsible for the success which the subject has made of his Navy career." The subject was in the Navy for more than 13 years; he joined while on parole from Lyman. He stated that his enlistment in the military changed his outlook on life: "In the Navy I was thrown in with guys from all over the country; some of them were well educated and had good backgrounds. I began to see that my thinking was way out of line and that I was probably wrong. I began to do things their way and things have gone well ever since."

This experience parallels that of another subject (Case #412) who also spent a considerable period of time in the Navy (seven and a half years) and had strong bonds to his wife and two sons. Similarly, other subjects in the study (for example, Case #600, Case #670, and Case #040) reported that they "matured in the service" or that the "Army taught me a few things." Like Elder (1986), we thus find that, for some men, serving in the military can help surmount childhood disadvantage.

Institutionalization as a Juvenile

According to narrative data in the case file, Case #230 admitted that he deserved to be sent to the Lyman School for delinquent boys and that his commitment convinced him to "respect the things that count in life." The subject insisted that the commitment to Lyman was "the best thing that ever happened" because it took him away from his family and placed him under "firm authority and close supervision," with the net result being a change in attitude. In fact, the subject believes he would not have reformed if it were not for the Lyman experience. The subject recounted: "I was a wise guy—I knew all the answers and no one could tell me anything. My father did the best he could, but I thought I knew more than he did. I thought I was tough and I wasn't afraid of anyone." The boy's family visited him frequently in Lyman, and this may have had a positive effect on his outcome.

When asked to give reasons for his reformation, Case #050 stated, "My houseparents at the Lyman School were wonderful to me. They often had long talks with me whenever they saw me thinking. I was their houseboy and I liked them. They really seemed interested in me. They impressed upon me that I owed my sister a lot for bringing me up. I made up my mind to stop going with the old gang when I came out and I did. I went to work and have never even been tempted to get into trouble since."

Finding a positive influence of institutionalization as a juvenile may appear somewhat surprising in light of earlier results showing the deleterious effects of juvenile incarceration on later adult development (see Chapter 7). It should be pointed out, however, that the two individuals discussed here served relatively short terms during adolescence (six months and eight months, respectively) compared with the total sample of delinquent subjects, where the average time served was one and a half years. This relatively short period of incarceration along with other aspects of the institutionalization (for example, closeness to house parents) may well account for any positive outcomes in later adulthood. It is also possible that because of other positive life events in adulthood, these subjects retrospectively reinterpreted their institutional experience as a significant turning point in their lives. As with the institutionalization experience of serving in the military, more attention needs to be devoted to understanding the effects of incarceration in a training school for juveniles on later adult development.

We turn next to the life histories of men that upon first examination do not fit our theory of crime and informal social control over the life course—desisters with weak social bonds. This subset of cases is potentially useful in illuminating weaknesses and gaps in our theoretical model. In the cases we examine below, the key dimensions of interest (weak marital attachment or weak job stability) were present during only one of the two follow-up periods. In other words, it was not easy to find cases that were inconsistent with our theoretical conceptualization.

WEAK MARITAL ATTACHMENT
AND DESISTANCE FROM CRIME

Claude Wilkins (born 8/28/27) had no official arrests during the wave 2 and wave 3 periods, yet according to the Gluecks' data he was characterized as having weak marital attachment. The question is: what accounts for his refraining from crime if not a strong marital bond?

At the wave 2 interview the subject was in the Army, having served 17 months up to that time. Prior to his military service the subject lived at his mother's home in Boston. The subject's father had been deported from the United States as a defective delinquent and an undesirable alien. According to narrative data in the interview, Wilkins had a strong attachment to his father and expressed hopes of visiting him in Europe while serving in the military. The subject wrote to his father regularly, and he was a frequent visitor while his father was confined in prison. The subject also appeared to have a strong attachment to his mother. He frequently sent letters, gifts, and money to his mother from Japan, where he was stationed prior to being sent to Korea. During the age 17–25 period, the subject remained single.

Prior to serving in the Army, Wilkins had a series of unskilled jobs—apprentice welder, milkman's helper, gum factory worker, mechanic's helper, ice cream man, farm worker, worker in a wool factory, and machinist's helper in an optical factory. He had at least seven jobs between 1944 and 1948, although he had worked at his last job for three years and from all accounts was a steady and reliable worker. The subject joined the Army in 1951 and later fought in the

Korean War, which extended his military service from two to three years. He was honorably discharged in 1954.

At the time of the wave 3 interview, Wilkins was living with his mother and brother. During the age 25–32 period, he suffered a nervous breakdown as a result of serious domestic difficulties. The subject was married in March 1954 and was divorced in January 1958. He was $26^{1}/_{2}$ at the time of marriage, while his wife was 15 years old. According to notes taken by the Gluecks' interviewer, Wilkins's wife was considered to be immature and incapable of handling children. As it turned out, she was the daughter of the subject's sergeant in the Army; the latter was described in the interview schedule as "alcoholic."

The couple's marital attachment was described as weak, and they eventually obtained a divorce. There was some speculation of adultery on the part of both parties. Also, it was noted in the interview schedule that Wilkins had a drinking problem and liked to avoid working. It appeared that he was exceedingly jealous of his wife, and she, in turn, was described as being afraid of him. There was constant friction in the home. The couple had three children—two boys and a girl. According to narrative data in the case file, the subject denied paternity of the last child. Overall, Wilkins was erratic in both financial and emotional support of the children. According to interviewer notes, he deliberately refused to make more money because he was not interested in having his ex-wife ask the court to increase the amount of weekly support he had to pay her.

With regard to his employment history during the period, Wilkins continued to work as an unskilled laborer (for example, a glass factory worker and a celery packer). He experienced frequent layoffs during the period because he was under psychiatric care for three months in 1957—the result of his domestic difficulties and excessive drinking. It was also the case that there were frequent seasonal layoffs in these kinds of industries. During the interview, the subject stated that "he does not care what he does—he just lives on a day to day basis." He also claimed that he got a "raw deal" from his wife.

WEAK JOB STABILITY AND DESISTANCE FROM CRIME

Joe Johnson (born 2/25/27) had no official arrests from age 17 to age 32. At the time of the wave 2 interview, he was living with his wife and child. The subject lived in a house owned by his sister, who had evicted a tenant for him; prior to that he had lived with his wife in his sister's apartment. The subject was married in March 1948. At the time of marriage, he was 21 and his wife was 23. According to narrative data, his wife was described as a good homemaker and a devoted mother. The couple had a child in 1949. The pair appeared to be compatible, and the subject was described as "devoted" to his wife. He was also portrayed as "financially responsible" in that all his debts were paid. The subject maintained at the time of the interview that "marriage has settled me down."

Johnson's employment entailed working on different shifts (some days, some nights) as an unskilled laborer—a centrifugal machine operator. At first he worked regularly and was quite industrious. For example, he had been employed for 53 months on his job at the age 25 interview. As if signaling his future intents, however, Johnson remarked that "I've got a dead end job." The subject also served for 31 months in the Navy during the World War II period. Previously he had joined the Army while on parole from Shirley, receiving an "Honorable Discharge."

At the time of the wave 3 interview, Johnson was living with his wife and children in the Boston area. By this time there had been a distinct change in the nature of their marital relationship and in his pattern of employment. According to narrative data found in the interview schedule, the subject's wife claimed that he was immature and irresponsible, "given to running up bills with no thought as to how he was going to pay them." It appeared that the subject liked to buy expensive clothes. He also bought a car, but he did not concern himself with how he would pay for these items. According to interviewer notes, his wife was expected to shoulder the burden of bills. The subject left all financial matters "up to her" to manage. The couple experienced temporary separations between ages 25 and 32.

During this period Johnson held several jobs—sugar factory worker, truck driver's helper, and day laborer. He experienced frequent layoffs because of the seasonal nature of his work. According to narrative data, during separations from his wife, the subject would deliberately loaf to avoid paying child support. The subject also stated that he lacked a trade skill, which made it difficult for him to get a decent job. He had worked at the job he had at the time of the age 32 interview for less than one month.

FURTHER ILLUSTRATIONS OF WEAK
SOCIAL BONDS AND DESISTANCE

We examined 14 additional cases of weak marital attachment or weak job stability yet little or no offending. Upon further scrutiny, however, fewer than half of these cases were true desisters. Moreover, although weak bonds to marriage and work did not lead to persistent offending in the form of arrests and incarceration for these men, we uncovered several negative consequences in adulthood. This is especially apparent when one extends the analysis beyond the official criminal record and examines unofficial data on crime and deviance. We explore three key areas—family, employment, and military service—where unofficial criminal and deviant behaviors surfaced. We also illustrate how these qualitative data highlight the importance of change over the life course.

Family

Although persistent offending did not occur in this subset of cases, there is still strong support for the basic idea that weak marital attachment increases criminality and deviance. Unofficial reports of domestic violence, nonsupport, and desertion emerged in several of the cases we examined, as did indications of other domestic disputes involving bigamy and adultery.

For example, Case #791 had a problem with alcohol; according to narrative data, he was considered an "alcoholic." This subject was bitter over the breakup of his marriage. According to his sister-in-law, the subject "became nothing but a bum after his wife left him." He deliberately loafed so that his wife would not be able to get any money from him to support their child. The subject lost all ambition once his wife and child left him. He worked only when he had to; for example, to pay pressing bills or to buy liquor. The subject began drinking excessively during his marital breakup, and was said to have been brought home several times in a police cruiser, "dead drunk."

Case #570 was married in 1949, and separated in 1951. The subject was $22^1/_2$ at the time of the marriage, and his wife was not yet 19 years old. In the interview schedule, the subject's wife was described as "a jailbird and a street walker." Prior to their separation, the couple had several arguments about money, and the subject left the community to avoid support payments to his wife and child. According to narrative data, there was evidence of domestic violence in this case. For instance, the subject threw a ladle at his wife and blackened her eye. He was eventually convicted of assault and battery on his wife as well as non-support. After his conviction, the subject deserted his wife and child and defaulted on support payments. According to interviewer notes, the subject received a severe beating from his wife's brothers for his actions.

Employment

By definition, the men we selected for in-depth analysis experienced little or no job stability as adults. However, these men were not persistent offenders according to their official criminal records. One factor not incorporated in our theoretical framework that nonetheless appears important in understanding this seemingly inconsistent outcome is physical health. For instance, Case #891 experienced both poor marital attachment and poor job stability. This subject was wounded during the Korean War, and the injury was deemed a "serious handicap to regular employment." In fact, the subject referred to his leg injury "as an excuse for a lack of stable work." Since he received some income from the Veterans Administration, there appeared to be no reason to secure a steady job. Despite his lack of job stability, this subject was not involved in criminal offending.

Other subjects experienced difficulties in work and family life and were involved in deviant behavior, especially drinking. For example, Case #393 was living with his second wife and three children at the time of the wave 3 interview. Their relationship was portrayed as "stormy" because of the subject's trigger temper, drinking, and industrial instability. As a result of excessive drinking and frequent personality clashes with his bosses and superiors, the subject was laid off several times. He also loafed following fights with his wife in order to get even with her by not giving her any money. The subject went on frequent "benders," followed by long periods of loafing financed by VA disability pension, unemployment compensation, or both.

The subject was in court for being drunk at age 22. According to his brother, the subject started drinking excessively at age 17, the year he entered the Marines. He drank even more heavily when he got out of the service, according to interviewer notes. His brother claimed that the subject drank because he saw himself as a failure in all of his family relationships.

Likewise, Case #680 was married and then soon separated because of incompatibility. The subject's wife drank excessively and frequently deserted the children. The marriage broke up after his wife left for the fourth time. Both the subject and his wife were described by the interviewer as "very immature, unstable, and extremely selfish." Each accused the other of adultery. The subject had a poor employment record and changed jobs frequently. At the age 32 interview, the subject was living on the west coast. He was involved in excessive drinking and was unwilling to support his minor child after divorcing his second wife. Again, although not a persistent offender, this subject failed to provide support for his family and was an excessive drinker. This case reflects the importance of domestic issues and deviance—especially abuse of alcohol. In addition, this relationship seems to provide support for the idea of "selective mating" as discussed by Caspi and Herbener (1990).

In a similar vein, Case #100 was living in Texas at the age of 32 with close friends from Boston who had recently moved there. The subject had separated from his second wife at the age of 26. He was charged with "begetting," and he deserted his second wife to go to Texas to flee from the charge. The subject was abusive both physically and verbally to his second wife. There is evidence that he would often beat up his wife and then go out with his "mistress." There is further evidence in the narrative data that this subject married for a third time, although this marriage occurred after the subject's 32nd birthday and was technically after the Gluecks' wave 3 interview. It was recorded that his third wife was pregnant at the time of marriage. This subject also had poor work habits and, although never arrested, was occasionally fired for stealing goods for resale. Again, this case points out the limitations of official records and the need to examine deviant behavior as well as crime itself.

Military Service

There is also evidence of misbehavior in the military among those men with weak marital attachment and/or weak ties to work. For example, Case #171 was already married by the wave 2 interview. At the time of marriage, the subject was almost 21, the same age as his wife. The couple met while the subject was in the Army and stationed overseas. According to narrative data found in the case files, there were several indications of strained relations. For example, the subject apparently did not discuss with his wife his intentions of re-enlisting in the Army. While in the Army and away from his family, the subject did not even correspond with his wife. He eventually deserted his wife for a short period of time.

The subject worked as a farm hand and a laborer before entering the Army, but he was depicted by the Gluecks' interviewer as an "irregular worker." He often pretended to have work when he didn't. On the job, he gave a good effort, but frequently became moody and disagreeable. The subject served in the Army for a total of 69 months during the age 17–25 period. He had three periods of enlistment. He eventually received an "Undesirable Discharge" from the Army for being AWOL. According to narrative data, the subject went AWOL when his request to stay in the United States was denied.

At the wave 3 interview the subject was still married, but it was reported that he frequently deserted his wife during the age 25–32 period. It appeared that the subject drank excessively and engaged in several extramarital affairs. The narrative data characterized the couple as having poor conjugal relations, and their child was placed in foster care because he was unruly and out of control. According to notes in the interview schedule, the subject's wife was impatient and cruel with their son. Moreover, it was believed that the child was neglected by both parents. During the age 25–32 period, the subject exhibited no job stability whatsoever—he had close to 60 jobs in 1956–1957. It appeared that he would quit a job on a whim or a spurt of temper. It is not surprising, then, that the subject was considered unreliable and irresponsible with respect to work habits.

The Importance of Change

Examining life histories that were apparently inconsistent with our theory further confirmed the importance of using longitudinal data that allow placement of key events in time. For example, the following case that was selected because it represented weak marital attachment at ages 17–25 and yet little or no offending at ages 25–32 in fact reveals the importance of causal ordering and change over the life course. Specifically, it turned out that Case #742 had five arrests during the age 17–25 period, including arrests for serious crimes such as armed robbery and burglary. This subject also served considerable time in penal institutions—32 months from ages 20 to 25.

Moreover, his marital situation at ages 17–25 was rocky at best. For example, when the subject was married in 1949, his marriage was described as "forced." The subject was 22 and his wife 17 at the time of the marriage. The subject's wife was in high school when she became pregnant. The couple separated on and off shortly after the marriage. Overall, the couple experienced very poor conjugal relations, and when the subject left prison he went to his parents' home rather than the home of his wife and child.

Despite the marital discord and record of crime as a young adult, this same person had no criminal record during the third wave, age 25 to age 32. What accounted for this change or life transition? Inspection of the life history material reveals a change in the marital relationship. At the time of the wave 3 interview, the family situation had changed dramatically, to the point where the couple's conjugal relations appeared to be good. The subject was described as a rather dependent type who clung to his wife. The wife was portrayed as a strong, sensible person whose interests were in the home and her family. There is no evidence of incompatibility in the narrative data collected for the third wave. The couple had two sons, and overall there was a strong "we feeling" in the household.

The subject also took a second, part-time job to supplement the family income and to prevent his wife from having to work. He worked as a tube machine operator for one employer during the entire period. On his second job, he was the foreman of a crew of eight people who cleaned office buildings. He worked from five to eight o'clock six nights a week. With respect to work, this subject appeared to be very responsible.

According to the subject, his reasons for reformation included the following: (1) "I have worked steadily"; (2) "I have family responsibilities now"; and (3) "I have learned my lesson"—the subject feared returning to prison. According to interviewer notes, his wife's strong influence was the most important reason for his reform.

This case illustrates the investment processes that are involved as social capital is formed through the development of strong marital ties. Marital investment is a reciprocal process between husbands and wives that, if successful, encourages desistance from crime and deviance because of the strength of the social relations that are built up in the family. This case, like many others in the Gluecks' study, also portrays *intra*individual change over the life course (see Farrington, 1988).

STRONG MARITAL ATTACHMENT AND PERSISTENT OFFENDING

George Seaver (born 1/8/27) experienced several arrests during the age 17–25 and 25–32 follow-up periods. In fact, between the ages of 17 and 25, the subject served 34 months in jail or prison. According to a newspaper clipping found in the case files, this subject was considered a professional burglar and was responsible for at least 20 burglaries in the greater Boston area.

At the time of the wave 2 interview, the subject was living with his wife and son. The subject married in 1950 when he was almost 24 years old. His wife was $16^1/2$ and a second-year high school student when they were married. According to narrative data found in the interview schedule, she was an excellent student and well disciplined. The couple had one child, who was born in 1951.

With regard to their marital attachment, the couple seemed devoted and affectionate toward each other. As evidence of his commitment to the marriage, Seaver worked at two jobs for 11 months prior to the couple's marriage to earn enough money to buy furniture and to fix up their apartment. All household bills were paid before the wedding. The subject was also strongly attached to his infant son. Finally, there is evidence in the case files revealing that the family frequently had visits with the subject's mother-in-law.

As for employment, the subject worked as a sheet metal worker, an unskilled job. He had been employed for 22 months at his job. According to narrative data, he was considered honest, sober, and hard working, but he did have a quick temper.

At the time of the wave 3 interview, Seaver was living with his wife and their three children, two boys and a girl. According to narrative data, the couple had exceptionally good conjugal relations; both parties were portrayed as being devoted to each other. Interviewer notes revealed that the subject's wife was a stable person who had established a good family environment. The subject was at times moody and refused to talk, but his wife appeared to be understanding of his difficulties.

During the age 25–32 period, Seaver worked primarily as an unskilled worker. His series of jobs included pressman, steamfitter's helper, factory worker, furniture mover, truck driver's helper, tonic factory worker, and meat-packing plant worker. From all the available data, it appears that the subject was an excellent worker who often was willing to hold two jobs to pay bills. However, Seaver had nine jobs during the age 25–32 period, and he experienced many layoffs—one employer even terminated him when he learned of his previous convictions. The subject did not appear to have any drinking problem. He had worked at his current job at a factory for about seven months, and he planned on remaining because he felt he had a good chance to advance. The subject claimed that he was "now there long enough so that I will have no more layoffs."

The narrative data suggest that the subject's involvement in burglaries and larcenies were the result of his lack of steady work and the pressing financial obligations of his own family. The narratives make it quite clear that his home life was a cause for optimism. It is ironic that although his wife had an unusual understanding of his difficulties, the subject seemed to take his family responsibilities so seriously that he became depressed when he was not working and unable to provide adequate support for his family. The subject also appeared to be the kind of person who had to keep busy when he was not working. This is evidenced by the fact that he completely renovated his apartment twice in five years.

STRONG JOB STABILITY AND PERSISTENT OFFENDING

Oscar Schell (born 5/16/27) was living with his wife and daughter in Boston at the time of the wave 2 interview. During the five years prior to the interview, the subject spent 15 months in penal institutions for several crimes including auto theft and larceny. During the same period, the subject did not serve in the military because he was rejected for physical reasons. Other narrative data found in the case file, however, indicated that subject was rejected because of his criminal record.

Schell was married in 1946. At the time of marriage he was almost 19 years old, while his wife was 17. According to narrative data, the marriage was apparently "forced" since their child was born three months after the marriage date. This couple seemed to get along very well. According to narrative data in the interview schedule, the subject matured with his marital responsibilities and generally took good care of his family. For employment, the subject worked as a building wrecker throughout the age 17–25 period, working regularly except when it rained or snowed. He worked for the same employer for the last three and a half years prior to the age 25 interview.

At the wave 3 interview, Schell was still living with his wife and daughter. During the age 25–32 period, he spent three months in a penal institution for operating under the influence—drunk driving. According to narrative data, the subject was upset over his marital difficulties and drank to escape those problems. In fact, during this follow-up period, the subject had two arrests for drunkenness. There is also evidence of some separations from his wife. It appeared that Schell's wife objected to the excessive drinking along with the seasonal nature of his work. According to interviewer notes, the subject drank excessively on pay days. There was no mention of abuse or adultery in the narrative data, although the subject's drinking did cause some economic hardship. Nonetheless, the couple were united in their love for their child. It should also be noted that the subject was extremely bitter over his criminal record and commitment to jail.

During the age 25 to 32 follow-up, Schell remained in the same line of work for the whole period—an unskilled laborer, specifically a building wrecker. According to narrative data, drinking was tolerated among the workmen in this type of employment as long as one did not drink while on the job. The subject was referred to as a "weekend drinker," although Schell's sister stated that sometimes his "drinking caused him to lose a day or two." Furthermore, she stated that "every guy who works as a wrecker drinks." The subject remained with the same employer for the period despite his excessive drinking and jail commitment. He kept working at this job because "it's the only thing that he knows how to do." According to his sister, he learned a good lesson when he was sent to jail, and he now appreciates his home and family and what he must do to keep them. The narrative data reveal that Schell started drinking to excess at age 18.

FURTHER ILLUSTRATIONS OF STRONG SOCIAL BONDS AND OFFENDING

We examined 15 additional cases of strong marital attachment or strong job stability coupled with persistent or occasional involvement in criminal offending. We uncovered three distinct patterns that may account for offending in adulthood among this group. The first is weak marital attachment coupled with alcohol abuse, despite the presence of strong job stability. The second is weak job stability coupled with alcohol abuse, despite the presence of strong marital attachment. The third and most common pattern is that of alcohol abuse overwhelming the effects of strong marital attachment or strong job stability. Examples of these patterns from the case histories are presented below.

Strong Job Stability, Weak Marital Attachment, and Alcohol Abuse

Case #203 was serving in the military at the wave 2 interview. The subject served for a total of 75 months during the age 17–25 period. According to an interview with his aunt, "He found a home in the military." At age 25, the subject was a staff sergeant and was described as being well adjusted. The subject did have two arrests prior to entering the service. He remained single during this time period.

At the wave 3 interview, the subject was still in the military. In addition to being a staff sergeant, he was an atomic, biological, and chemical warfare specialist. He served in the military throughout the 84-month period and, from interviewer notes, it appeared that he re-enlisted again in 1961. This subject was noted as having a problem related to alcohol—he was described in the interviewer notes as "wild" and as drinking to excess on occasion. He was also characterized as being "difficult to get along with." During the age 25–32 period, the subject was arrested for assault and battery. This charge was ultimately dismissed at the request of the complainant.

Although the subject was married at the age of 26, his marriage was annulled six years later. According to narrative data in the interview schedule, the marriage was illegal because his wife married the subject before the divorce from her first husband was final. There appeared to be much friction in their relationship, including accusations of adultery. In addition, the subject's wife did not have custody of her four children from her first marriage and wanted to adopt these children against the subject's wishes. The subject was depicted as extremely bitter over his failed marriage.

Another subject (Case #223) also served in the military for a good portion of the wave 2 time period (75 months). This subject enlisted in the Army for six years and re-enlisted for another six-year period. He worked as a draftsman and a statistical clerk in the Army. At the wave 2 interview, this subject was separated with a divorce pending. At the date of marriage the subject's wife was four months pregnant. According to narrative data, the subject met his wife in a house of prostitution. She was described in the narrative data as "a professional prostitute." The subject was seeking a divorce at the time of the interview on the ground that his wife had adulterous relationships with other men. There is some evidence in the case file of the subject's physical abuse of his spouse when he discovered her continuous sexual relations with his Army buddies.

At the wave 3 interview date, the subject was still living with his wife and four children. He was in the Army for a total of 142 months, with 67 months occurring during the age 25–32 period. The subject was arrested once during this period for drunkenness, although according to narrative data, he began drinking excessively at age 22. At the time of the interview, the subject had a gambling debt of over $1,300. He was also AWOL in the service.

Although the subject was still married to the same spouse, the couple were temporarily separated when the subject was discharged from the service. There appeared to be much friction in the marriage, and it was believed that the subject was not the father of his wife's fourth child. According to interviewer notes, the major problems were his wife's infidelity and the subject's drinking. There is also some evidence of physical abuse by the subject, who apparently committed assault and battery on his wife. The subject learned of his wife's affair while serving in the military, and when he came home on a furlough he gave her a severe beating in which he blackened both of her eyes. From the narrative data, there is further evidence of several severe beatings over the period. As for post-military employment, the subject "loafed" following his Army discharge.

Finally, Case #591 had two marriages during adulthood. At age 32, he was living with his second wife and four children (including his oldest child from his first marriage). The subject drank to excess, usually "weekend benders." The subject blamed his wife for his lack of material progress because she was a "poor manager" of the finances. He was bitter because he worked so hard and yet did not get ahead. The couple experienced several separations due to incompatibility caused by the subject's drinking and his wife's poor management of the finances. According to narrative data, each Saturday the subject along with his co-workers (who were also truck drivers) went to hang out at a tavern in town. They would arrive at about one o'clock in the afternoon and stay until midnight. Then the subject would pick up prostitutes or start fighting with other patrons in the bar. The subject remained with his present employer because this employer tolerated his weekend benders.

Strong Marital Attachment, Weak Job Stability, and Alcohol Abuse

At the wave 2 interview, Case #861 was living with his wife and children. During the age 20–25 period, this subject spent 16 months in penal institutions. He did not serve in the military. As he stated, "I was in the can when they called me up." The subject was married in 1951; he was $21^1/2$ and his wife was $18^1/2$. According to interview notes, this was a "forced" marriage since the child was born six months after the date of the marriage. The subject claimed to be very fond of his wife and stated that she was solely responsible for his reformation. There appeared to be no friction between the subject and his wife, and there were no reports of abuse or adultery in the narrative data. The subject was depicted as being devoted to his wife and children, and it was recorded that he took his responsibilities as a father and husband seriously.

At the wave 3 interview, the subject was in prison. In fact, he had spent 30 months in penal institutions since the age 25 interview. The subject was described by the interviewer as "emotionally unstable" and "aggressive." He claimed that his larcenies were motivated by his desire to provide for his children and wife. The subject was in the community for 48 months with frequent periods of "loafing." In addition, he was frequently laid off from his job. There was some evidence of excessive drinking, but the subject claimed that it was not chronic and did not interfere with his work. According to the subject, the future appeared dismal since he had been given a life sentence and would not see the parole board for at least five years. His current offenses included assault and battery with a deadly weapon, kidnapping, assault with intent to murder, armed robbery, and escape. This subject had had 16 arrests as a juvenile.

Strong Marital Attachment, Strong Job Stability, and Alcohol Abuse

Case #131 was living with his wife and child at the wave 2 interview. The subject spent 46 months in the Army during World War II and received an "Honorable Discharge" with some misbehavior. According to narrative data, his Army misconduct was tied up with drinking—his offenses were being AWOL, assault and battery, and drunkenness. Since his discharge, the subject had been arrested four times, three of which were for drunkenness.

The subject was married about seven months before his discharge from the Army. His conjugal relations were described as good in the narrative data. He took his marital responsibilities seriously and was characterized as a hard worker who diligently sought better job opportunities (with his wife's encouragement). The subject was employed as a civil service worker for almost two years. He worked steadily and improved himself on each assignment he had. However, he was a fairly steady drinker.

Although the subject generally had good conjugal relations at the wave 3 interview, his drinking was again the cause of some difficulty. The subject had repeatedly worked at part-time jobs to supplement his regular week's salary. He was described as being very conscientious about his paternal duties. The subject was still employed as a civil servant and had good work habits throughout the follow-up period. At the start of the third wave follow-up period, he was arrested for drunk driving. According to narrative data found in the interview schedule, the subject only drank out of town because he was aware of the fact that his job was dependent upon good behavior. He was pictured as being very worried about his past criminal record and drank only when he was not working and outside of his city of residence. Evidently, the subject's wife was a strong positive influence on his reform (note that this subject was also classified in the strong marital attachment dimension).

Case #926 was working as a seaman in the U.S. Merchant Service at the time of the wave 2 interview. He joined the U.S.M.S. when he was 19. He entered this branch of service because of his poor educational background; the requirements of the U.S.M.S. were minimal. During the age 17–25 period, he worked for various shipping lines except for short intervals between trips. He also spent almost six months in penal institutions during the age 20–25 period. The subject had eight arrests between ages 17 and 25, including arrests for burglary, larceny, and auto theft. He served jail time for larceny. The subject remained single throughout the period.

At the wave 3 interview, the subject was again at sea in the U.S.M.S. The subject had married when he was nearly 29 years old and lived with his wife and her children when he was not at sea. His wife had three children from a previous marriage. The couple's conjugal relations were described as good. In his work as a merchant seaman, the subject was employed in various jobs (mess boy, seaman, steward). When ashore the subject worked as a furniture mover and as a truck driver's helper. All of these jobs were classified as "unskilled" by the Gluecks' research team. It appeared that the subject had taken several temporary jobs to support his family, and the narrative data suggested that his work habits had improved since his marriage because of his wife's positive influence coupled with the fact that he now had three dependent children. According to the narrative data, prior to his marriage the subject would simply live off Seaman's Unemployment Benefits between trips. The subject had two arrests during the age 25–32 period—one for drunkenness and the other for disturbing the peace. The subject appeared to have an alcohol problem, although the narrative data were inconsistent as to whether he was a frequent or an occasional drinker.

Another subject (Case #551) was arrested once during each of the follow-up periods (each time for drunkenness). At the wave 2 interview, the subject was living with his wife and two children. The subject was married at age 22; his wife was 23. At the date of marriage, his wife was pregnant. The subject worked as a porter at a hospital, and his wife worked there as a nurse. The couple was described as having good conjugal relations. At his wife's request, the subject took courses to improve his occupational status. However, the subject had a serious drinking problem.

For employment, the subject worked in unskilled jobs (for example, as a porter). He was considered a steady worker, and his drinking did not interfere with his work record. In total, he was employed for eight years as a porter—interrupted only by a stint in the military. The subject was inducted during World War II and served for 26 months. He received an "Honorable Discharge" from the Army. According to narrative data found in the interview schedule, the subject claimed that he graduated from a 16-month course in refrigeration and electricity at a technical school in Boston. He attended this school afternoons from one o'clock to six o'clock, five days a week, for 16 months under the G.I. Bill. According to the Gluecks' interviewer, however, his drinking problem seemed to hamper his making a significant career advancement. By contrast, the subject felt that his criminal record was preventing him from obtaining a better job than his current position as a linoleum cutter in a department store.

Finally, Case #490 appeared devoted to his wife. He claimed that "she straightened me out and stuck by me" during his adult criminality.

The subject was fond of his baby daughter and seemed serious about his family obligations. At the wave 3 interview, the subject expressed worries about his family and was especially concerned about his ability to support them. This subject drank excessively when he felt discouraged.

DISCUSSION

John Clausen (1990) contends that the idea of a turning point is an important concept for those interested in the study of lives. Some key turning points in the life course are marriage, meaningful work, and serving in the military. The idea of a turning point is closely linked to role transitions, and, conceptually, turning points are helpful in understanding stability and change in human behavior over the life course. We adapted this perspective to ask in this chapter: what were the turning points in the lives of a disadvantaged sample of adolescent delinquents? What led the Gluecks' delinquents away from continued involvement in crime? Conversely, what were the turning points (or lack of turning points) that facilitated continued involvement in crime?[7] These are the theoretical questions that led us to examine in more depth the longitudinal case-record data collected by the Gluecks' research team.

Overall these qualitative data support our central theoretical idea that there is both stability and change in criminal and deviant behavior over the life course, and that these patterns are systematically linked to the institutions of work and family relations in adulthood. Specifically, through an analysis of the qualitative data found in the Glueck case files, we found that poor job stability and weak attachment to one's spouse increase the likelihood of criminal activity and deviant behavior. Conversely, these case records affirmed that strong job stability and marital attachment reduce the likelihood of involvement in criminal and deviant behavior.

To further assess this general conclusion, we examined the criminal records at ages 32 to 45 of the eight men for whom we analyzed detailed life histories from ages 17 to 32. We again found agreement with our theory—men selected because of their strong marital attachment and/or job stability at waves 2 and 3 revealed no record of offending between ages 32 and 45, regardless of their offending pattern at waves 2 and 3. Similarly, men with weak marital attachment and/or job stability at waves 2 and 3 did generate a record of offending at ages 32 to 45, regardless of their pattern of offending at waves 2 and 3. In other words, the cases we selected as consistent with our theory remained consistent, and the cases we selected as inconsistent with our theory were now totally consistent on the basis of an examination of criminal records at ages 32 to 45.

Nevertheless, one issue did emerge in the qualitative data analyses that complicates our theoretical model—namely, the fairly consistent finding that serious drinking contributes to poor marital attachment and weak job stability. In addition, for some individuals a reverse causal order is suggested for crime itself; that is, involvement in crime leads to poor job stability and weak marital attachment. These findings are consistent with the "selection effect" and are illustrated in the following examples.

Case #802's weak marital attachment was characterized as a consequence of the subject's drinking. According to narrative data in the interview schedule, the subject's sister claimed that his "wife frequently gets fed up with [the subject's] chronic drinking and returns to live with her parents." The couple eventually separated permanently after several temporary separations over a nine-year period. This subject's drinking also affected his job stability. Working in primarily unskilled jobs, the subject held six jobs in 28 months. According to narrative data, the subject was described as "a chronic alcoholic who would go on sprees and disappear for weeks and months at a time from his wife and son." His wife claimed that the subject was "frequently let go" because he was unreliable in the work setting.

Similarly, Case #021 was wounded in the Korean War while serving in the Army, and this injury subsequently affected his employment. In fact, subsequent to his Army duty this subject had no steady work. During the age 25–32 period, for example, the subject had five jobs ranging in length from three to sixteen months. He also experienced long periods of idleness between jobs. There is evidence from the narrative data that his drinking led to absenteeism from work, which then led to firings. The subject also quit some of these jobs.

Furthermore, Case #001 exhibits data suggesting that deviance is sometimes the cause of weak marital attachment *and* poor job stability. This subject was married at the age of 22 and divorced three years later. His confinement in prison meant that he was able to live with his wife for only four months. The subject was given a 15 to 20 year prison sentence, and he "urged his wife to forget him and go out with others." His criminal offending also led to poor job stability. For example, according to narrative data found in the interview schedule, this subject deliberately chose to have periods of unemployment and seasonal work like the U.S. Merchant Service in order to further his opportunities for theft and to elude police attention.

The nature of the qualitative data in the Gluecks' study does not permit us to rule out definitely these sorts of "selection effects" as a possible explanation of our findings. Nevertheless, on the basis of our overall analysis of 70 of the Gluecks' qualitative life histories drawn from several independent data sources, we believe our findings regarding continuity and change in criminal behavior over the life course underscore the importance of social capital—social ties embedded in work and family institutions. Moreover, variations in the strength of social bonds with respect to the formation and development of social capital appear to account for differential outcomes in adulthood despite selection effects and prior propensities to deviance.

This finding from the qualitative data corresponds to our efforts to take into account selection effects in the quantitative analyses presented in Chapters 7 and 8. Recall that even though we did find clear evidence that early childhood delinquency and adult deviance—especially drinking—attenuated adult social bonds, the data also confirmed that adult social bonds had both concurrent and lagged inhibitive effects on crime and deviance. Consequently, the qualitative and quantitative data converge in suggesting the complex and sometimes simultaneous interplay between social bonding and deviant behaviors over the life course. Put more broadly, both social selection and social causation (in the form of social capital) seem to be at work in the unfolding of human lives over time.

SUMMING UP
AND
LOOKING
AHEAD

This book has been driven by the following challenge: can we develop and test a theoretical model that accounts for crime and deviance in childhood, adolescence, and adulthood? To answer this question we first synthesized and integrated the criminological literature on childhood antisocial behavior, adolescent delinquency, and adult crime with theory and research on the life course. This strategy led us to develop a theory of age-graded informal social control to explain crime and deviance over the life span.

The second element of our answer involved the resurrection of a classic data set in the field of criminology, consisting of two large samples of delinquent and nondelinquent boys followed from childhood and adolescence into their forties. We have reconstructed and reanalyzed both quantitative and qualitative data from the Gluecks' longitudinal study of juvenile delinquency and adult crime (Glueck and Glueck, 1950; 1968). These heretofore unavailable data represent an extraordinarily rich body of information and provide an important comparative base for contemporary studies of crime and crime control.

SUMMARY OF THEORETICAL MODEL

Our theoretical framework has three major themes. The first is that structural context is mediated by informal family and school social controls, which in turn explain delinquency in childhood and adolescence. The second theme is that there is strong continuity in antisocial behavior running from childhood through adulthood across a variety of life domains. The third theme is that informal social capital in adulthood explains changes in criminal behavior over the life span, regardless of prior individual differences in criminal propensity. In our view, childhood pathways to crime and conformity over the life course are significantly influenced by adult social bonds.

Although we reject the "ontogenetic" approach dominant in developmental psychology (see Dannefer, 1984), our theoretical framework nonetheless follows a developmental strategy (see Loeber and LeBlanc, 1990; Farrington, 1986b; Patterson et al., 1989). Loeber and LeBlanc (1990: 376) define "developmental criminology" as strategies that examine within-individual changes in offending over time. Moreover, the developmental approach that we take views causality as "best represented by a developmental network of causal factors" in which dependent variables become independent variables over time (Loeber and LeBlanc, 1990: 433). Developmental criminology recognizes continuity and change over time and focuses on life transitions as a way of understanding patterns of offending. This strategy has also been referred to as a "stepping stone approach," where factors are time ordered by age and assessed with respect to outcome variables (see Farrington, 1986b).

A similar perspective can be found in interactional theory (see Thornberry, 1987 and Thornberry et al., 1991). In our theoretical

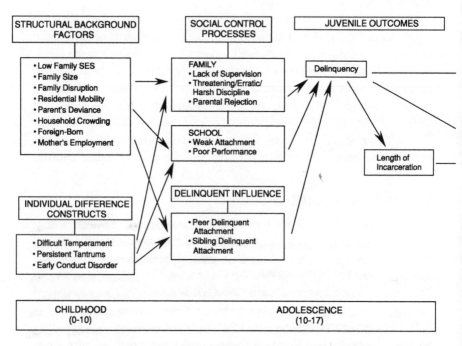

Figure 10.1 Dynamic theoretical model of crime, deviance, and informal social control over the life course of 1,000 Glueck men, circa 1925–1975. (In the *UJD* design, delinquent and nondelinquent males were matched on age, race/ethnicity, neighborhood SES, and IQ.)

framework, we draw on the key idea of interactional theory that causal influences are bidirectional or reciprocal over the life course. Interactional theory embraces a developmental approach and argues convincingly that delinquency may contribute to the weakening of social bonds and informal social control over time. In particular, Thornberry maintains that interactional theory offers an explanation for continuity in criminal trajectories over time: "The initially weak bonds lead to high delinquency involvement, the high delinquency involvement further weakens the conventional bonds, and in combination both of these effects make it extremely difficult to reestablish bonds to conventional society at later ages. As a result, all of the factors tend to reinforce one another over time to produce an extremely high probability of continued deviance" (Thornberry et al., 1991: 30).

Thornberry's perspective is also consistent with a person-centered approach to development as described by Magnusson and Bergman

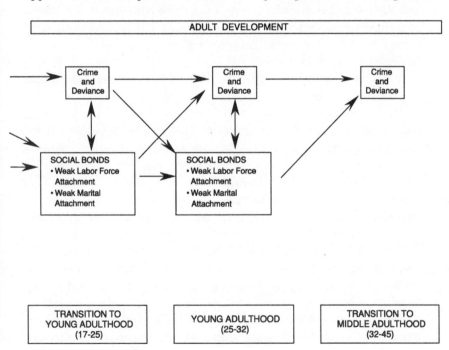

(1988: 47). In our analysis of the Gluecks' qualitative data we focused explicitly on "persons" rather than "variables" by examining individual life histories over time (see Magnusson and Bergman, 1988 and 1990). This focus complemented our quantitative analyses and offered insight into the social processes of intraindividual developmental change in criminal behavior over the life course.

A summary representation of our sociogenic developmental theory as applied to the Gluecks' data is presented in Figure 10.1.[1] In essence, this model explains probabilistic links in the chain of events from childhood to adult criminal behavior. It is our view that family and school processes of informal social control provide the key causal explanation of delinquency in childhood and adolescence. Structural background characteristics are important in terms of their effects on informal family and school processes, but these same characteristics have little direct influence on delinquency. Individual characteristics like temperament and early conduct disorder are also linked to both family and school social control processes as well as delinquency itself, but these same factors do not significantly diminish the effects of social bonding in family and school on delinquency.

The theory embodied in Figure 10.1 explicitly links delinquency and adult crime to childhood and adolescent characteristics as well as socializing influences in adulthood. Early delinquency predicts weak adult social bonds, and weak adult social bonds predict concurrent and later adult crime and deviance. The process is one in which childhood antisocial behavior and adolescent delinquency are linked to adult crime and deviance in part through weak social bonds. We also believe that salient life events and socialization experiences in adulthood can counteract, at least to some extent, the influence of early life experiences. For instance, late onset of criminal behavior can be accounted for by weak social bonds in adulthood, despite a background of nondelinquent behavior. Conversely, desistance from criminal behavior in adulthood can be explained by strong social bonds in adulthood, despite a background of delinquent behavior. In contrast to many life-course models, our theory emphasizes the quality or strength of social ties more than the occurrence or timing of life events (cf. Loeber and LeBlanc, 1990: 430–432). Thus, our theory provides a sociological explanation of stability and change in crime and deviance over the life course with an explicit focus on within-individual changes in offending and deviance.

SUMMARY OF EMPIRICAL FINDINGS

Causes of Delinquency

We found that the strongest and most consistent effects on both official and unofficial delinquency flow from the social processes of family, school, and peers. Low levels of parental supervision, erratic, threatening, and harsh discipline, and weak parental attachment were strongly and directly related to delinquency. In addition, school attachment had large negative effects on delinquency independent of family processes. Moreover, attachment to delinquent peers had a significant positive effect on delinquency regardless of family and school process. Despite this finding on peer influence, further analyses of delinquent siblings and attachment to peers revealed that family and school processes appear most important in the causal chain.[2]

At the same time, we found that structural background factors have little direct effect on delinquency, but instead are mediated by intervening sources of informal social control. Moreover, whereas difficult children who display early antisocial tendencies (for instance, violent temperament) do sort themselves into later stages of delinquency, the processes of informal social control explain the largest share of variance in adolescent delinquency.

Overall, the results support our integrated version of social control theory that recognizes the importance of both structure and process. When the bonds linking youth to society—whether through family or school—are weakened, the probability of delinquency is increased. Negative structural conditions (such as poverty or family disruption) also affect delinquency, but largely through family and school process variables.

Stability and Change in Criminal Behavior over the Life Course

Independent of age, IQ, neighborhood SES, and ethnicity, the original delinquents and nondelinquents in the Gluecks' study displayed behavioral consistency—both homotypic and heterotypic—well into adulthood. Indeed, delinquency and other forms of antisocial conduct in childhood were strongly related to troublesome adult behavior across a variety of life's domains (for example, crime, military offenses, economic dependence, marital discord).

Consistent with a sociological theory of adult development and informal social control, however, we found that job stability and marital attachment in adulthood were significantly related to changes in adult crime—the stronger the adult ties to work and family, the less crime and deviance occurred among both delinquents and controls. We even found that strong marital attachment inhibits crime and deviance regardless of the spouse's own deviant behavior, and that job instability fosters crime regardless of heavy drinking. Moreover, social bonds to employment were directly influenced by State sanctions—incarceration as a juvenile and as an adult had negative effects on later job stability, which in turn was negatively related to continued involvement in crime over the life course. Although we found little direct effect of incarceration on subsequent criminality, the indirect "criminogenic" effects appear substantively important.

Despite differences in early childhood experiences, adult social bonds to work and family thus had similar consequences for the life trajectories of the 500 delinquents and 500 controls. In fact, the parameter estimates of informal social control were at times nearly identical across the two groups, and the predictive power of early individual-difference constructs was virtually nonexistent once differences in juvenile delinquency were accounted for. These results were consistent for a wide variety of outcome measures, control variables (for example, childhood antisocial behavior and individual-difference constructs), and analytical techniques, including methods that account for persistent unobserved heterogeneity in criminal propensity.

Our strategy also included a new way of portraying life histories of individuals in context. Namely, our quantitative findings were systematically challenged through an intensive examination of qualitative data drawn from the Gluecks' original case files. Integrating divergent sources of information on life histories, the qualitative analysis supported the central idea of our theoretical model that there are both stability and change in behavior over the life course, and that these changes are systematically linked to the institutions of work and family relations in adulthood. Specifically, through an analysis of the narrative data found in the Gluecks' case files, we found that poor job stability and weak marital attachment to one's spouse increase the likelihood of criminal activity and deviant behavior. Conversely, the case records supported the idea that strong job stability and attachment to one's spouse reduce the likelihood of involvement in criminal and deviant behavior.

Taken as a whole, then, our qualitative and quantitative findings suggest that social ties embedded in adult transitions (for example, marital attachment, job stability) explain variations in crime unaccounted for by childhood propensities. This empirical regularity supports our dual concern with continuity and change in the life course (see also Rutter et al., 1990).

Limitations

To be sure, one issue emerged in our qualitative data analyses that complicates our theoretical model—namely, that frequent drinking tends to undermine marital attachment and job stability for some sample members. We also observed for some individuals a reciprocal causal order—crime itself leading to poor job stability and weak marital attachment, which in turn leads to more crime. Consistent with these findings, Vaillant's extensive research on alcoholism has revealed that alcoholics create bad marriages far more often than bad marriages create alcoholics (1983: 97). Vaillant (1983: 6) has further noted that previous studies of delinquent populations have found that *"premorbid* antisocial behavior is associated with *subsequent* alcohol abuse"* (see also Robins, 1966; McCord and McCord, 1960; Glueck and Glueck, 1968).

Unfortunately, the nature of the Gluecks' data precludes a definitive analysis of the reciprocal linkages among drinking, social bonds, and crime. As Vaillant (1983) notes, the overrepresentation of antisocial children in the Glueck studies makes it difficult to separate out the antecedents of alcoholism and antisocial behavior. Yet, suggesting support for our informal social control framework, Vaillant (1983: 191) maintains that those alcoholics with the most to lose (for example, a job, spouse, or friend) have the best chance at recovery. Alcoholics with social ties to work and marital or other intimate relationships have a base of social support and are under continual supervision and monitoring. Moreover, on the basis of detailed quantitative analyses, we found that although drinking does seem to foster disrupted marriages and job instability, this relationship does not explain the role of these two factors in fostering crime. Though limited in scope, analysis of simultaneous equation models also revealed that the concurrent effect of adult social bonds on adult crime remained when the reciprocal effect of crime itself

was controlled.[3] Therefore, while there is certainly much to be learned
about the complex interactional nature of social bonding and drinking
(see also Thornberry, 1987), the essential elements of our theoretical
model appear robust.

FUTURE DIRECTIONS IN THE STUDY OF INFORMAL
SOCIAL CONTROL AND THE LIFE COURSE

The Need for Longitudinal Data on Life Transitions

Advances in knowledge about crime and delinquency over the life
course require a fresh infusion of data capable of measuring key life-
course transitions. In particular, we need to learn more about transitions from childhood to adolescence and from late adolescence to adulthood. Although our theoretical model and data emphasized family and
school social control processes, we cannot ignore the strong peer effects
on delinquency in our analysis, and we recognize the need to examine
more carefully the role of peer influences (see also Akers, 1985, 1989;
Elliott et al., 1985). The transition from family to school along with
changes in friendship networks as children move into adolescence
seems to be a promising area of exploration for criminologists. It is
especially important to learn how peer attachments are influenced
by structural background factors and if peer influence can neutralize
informal social bonds formed in the family and school. Similarly, learning more about the transitions from adolescence to adulthood is critical
for understanding the development of social ties in adulthood. For
instance, what predicts strong marital attachment in adulthood? How
do adolescent relationships influence marital relationships in adulthood? Along the same lines, how do disadvantaged youths achieve job
stability and strong commitment to work? What role do structural
factors play in determining strong bonds to family and work? Is military
service a vehicle out of poverty for disadvantaged youth with troubled
backgrounds?

Another implication of our findings is the need for better measurement of the timing and sequencing of changes in salient life events over
the life course. Quantitative measurement of the timing, duration, and
ordering of life transitions has the further advantage of permitting
substantive applications of event history analyses (see Featherman and
Lerner, 1985), growth curve trajectories (Rogosa et al., 1982), hierarchical models for the assessment of change (Bryk and Raudenbush,

1987), and recent methods for detecting resemblance in career sequence data (Abbott and Hyrack, 1990). In particular, longitudinal research in criminology has focused almost exclusively on the consistency of individual differences over time rather than the consistency of individual behavior. But as Rogosa (1988: 172) argues, research questions about growth and development "center on the systematic change in an attribute over time," and thus individual growth curves are a natural foundation for modeling longitudinal data.

Similarly, Caspi and Bem (1990: 569) argue that when the term *change* appears in the literature, it frequently refers to the absence of continuity. Caspi and Bem call for the development of theory and data to account for "systematic" change as opposed to the mere absence of continuity. Accounting for developmental trajectories in crime and deviance will help to distinguish between true systematic change fostered by life transitions and the absence of continuity. A focus on growth curves and systematic change also parallels Farrington's (1988) argument that criminology has neglected the study of changes within individuals in favor of between-individual analyses.

In short, longitudinal data on life-course transitions are needed to make proper inferences about individual trajectories of stability and change (Rutter, 1988; Rogosa, 1988). We would like to emphasize, however, that longitudinal studies do not necessarily entail large expenditures of funds (see especially Gottfredson and Hirschi, 1987), for there are excellent data archives capable of supporting research on the life course in different historical and macro-level contexts (see, for example, Elder, 1974; Caspi et al., 1987; McCord, 1979; Vaillant, 1983; and Featherman et al., 1984).

Merging Quantitative and Qualitative Data

Research questions on the life course also demand that data collection efforts include both quantitative and qualitative data. A strong point of the Gluecks' research was that their data collection included qualitative and quantitative data on both variables and persons (Magnusson and Bergman, 1990; Cairns, 1986). Qualitative data derived from systematic open-ended questions or narrative life histories are crucial in uncovering the social processes underlying stability and change in criminal and deviant behavior. These data can also help confirm results derived from quantitative analyses, especially if the quantitative analyses are used as a guide to case selection as we did here.

Qualitative data are particularly useful in suggesting important areas for future research consideration. From our analyses, the following areas stand out as worthy of attention in future research: the consequences of domestic violence for developing social ties in families, work, and neighborhoods; substance abuse—especially excessive drinking—and its reciprocal relationships with social bonds to family and work; exits from poverty among disadvantaged children and youth (for example, employment opportunities, marital selection, and community support networks); and institutionalization experiences (for instance, prison and the military) in adolescence and adulthood and their consequences for subsequent development. We also need to identify subjective transitions in the life course independently of behavioral transitions in understanding patterns of crime (Gartner and Piliavin, 1988: 302). Qualitative data may be especially useful in this regard because social transitions (such as marriage or full-time work) probably do not have the same meaning for everyone (Rutter, 1989: 20).

Further Understanding of Age and Crime

A major limitation of prior research on age and crime is the narrow focus on legally defined categories of crime. As we have documented, one of the staples of developmental research is the heterotypic continuity of antisocial behaviors. Consequently there is a need to measure a wide spectrum of behaviors, both legal and illegal, that are relevant to the study of crime. This strategy permits addressing the question of whether there are individuals for whom antisocial behavior, regardless of the actual sphere in which the activity occurs, does not decline with age (for example, absenteeism at work as an adult might be conceptualized as the theoretical equivalent of truancy in childhood). Other life domains ripe for inquiry include occupational mobility, educational attainment, poverty, physical health, mental health, and even homelessness. More generally, we need to broaden our conceptualization to investigate the impact of childhood delinquency on a wide range of non-crime outcomes that nonetheless have significance for adult development.

In a similar vein, explanations of the age-crime curve have focused mostly on official accounts of crime. For example, in investigations of whether crime declines with age, it is not known whether adults are disproportionately involved in crimes typically not counted in official statistics, especially white-collar offenses (see Braithwaite, 1989: 46).

It is conceivable that while street crime declines with age, white-collar offending and other antisocial but "hidden" behaviors (family violence, alcohol abuse) take up the slack (see also Moffitt, 1991). This concern highlights the need to link age and crime with the life-course framework by investigating how age-graded transitions (such as work and family) create both opportunities for crime and differential probabilities of detection and labeling by official agents of social control.

Societal reactions to crime may also interact with age (Gartner and Piliavin, 1988: 302; Shover, 1985; Shover and Thompson, 1992). For example, Shover (1985) reports that aging interacts with the stigma of a criminal record; for those offenders in his sample who desisted in later life, there was an erosion of the original stigma, while for others the process of aging compounded the effect of the original stigma. Research should thus examine how labeling, particularly formal labeling by the criminal justice system, affects life-course development relating to crime and non-crime outcomes.

Finally, in implementing all of these strategies, we need research that better "unpacks" the meaning of age. Rutter (1989) argues that in order to understand age changes in behavior, chronological age must be broken down into its component parts. Without this separation, "age is devoid of meaning" (1989: 3). According to Rutter, from a developmental perspective age reflects at least four components: cognitive level, biological maturity, duration of experiences, and types of experiences. Separating these and other components of age (for example, biological versus chronological age) will help to resolve conflicts over the direct and indirect effects of age on crime.

PUBLIC DEBATE ON CRIME AND CRIME POLICY

A researcher who takes on secondary data analysis is often confronted with the comment that the data are "old" and no longer useful for addressing important contemporary questions, especially those concerning policy. This has been particularly true for us with the Glueck project because the subjects (white males) grew up during the 1930s and early 1940s and reached adulthood in the late 1940s and early 1950s. In this social and historical context, drugs like "crack" cocaine were not even known, and the level of criminal violence, especially gun use, was far lower than what we see today. The role of alcohol abuse coupled with the virtual absence of other drug use thus suggests a period effect. Moreover, there is a sense that the responses of the juvenile justice and criminal justice systems to crime were far different then from what they are now. So the question is raised: how can these data possibly be of any practical utility now?

We argue that precisely because these data are "old" they provide an unusual opportunity to assess whether the causes of juvenile delinquency and adult crime are specific to a historical period. Because of this opportunity, combined with the fact that the range of measures collected by the Gluecks will in all likelihood never be replicated in social science research again, we believe that the "age" of the Glueck data becomes a strength, not a weakness. For example, a focus on data from the 1930–1960 time period leads to several interesting questions relevant to an understanding of current patterns of crime. Are the risk factors associated with crime similar across different structural contexts? Were characteristics of today's "underclass" (for example, chronic joblessness, family disruption, poverty, criminal behavior) in fact found among earlier immigrant/ethnic groups?

Our analyses suggest that crime in the Gluecks' era was not all that different from today in terms of its structural origins and underlying nature. Consider that the men in the Gluecks' delinquent sample were persistent, serious offenders, yet all were white ethnics in structurally disadvantaged positions in a major urban center. Moreover, even though drugs like cocaine and heroin were not pervasive, crime and alcohol abuse were widespread, and violence—especially among family members—was common (see Chapter 9). The fact that sample members were all white provides an important comparative statement on current concerns with race, crime, and the underclass (see Kotlowitz, 1991). That is, we are analyzing a sample which is largely an "underclass" by today's economic definition, but in which race is not an explanation (see Jencks, 1992). In itself this fact undermines some of the prominent conceptions about crime that are advanced today.

Our findings based on the Glueck data thus become a window from which to view contemporary research and begin a dialogue on crime and crime policy, especially in a non-race-specific context. In a discussion of persistent poverty among various racial and ethnic groups in the United States, Lemann argues that "to seek an explanation for poverty among Puerto Ricans rather than blacks may make possible a truly deracialized grasp of what most experts agree is a non-race-specific problem" (1991: 97). Similarly, the Glueck data allow us to discuss crime in a "deracialized" and, we hope, depoliticized context. In this regard we believe that the causes of crime across the life course are rooted not in race, and not simply in drugs, gangs, and guns—today's policy obsessions—but rather in structural disadvantage, weakened informal social bonds to family, school, and work, and the disruption of social relations between individuals and institutions that provide social capital.

The life-course perspective of our book also has implications for specific crime policies. It appears that the major thrust of current crime control policy—whether aimed at drugs or violence—is to lock up offenders regardless of age. For those offenders with extensive prior records, even longer sentences of incarceration are being called for. Finally, the most extreme formal sanction by the State—the death penalty—is being made available and increasingly used. Such policies assume that either individual deterrence or incapacitation will reduce further violence. Yet rates of violence have recently risen in many of our nation's cities despite unprecedented rates of imprisonment and executions (Hinds, 1990; James, 1991; Koop and Lundberg, 1992). How can this happen?

One clear possibility is that current policies are producing unintended criminogenic effects. From our perspective, imprisonment may have powerful negative effects on the prospects of future employment and job stability. In turn, low income, unemployment, and underemployment are themselves linked to heightened risks of family disruption (Wilson, 1987; Sampson, 1987). Through its negative effects on male employment, imprisonment may thus lead indirectly through family disruption to increases in future rates of crime and violence (Sampson, 1987). The extremely high incarceration rate of young black males (see Mauer, 1990) renders this scenario very real.

In our reanalysis of the Gluecks' data, we have shown how long-term developmental effects of incarceration on crime and deviance may come about. Length of incarceration in both adolescence and adulthood has negative effects on job stability, which in turn leads to later crime and deviance. At the same time, our analysis revealed that intraindividual change is possible, and therefore it is critical that individuals have the opportunity to reconnect to institutions like family, school, and work *after* a period of incarceration (see also Cook, 1975; Braithwaite, 1989). Perhaps the most troubling aspect of our analysis is that the effects of long periods of incarceration appear quite severe when manifested in structural labeling—many of the Glueck men were simply cut off from the most promising avenues for desistance from crime.

Although our view may be currently unpopular, we believe it is time to take a renewed look at social policies that focus on *prevention* as opposed to after-the-fact approaches that ignore the structural context of crime and neglect the basic institutions of society, such as family, school, and work, that provide informal social control and social capital. We are not suggesting that imprisonment is unnecessary or undeserved in all cases, nor even that it has no deterrent effect on crime. Rather, we are saying that it is time to base crime policy on more than formal social control by the criminal justice system. Thus, it is time to take a more complex and long-term perspective that recognizes the linkages among crime policies, employment, family cohesion, and the social organization of inner-city communities. While we admit these more complex crime policies are not easily translated into specific program initiatives, the costs of current crime policies are quite high and their effects will be felt over the long term. As we write this book, a generation of adolescent and adult offenders are being locked up and are at risk of being permanently cut off from society. These offenders are being relegated to the structural role of the "dangerous, criminal class" (Brace, 1872; Hagan and Palloni, 1990), with the promise of a future life course that is very bleak indeed. We question the wisdom and foundation of such a devastating and costly crime policy.

CONCLUSION

We recognize that all of the empirical findings in this book are technically limited to the specifics of the Gluecks' research design and the measures we adapted from their study. However, we believe that our findings cannot be dismissed, like the Gluecks, as relics from the past or as disciplinary outcasts (see Chapter 2; Laub and Sampson, 1991). This seems especially true to the extent that several of our findings regarding the sources of delinquency and adult crime have been corroborated by other empirical research, most of which uses more "contemporary" data. Indeed, the Gluecks' research on such key issues as families and delinquency, criminal careers, and the importance of longitudinal data turns out to have been more correct than common wisdom allows, and has in fact set the stage for contemporary debates in the study of crime. We thus hope that our book will serve to reestablish the fundamental contributions of the Gluecks to criminology, especially with respect to data gathering and research design.

Most important, our analyses of the Gluecks' data undergird a much larger effort—the explication of a coherent theory of crime and deviance over the life course that is applicable not only to the 1940s but also to the 1990s and beyond. In this sense the goal of this book has been to expand the focus of criminological theory and research, as well as public dialogue on crime policy. The ultimate result is a theoretical model of crime and informal social control that brings the formative period of childhood back into the picture while recognizing that individuals can change through interaction with key social institutions as they age. By redirecting attention to the significance of both pathways and turning points in the life course, a new research agenda is opened up that has the potential to unify heretofore divergent conceptions of stability and change in the making of crime. We are thus optimistic that future efforts will continue to unravel the mysteries of crime, deviance, and social control in the course of human development.

INTERVIEWS WITH THE GLUECKS' ORIGINAL RESEARCH STAFF

a
p
p
e
n
d
i
x

As part of a larger project, we tried to locate and interview the original participants from the Gluecks' research team. We were successful in conducting detailed oral history interviews with three members of the team—Sheila Murphrey, a secretary for the Gluecks for 30 years, Mary Moran, a case investigator, and Richard LaBrie, a computer programmer and statistician. Although our interests were catholic, the edited interviews presented below focus on the methodology of the *Unraveling Juvenile Delinquency* study and the overall quality of the data.

The first excerpt is from a joint interview with two members of the Gluecks' staff—Mary Moran (MM) and Sheila Murphrey (SM). Mary Moran worked as a case investigator on the *UJD* project for 25 years (1942 to 1967). Sheila Murphrey worked as a secretary for both Sheldon and Eleanor Glueck for nearly 30 years. This interview was conducted by John Laub at the Murray Research Center of Radcliffe College, November 20, 1987.

JL: Mrs. Moran, what actually did you do on the *UJD* project? I have seen your title listed as an "Investigator." I'm not quite sure what that means.

MM: I don't know what it means, but in my case it meant investigating lives of many people. The work for me began after these families (there were over 1,000 in the beginning) had been checked through the Social Service Index. From these replies we learned the names of the family members and the agencies where they were known. At that time, in 1942, Mrs. Ava Burrows supervised work pertaining to the nondelinquents and Mrs. Mildred Cunningham worked on the delinquents. After Mrs. Burrows left, Mrs. Cunningham worked on both groups. I went to agencies, requested the record I wanted, and took notes on what I had read. I was looking for information about the physical and mental health of the family, about their education, employment, routine of family life, who disciplined the children, any police records, etc. I was also interested in the home itself—size, condition, etc., as well as the relationships within the family.

These offices were scattered—some in the downtown area, others in the districts. The personnel in these offices were always helpful. I appreciated this. It made my work more pleasant. After all, I was an intruder—someone who interrupted a worker to locate a record and find a desk where I could work. Not all of these records were in Boston offices. I remember going to Newton, Watertown, Cambridge, Somerville, Malden, and Chelsea. As time went on some records were on microfilm, but I found these difficult to read.

Besides getting information from the case records, I spent many hours in the Bureau of Vital Statistics in a small busy office in the State House. There I looked up births, deaths, and marriages, giving further proof regarding data we already had; cleaned up some things that seemed contradictory; and sometimes obtained new information.

JL: There was a lot of information collected about these families.

MM: We would not be able to do a project like this now because records are private and the Social Service Index is not available. I doubt if social agencies would be inclined to offer their records in these trying times or schools would be permitted to have *UJD* staff come in to do our tests as was done in the 1940s.

JL: Did you do this kind of record checking for the follow-up studies as well?

MM: I never knew if I was working on a follow-up case or not.

JL: Did Eleanor Glueck do any of the home visits or record checks?

SM: Oh God, no. George McGrath was the main person in the field. George got them permission to go into the schools. Only George McGrath was able to do that. The Gluecks did not show their face, that would have been the kiss of death if they went to the Boston School Committee. Absolutely. They even tried to downplay Harvard as much as possible. It was all George McGrath. He could talk to anyone. He was persuasive and he empathized with everybody.

JL: So because of George McGrath there was a *UJD* study?

SM: Absolutely. Without him they never would have had the physique study, they would have never got Selective Service cooperation. George was largely responsible for that, but George could never have coordinated the project the way Eleanor did.

JL: Was Eleanor the principal architect behind the study?

SM: She was the organizer and she was persistent. She was dedicated, her whole life was dedicated to this work. On a personal note, both of their lives were dedicated to this project. Especially Eleanor but Sheldon too. Everything else in their lives got pushed away.

JL: Mrs. Moran, there has been concern among some researchers about the quality of data collected for the *UJD* study. What is your sense of the data, given that you were one of the original data collectors? Are these good data?

MM: Well, I got it second hand, of course. I got it out of somebody else's reports.

JL: Was there any attempt to verify those reports?

MM: When a social worker from one of the agencies interviews somebody, you have to rely on what is written in the report. Of course, that is his or her opinion. These were professional people and you have to assume that they sized the situation up the best they could. The information was then matched to the information collected in our home investigation. Also, these families were known to more than one agency—public welfare, the family society, Judge Baker, etc. You had a variety of sources of information, and one sifted through them to find the truth. Mrs. Cunningham was very thorough in cross-checking information.

SM: All of the coding was done by Eleanor Glueck. She made the assessments. When everyone was through with a case and everything was collated, she would code it.

JL: How complete were the records that you looked at?

MM: Well, they were complete in a way. If a social worker hadn't done a recent interview, the information I was relying on may not have been up to date. On the other hand, I could go to an agency and they would tell me that the record is out: "So-and-so has it. It will be back in the file in a few days." I would then come back and that information would be recent. I think that overall the agencies did a good job.

SM: Considering the Gluecks' method of collecting information, I think that overall things came out pretty well. In an individual case here and there may be a problem, but on the whole things look pretty good. Remember, there are many sources of information.

The second excerpt is taken from an interview with Richard LaBrie (RL), a computer programmer and statistician with the Glueck staff during the 1960s. LaBrie worked with the Gluecks for nearly eight years and published two statistical analyses using the Gluecks' data (see LaBrie, 1970a and 1970b).

JL: Could you describe your work on the Glueck project, *Unraveling Juvenile Delinquency?* For instance, what tasks did you perform?

RL: I was at the Harvard Statistical Laboratory, which became the Harvard Computing Center when Harvard got its own computer. In those days the machine we were using was billed as the first commercial computer—the IBM 704. The Gluecks had a whole set of data that they had collected which were on multiply punched cards. The Gluecks had been using a simple card sorter to get at the information and to do counts, effectively all you can do with a sorter. Sorters had gotten pretty fancy just before the introduction of computers because all of that business equipment had gotten about as highly technologically developed as it could. So sorters were able to count on more than one column at a time, and they could count all the punches in the cards in one pass and so forth. However, the Gluecks realized the limitations of the card sorters especially in terms of managing the data—you still had to put the cards in each time to be read, cards were always jamming or getting lost, etc. So their first need was data processing to convert multiply punched cards into single variables. The Gluecks came to the Statistical Laboratory to get some help. Just about that time I was leaving the Statistical Laboratory to become a consultant on my own, so they hired me as a consultant.

One of the first things we did—I worked principally with Rose Kneznek, who was in charge of shaping up the data; she had been working for the Gluecks on and off for several years—was to recode all of the basic Glueck data into yes/no categories. Remember a lot of the Glueck questions had five or six responses and these have since been recoded into yes/no categories—is it associated with delinquency or not? Those decisions were made based on published work that had already existed, for example, *Family Environment and Delinquency* (1962). So, when we went through each of the items, sometimes we created a single item (yes/no) and sometimes we created several items. We translated them all into binary variables for good reason. I think a lot of the original measures were somewhat confusing and they weren't necessarily linear. An item like "Does the father live at home?" might have five or six responses to it—yes, he does; no, he doesn't; he only shows up on weekends; he is there once in a while; there is a father there, but we are not sure whose it is; etc. These were all coded as one item, although there is no particular linearity to them. So that recoding was the first project—to get the variables untied from their previous format and create a new format that was suitable for processing on the then modern computer.

JL: How did your work on prediction get started?

RL: Publications were starting to appear that were critical of prediction generally as well as critical of the Gluecks themselves and their research methodology. We sat down one afternoon, Sheldon, Eleanor, and myself, to discuss the situation. I had suggested to them that techniques existed, multivariate analyses, something I was studying at the time, that could be used independently of the researchers' heuristics, so that you could effectively be led by the data to a conclusion, developing a prediction table, for example. Then the suitability, the comparability, the similarity between a mathematically generated model and a model that they had generated would be interesting to look at. The risk here being that the mathematical model would come up with a completely different set of variables. The benefit being that if we had agreement then we would have independent confirmation that the way in which the Gluecks had come upon their model would be founded on something better than their methodology, which wasn't bad, but wasn't terribly sophisticated. The Gluecks had principally taken measures from each of several areas, family environment, characteristics like intelligence and so forth, early experience, early school experience, etc. They had categories of measures and their prediction table generally sampled from those categories, and then they effectively sought to weight them based on relative frequencies, which is about the way you do things, whether you do it mathematically with the help of the computer or whether you do it by knowing the data intimately. It probably doesn't make much difference. There is an old saw that says "Statistics only prove what you already know!"

I had convinced the Gluecks that statistics were not magic, and the Gluecks knew the data well enough that it was probably worth taking this risk. I then offered them my help in being very scrupulous about the way things were done. I felt very removed from their biases and any of their favorite variables, and I would conduct an independent study leading to a prediction equation to see how closely it resembled the Glueck prediction table. We would then effectively publish this and hopefully put the critics to rest. The Gluecks thought that this was a good idea. I then began this study which leads up to that paper delivered at the International Congress on Criminology meeting in Montreal, "The Validation of the Glueck Prediction Table." It was also published in the *Journal of Criminal Law, Criminology, and Police Science* (1970). The exercise was not as simple as that paper might appear. I had been given a free hand and had been told to use whatever resources were necessary, but it didn't always work out that way. But the point was that the Gluecks wanted me to exercise just as much as care in doing this as I could so they would be clean if the validation worked out to be supportive.

I finally finished up the discriminant function analysis, and lo and behold there was very little difference between the prediction equation and the weighting system used by the Gluecks compared with a similar system and weighting system the modern computer would have selected. The Gluecks were very pleased, and I was very pleased too because I had thought that this was a validation of my own bias—if you do things right, you don't need statistics in a sense. And similarly, if the statistician does things right, if given enough resources, he can emulate in-depth knowledge of the data. So it is a validation both ways.

JL: Some of the major critics of the Gluecks' research have questioned their basic data, for example, raising questions about whether the data are fudged or manipulated in some fashion to reinforce their own biases.

RL: Well, you have seen the actual records and I have seen the actual records—the data that are coded from these records are clearly correct. Some of the data that were really off the wall, like the morphological data or the Rorschach data, really didn't influence them all that much. Sheldon's influence on Eleanor's interpretation as well as our coding in a binary way was to make things as clear as possible and not play games with the data.

The Gluecks were not capable of fudging. Sheldon was most honorable. He was asked to sit on the Nuremberg Trials because of his reputation for honesty as much as anything else. I think that's a myth that has no support. I think the study I did clearly shows that as well. I had to be just as scrupulous and I came out with the same answer as they did. The basic data being fudged that would only lead you to that answer—unlikely! They had a lot of people helping them. Two or three people working on the coding and cross-checking the coding. They would not, any of them, be party to any fudging of the data. There are circumstances that give you a feeling for the reliability, the accuracy of what they did. It is a lot different from taking the data from a laboratory and then going off somewhere and writing a paper and not letting anyone know about it. We have a whole group of people here that have been milling around these data for 25 to 30 years. There was little or no opportunity to fudge if they wanted to. Somebody would have said "That's not right." The basic Glueck data are sound.

NOTES

1. An Age-graded Theory of Informal Social Control

1. Of course, the concept of "antisocial behavior" is not without problems. Cultural deviance theorists in criminology argue that crime is social behavior learned in groups (see especially Sutherland and Cressey, 1978). Our use of the term follows convention in referring to destructive behavior that violates generally accepted norms of society (see Robins, 1966; Kornhauser, 1978) and is not meant to convey a particular etiological theory.

2. We follow convention in defining *crime* as violation of societal rules of behavior that are embodied in law. When officially recognized, such violations may evoke sanctions by the State. A wide-ranging body of research has demonstrated general consensus underlying most definitions of crime (see Kornhauser, 1978: 214–218; Gottfredson and Hirschi, 1990: 151). On the other hand, we are also interested in the more general conception of *deviance*, defined as violations of social norms or accepted standards of society (that is, institutionalized expectations; see Cohen, 1959: 462). By uniting crime and deviance in a single theoretical explanation, we avoid many of the definitional problems encountered by criminologists in the past, especially the tendency to define their dependent variable solely in reference to legal codes (see Gottfredson and Hirschi, 1990: Chapters 1 and 2). Moreover, we generally avoid crime-specific analyses because they are inherently inconsistent with our general theoretical approach and the nonspecialized nature of criminal offending (see Chapter 3).

2. *Unraveling Juvenile Delinquency* and Follow-up Studies

1. This work was honored by three symposia of reviews that appeared in the *Harvard Law Review* (1951), the *Journal of Criminal Law, Criminology, and Police Science* (1951), and *Federal Probation* (1951). See also S. Glueck (1960) for a response to the various reviews of *Unraveling Juvenile Delinquency*. Additionally, in an assessment of the quality of criminological literature in the United States, it was found that from 1945 to 1972 *Unraveling Juvenile Delinquency* was the most heavily cited work in the field (Wolfgang et al., 1978).

2. For example, approximately 30 percent of the delinquent group had a juvenile court *conviction* at age 10 or younger, and the average number of convictions for all delinquent boys was 3.5 (Glueck and Glueck, 1950: 293). Further, about two-thirds of the offenses were personal and property crimes (for example, burglary, larceny, assault) (Glueck and Glueck, 1950: 29).

3. See also Vaillant (1983: 245–247), who used the control group sample from the Gluecks' study in a highly regarded investigation of alcoholism.

4. National University Law School was affiliated with George Washington University and is now known as George Washington University Law Center. It appears that Sheldon Glueck chose this school because it offered classes at night.

5. Both Sheldon and Eleanor Glueck were given honorary doctorates by Harvard University in 1958, the first husband and wife team to receive such an honor in the history of the university.

6. Eleanor Glueck received her doctorate in educational sociology at the Harvard Graduate School of Education, at the time the only school at Harvard to admit women.

7. Harvard Law School did not admit women as students until 1950, the last Ivy League law school to do so. Even then, it has been noted that during the 1950s and 1960s women at Harvard Law School were "treated like members of an alien species" (Abramson and Franklin, 1986: 10).

8. Although the Gluecks' research was carried out under the auspices of the Harvard Law School, their research was funded by numerous private foundations. Eleanor Glueck spent an enormous amount of time on this fund-raising activity.

9. Harvard sociology in the 1930s has been described as "intellectually ill-defined" (Camic, 1987: 425). Although Sheldon Glueck's criminology course was offered to sociology students, the powers that did exist (for example, Pitirim Sorokin and later Talcott Parsons) certainly did not consider the study of crime to be central to the mission of sociology (see Faculty Committee Report, 1954 and Cohen's interview with Laub, 1983b). It should also be noted that both Sheldon and Eleanor Glueck were Jewish. One can speculate that discrimination against Jews at Harvard University (see Laub, 1983b: 185) may have also contributed to isolating the Gluecks from the mainstream academic community.

10. Other major problems with the Gluecks' attempt at predicting delinquency include the absence of a validation sample. For a general review of this issue see Farrington and Tarling (1985: 7–8).

11. It should be recognized that in later works—*Physique and Delinquency* (1956) and *Family Environment and Delinquency* (1962)—the Gluecks used a relatively new methodology developed by John W. Tukey that allowed

for "multiple comparisons" of variables in their contingency tables. This methodology was recommended to the Gluecks by Frederick Mosteller (for more details see Worcester, 1956: 276–283).

12. It is not clear, however, that the presentation of data in *UJD* was necessarily wrong given the nature of the case-control design. See, for example, Loftin and McDowall's (1988) discussion of case-control data in criminology and the calculation of odds ratios from tables where cases and controls are traditionally column rather than row variables.

13. For an overview of prediction research in the criminal justice area, see Glueck and Glueck (1959); for an application of the prediction tables in the military, see Schneider, LaGrone, Glueck, and Glueck (1944).

3. Restoring, Supplementing, and Validating the Data

1. These self-reported data sometimes resulted in eliminating a previously designated nondelinquent boy from the study. In fact, 36 cases originally selected as nondelinquents were eliminated from the study. This is not to say that the boys in the nondelinquent group were "pure" nondelinquents—about 25 percent reported some misbehavior during the interview (Glueck and Glueck, 1950: 29). Given that there is also considerable variation on self-reported delinquency *within* the original delinquent group, the self-reported data emerge as an important validation tool.

2. Still, there could be variation among teachers, parents, and the boys themselves in the interpretation of the behavioral characteristics asked about in the study. There may also exist differential validity among the various respondents. The Gluecks themselves stated: "The delinquents' parents certainly knew far less, or were perhaps unwilling to admit what they actually knew, than the parents of the non-delinquents in regard to the bad habits of the boys" (1950: 130). Fortunately, this issue can be addressed empirically through construct validation.

3. Nevertheless, it should be noted that no matter how the unofficial scales were created, they were highly intercorrelated. The use of different scales also did not affect substantive results.

4. Of course, it is not possible to trace patterns of communication between parents and teachers regarding each boy's behavior. If such communication occurred, it could have influenced reporting practices, and our interpretation of the parental and teacher reports as independent measures of delinquency and other misconduct would be inaccurate.

5. This issue is also addressed in later chapters through the longitudinal analysis of change in delinquency within both the delinquent and nondelinquent groups. Obviously, patterns of relationships within the two different groups cannot be attributed to the fact that investigators knew whether the subject was a delinquent or a control group member.

6. Unfortunately, the original records for 20 cases were apparently lost. We thoroughly searched the Harvard Law School Library storage area to no avail. As a result, the detailed criminal histories for the delinquents are based on the 480 men for whom we have records. Further analyses revealed nothing unusual about the 20 lost cases.

7. We coded the three most serious charges for each arrest. This decision was based on a pretest of 50 randomly selected cases wherein we discovered that 99 percent of the cases had three or fewer charges per incident. We also coded the total number of charges for each event for those with more than three.

8. We allowed up to three incarcerations resulting from parole revocations without a new arrest. This decision was also based on a pretest of 50 randomly selected cases which revealed that over 99 percent of cases fit this scheme.

9. The full criminal history data were extensively validated. For example, in addition to numerous logical validity checks, comparisons to other research, and internal validation, the complete criminal histories of a random sample of 20 cases were checked by hand against the computerized files.

10. We gratefully acknowledge Dr. Vaillant's assistance in allowing us to code these data.

11. All arrests were coded except minor traffic offenses (such as speeding or not slowing down) and technical violations of the motor vehicle code (for example, improper license; expired insurance).

4. The Family Context of Juvenile Delinquency

1. For the sample as a whole, 24 percent of the cases of family disruption involved parental death. The remainder entailed desertion, separation, or divorce (Glueck and Glueck, 1950: 122–123). Although there is some literature regarding differential effects by type of family disruption on serious delinquency (see Rutter and Giller, 1983: 190–191), from a social control perspective any break in the home should have detrimental effects. Thus, we conceptualized family disruption broadly to include any break in the home. In a separate analysis we found no relationship between death of parent and son's delinquency (phi = .03), while the relationship between parental divorce / separation and delinquency was strong (phi = .62). Nevertheless, experimentation with different measures of family disruption did not change the general pattern of results in the multivariate analyses reported in this chapter.

2. The Gluecks did not collect data on the father's supervision of children, and we are thus limited to an examination of the mother's supervision. This rather narrow focus by the Gluecks reflects the era in which this study was conceived, wherein mothers assumed primary responsibility for the supervision of children.

3. We are not suggesting that measurement error is absent in the Gluecks' data, only that it is not of the type typically found in modern survey research. Consequently, throughout this and other chapters we address in detail the various measurement issues that may confound the results (for example, retrospective bias, unreliability, differential validity) and the procedures we use to counteract them. Moreover, we do in fact employ covariance structure models for some analyses (see, for example, Chapter 8).

4. This specification is further supported by Liska and Reed's (1985: 557) simultaneous analyses wherein the relationship between parental attachment and delinquency "comes about because of the effect of parental attachment on delinquency."

5. Statistical significance tests—including the use of one-tailed hypothesis tests appropriate for our theoretical predictions—are not strictly applicable given the Gluecks' non-probability sampling scheme. As a general rule of thumb, we therefore focus in this chapter and throughout the book primarily on coefficients that are greater than twice their standard errors, which approximates a traditional .05 level of significance. We also use the .05 level for bivariate Pearson correlation coefficients. Among "significant" coefficients, our interest lies in their relative *magnitude* (for example, standardized beta coefficients). Given the theory-based nature of our analysis, these procedures are conservative and may underestimate the significance of variables. However, they do protect against type 1 error.

6. Hirschi (1991) has argued that single-parent households are less able to provide adequate supervision and monitoring than are two-parent households. Although in the Glueck data the bivariate relationship between family disruption and supervision is significant and in the predicted direction (-.30), our multivariate analysis reveals an insignificant weak effect of family disruption on parental supervision ($\beta = -.05$).

7. Bearing in mind this historical context, the Gluecks' concern with working mothers and single parents was that children would be deprived of maternal supervision (1950: 112; see also "Working Mothers and Delinquency," reprinted in Glueck and Glueck, 1964: 31–59). Such views reinforce traditional gender roles of women as housewives and mothers by defining their primary role as that of nurturing children. For a recent assessment see McCord (1990) on the quality of family life in understanding crime.

8. Multicollinearity or redundancy among variables is not a major problem in these models. The largest intercorrelation among predictors was .52, and that was between mother's and father's erratic/threatening discipline, both of which had *independent* effects on delinquency. Variance inflation factors (for details see Fisher and Mason, 1981) were therefore much below levels of concern (for example, the largest was less than 2.0).

9. The tantrum measure is taken from a combined parent/teacher-reported

interview. As Lytton (1990) notes, the fact that it is typical to derive ratings of a child's early temperament and of parental practices from the parent interview alone makes for methodological confounding. We avoid this wherever possible through multiple sources of measurement (that is, self, parent, *and* teacher).

10. For reasons of theoretical and empirical parsimony in the "trimmed" models, we created a standardized scale that combines mother's and father's disciplinary styles. Although these two variables did have independent effects in prior analysis, they are correlated over .50, tap conceptually similar dimensions, and in fact have a similar magnitude of effect. Creating a composite index also helps us to identify more cleanly the independent effects of discipline, supervision, and attachment. In terms of our theory, this goal is more important than the precise partitioning of mother's and father's effects when the results show that both are important.

11. Of course, the base rate of official delinquency is artificially high because of the Gluecks' research design. As a result, estimating proportional change in the dependent variable from logistic models (see, for example, Petersen, 1985) is somewhat misleading. This problem is akin to the Gluecks' efforts at prediction using the *UJD* data. Nevertheless, one can compare relative magnitudes among variables.

12. As expected on the basis of the Gluecks' matching design, both IQ and age had insignificant effects on official delinquency. Also as expected from the findings in Glueck and Glueck (1950), mesomorphy had a significant positive effect on official delinquency. Interestingly, however, mesomorphy had no effect on unofficial delinquency, suggesting that the Gluecks' original finding may have resulted from selection biases in the pattern of official reaction by agents of the juvenile justice system.

13. Rutter and Giller (1983: 186) have stated that "the mechanisms underlying the link between large family size and delinquency remain rather obscure." The conventional account of this relationship is the linkage of family size to disadvantaged socioeconomic status and/or educational deficiencies (for example, low IQ, poor reading scores; Rutter and Giller, 1983: 185–186). However, these variables are controlled either through the matching design or in our analysis. An alternative explanation is that within large families there is an increased probability of sibling influence on delinquent behavior (see Offord, 1982). This issue is taken up in the next chapter.

5. The Role of School, Peers, and Siblings

1. Research by Liska and Reed (1985: 557) suggests that "most of the observed negative relationship between school attachment and delinquency comes about because of the effect of delinquency on school attachment." Given the design of the Gluecks' study, we are unable to address fully the issue

of reciprocal effects. However, as in Chapter 4, we can assess the extent to which childhood antisocial behavior confounds the relationship between school attachment and adolescent delinquency.

2. Although we control for family SES, it should be noted that there is very little variation in parental education. Not surprisingly, given the time period and lower-class nature of the sample, the vast majority (> 75 percent) of parents had not even graduated from high school.

3. "Grades repeated" was rescored such that the resulting scale takes on a higher value when school performance increases.

4. Those with no siblings obviously cannot be measured in terms of their sibling attachment. Fortunately, only 71 of the boys (< 10 percent) had no siblings, and hence they are excluded from analysis.

5. Not surprisingly, there is a strong relationship between a boy's family size and delinquency among siblings (gamma = .57). As in previous analyses, family size is controlled when assessing the effects of sibling delinquency on the boy's own delinquency.

6. With respect to sibling spacing, we do know that of those in the study with siblings, 66 percent were within three years or less of their closest sibling in age. We also know that 170 of the subjects were the eldest child in the family. Of these 170, 74 were delinquents and 96 were nondelinquents. Moreover, a total of 71 subjects in the study were without siblings, that is, the only child. Of these 71, 28 were delinquents and 43 were nondelinquents. We should also note that delinquency among siblings is linked to birth order: the middle child is most likely to have delinquent siblings. Whether this relationship is due to birth order or family size is not clear.

7. We also examined a series of regression models that investigated the interaction of school process with structural background and also family process variables. In general, interaction terms did not improve the fit of the models. More specifically, interactions of school attachment with key family process variables from Chapter 4 were not significant. The effect of school attachment, as with family process, thus appears to be additive.

8. If we consider the delinquency of siblings regardless of attachment, the significant predictors are mobility, family size, crowding, mother's employment, foreign-born status, and parental deviance (data not shown).

9. For the final models we estimated a series of higher-order interactions. As in previous analyses, the interaction terms were highly correlated with constituent terms and did not improve the overall explanatory power of the models.

10. We also re-estimated models of school attachment as a dependent variable by adding age, IQ, and ethnicity (dichotomous variables for Irish, Italian, and English background) as predictor variables. Not surprisingly, IQ was significantly related to attachment (r = .36) but was weakly related to the

other independent variables in our analyses ($r = .10$ or less). Age was negatively related to attachment ($r = -.15$), but it too was weakly correlated with exogenous variables. Ethnicity was unrelated to school attachment. Accordingly, the addition of age, IQ, and ethnicity did not change the substantive picture of our main results.

11. We acknowledge that ours is not a definitive test of differential association theory because we do not have direct measures of attitudes toward deviance and the ratio of definitions favorable to law violation to those unfavorable. For example, in Matsueda's (1982) analysis, delinquent definitions (that is, attitudes) were found to mediate the effect of background exogenous characteristics on delinquency. On the other hand, it would be surprising indeed if attachment to delinquent peers were not highly related to differential association with delinquent values and attitudes.

7. Adult Social Bonds and Change in Criminal Behavior

1. Of course, this process may well be one in which transitions in objective contingencies—marriage, employment, and so forth—lead to changes in subjective contingencies—such as self-concept, motivations, aspirations (Gartner and Piliavin, 1988: 299–300). Moreover, there is some evidence that objective and subjective contingencies interact with age (Shover, 1985; Shover and Thompson, 1992). We address these issues when we merge our quantitative and qualitative data analysis in Chapter 9.

2. For job stability and several other measures (such as general deviance and drinking) the data at wave 2 refer to the previous five years—ages 20 to 25—or to most recent job rather than the entire age 17–25 span. Even though measurement lags in our analysis do not necessarily correspond exactly to causal lags (see also Plewis, 1985: 60), we do not believe that this is a major problem because the Gluecks' research strategy was designed to reflect average levels during the age periods 17–25 and 25–32.

3. This does not imply that we reject the use of measurement models and structural equations (for example, LISREL) or other methods for longitudinal data (such as random-effects models). In fact, these and other techniques are considered and used where appropriate (see also Chapter 8).

4. This strategy confronts head on the claim that correlations among adult factors (for example, job stability and crime) are spurious because of propensities to delinquency formed in childhood. In other words, if the spurious (or common third cause) argument is correct (see Gottfredson and Hirschi, 1990), our research design will yield insignificant relationships between adult social bonds and crime.

5. In Table 7.1 only, job stability is trichotomized and commitment is dichotomized to permit visual display of the pattern and magnitude of the relationships. Because of extreme skew, the attachment measure at wave 2 is

dichotomized here and in later multivariate analyses. The number of cases ranges from a minimum of 224 for the ever-married subsample at wave 2 to 437 for occupational commitment at wave 2. The corresponding number of cases for wave 3 is 314 and 292. It is important to note that all of the percentages are based on at least 30 cases, and this holds for the control group percentages presented in Chapter 8 as well (see Table 8.1).

6. For the purposes of this book, the transition to young adulthood is generally defined as ages 17–25, while ages 25–32 and 32–45 refer to the stages of young adulthood and the transition to middle adulthood, respectively. We recognize that these distinctions are somewhat arbitrary and relative to our sample, but they do highlight the different stages of adulthood covered by the Gluecks in an earlier historical period.

7. As Plewis (1985: 59–60) notes, in the equation $y_2 = a + b_1 y_1 + b_2 x_1 + e$, the parameter b_2 measures "the effect of x_1 on a change in y." The idea that change is examined only with the computation of change scores (for example, $y_2 - y_1$) is simply incorrect; in fact, the latter can have serious disadvantages, especially when the measurement schemes differ across time (see also Kessler and Greenberg, 1981). In this regard note that our research design differs from the usual situation in panel data where short (for example, yearly) lags using identical measurement schemes often induce autocorrelation, leading to biased estimates (see also Matsueda, 1989; Plewis, 1985: 136; Markus, 1979). For example, the wave 1 measures refer to behavior in childhood and adolescence (both parent/self/teacher-reported and juvenile-justice recorded), whereas the wave 2 measures refer to adult behavior in the late teens and early twenties as recorded in adult interviews and by the adult criminal justice system. Moreover, preliminary two-stage least-squares regression of wave 3 crime/deviance, using wave 1 delinquency as an instrumental variable for wave 2 crime/deviance, produced substantively consistent results with those presented in this chapter. Chapter 8 also shows that correction for autocorrelation in random-effects models does not materially alter the substantive parameter estimates. Because of these results, the long-term nature of the follow-ups, and the theoretically based model specification that assigns a substantive role to prior crime/delinquency in generating later behavior, we conceptualize our wave 1 crime/delinquency measures as independent variables.

8. For a detailed discussion of sample selection methodology, see the seminal work by Heckman (1979). Excellent explications with examples relevant to criminology may also be found in Berk (1983) and Berk and Ray (1982).

9. In practice it appears to make little difference whether the bivariate logistic or bivariate normal distributions are assumed. For example, Berk (1983: 394) found that hazard rates constructed using probit and logistic specifications were correlated at least .98. We prefer the logistic model because of

its computational ease and its congruence with the maximum-likelihood logistic models analyzed throughout this book. Moreover, the logistic procedure produces results virtually equivalent to Heckman's (1979) probit-based hazard instrument (see note 11 below).

10. Although juvenile arrest frequency has a surprising negative effect on later exclusion, the effect of unofficial delinquency is insignificant. Moreover, as we discuss later, incarceration and crime frequency in adulthood are highly correlated, so it is still the case that crime-prone adults were more likely to be excluded. What Table 7.2 tells us is that the *independent* effect of juvenile delinquency is both less salient and of the opposite sign than the more proximate effect of adult incarceration.

11. Of course, sample selection methods are not foolproof, and caution is still necessary in the interpretation of results (Berk, 1983; Stolzenberg and Relles, 1990). To guard against incorrect conclusions, we took several steps to investigate the sensitivity of results. First, all models were estimated both with and without the hazard rate correction instruments. Second, several different hazard rate instruments were constructed to assess the variability of results to different model specifications of exclusion risk (for example, alternative predictors in the first-stage exclusion equation). As reported in more detail later, these various procedures converged. Third, we re-estimated all models substituting Heckman's (1979) "lambda" in lieu of our logistic-based hazard rate. The major difference is that a probit model was used to construct the hazard rates (that is, predicted probit values were multiplied by −1 and the density and distribution values calculated; see Berk, 1983 for details). Similar to results reported by Berk (1983: 394), the probit-based results were identical to the logistic-based procedures. Overall, then, our logistic model of exclusion risk appears robust to alternative model specifications and correction procedures (for example, distributional assumptions) for sample selection bias.

12. The dichotomous nature of these measures violates the assumptions of ordinary least squares (OLS) regression. Hence maximum-likelihood (ML) logistic regression is used, which, unlike log-linear analysis, preserves the interval nature of the majority of our predictor variables (see Aldrich and Nelson, 1984). The unstandardized logistic coefficients in Table 7.3 represent the change in the log-odds of exhibiting antisocial behavior associated with a unit change in the exogenous variable. Because the units of measurement of the independent variables are not consistent, we also present the t-ratios of coefficients to standard errors (Aldrich and Nelson, 1984:55).

13. Our measure of income for each subject is an ordinal scale of the weekly gross earnings derived from legitimate occupations (Glueck and Glueck, 1968: 95). A dummy variable for marital status indicates whether marriage

alone is an inhibiting factor in adult crime. In preliminary analysis we also examined several other socioeconomic factors such as economic dependence and education, but these results were substantially similar. Because it is the most direct indicator of SES, we focus on wages as a primary control variable.

14. Our previous analyses of these measures (Sampson and Laub, 1990) focused mainly on the concurrent effects of social bonds on crime. Those results mirrored Table 7.3. For example, the t-ratios reflecting the effects of age 17–25 job stability on age 17–25 deviance, drinking, and arrest were –2.72, –3.12, and –2.44, respectively (all $p < .05$). The corresponding t-ratios for marital attachment were –2.26, –2.42, and –2.31 (for further details see Sampson and Laub, 1990: 619). Although these concurrent effects are consistent with our theory of informal social control, they may be biased by reciprocal effects. So while we sometimes display both concurrent and predictive effects for comparative purposes (as in Table 7.4), we place the greatest emphasis on the predictive effects of adult social bonds on later crime to reduce the possibility that crime itself may have influenced observed levels of attachment and job stability.

15. Because the frequency of arrests is positively skewed, we analyze the natural logarithm (+1) of an annualized measure of arrests per day free, using ordinary least squares (OLS) regression. The equations with the unlogged rates produced nearly identical results, although the explained variances were usually less. Poisson regression-based models for raw frequency counts are discussed later in this chapter.

16. To verify the robustness of this finding, we reanalyzed all models using different instrumental variables for the hazard of exclusion among the subsample of married men. In particular, income and job stability have been posited to influence marriage decisions because men with low incomes and unstable job histories may make relatively undesirable mates (see, for example, Wilson, 1987). We thus re-estimated the sample selection equations using wages and job stability as additional predictors. Higher income, but not job stability, was a consistent predictor of marriage, thereby increasing the multicollinearity in the final model-2 substantive equations. Still, the results were virtually indistinguishable from those presented earlier. For example, the t-ratios reflecting the independent effects of job stability and marital attachment on crime frequency at ages 25–32 were –2.90 and –2.95, respectively (cf. model 2, Table 7.4). Similarly, marital attachment retained its strong negative effect on arrest, unofficially reported deviance, and excessive alcohol use at ages 25–32 (see Table 7.3). Marital attachment at ages 25–32 also had the exact same effect on later crime at ages 32–45 (beta = –.36) when we substituted the alternative sample-selection exclusion risk (cf. Table 7.5). Analyses of the married

subsample are thus robust to two different methods for accounting for sample selection bias.

17. For further details on the statistical properties of Poisson regression, see King (1988) and Greene (1989: 243–254). Our purpose in using these models is driven by substantive and pragmatic concerns: do the basic results change under alternative methodologies (cf. Cook, 1985)?

18. Because the negative binomial model takes into account the skewed distribution of arrest counts, we were also able to estimate crime-specific models of rarer events. Namely, we estimated negative binomial models for property crime, violent crime, and drunkenness arrests. Except for violent crimes—where *no* variable was significant at $p < .05$—the results were consistent. For example, the t-ratios reflecting the effects of job stability on arrests for property crime and drunkenness were –3.55 and –2.32, respectively.

19. Marital attachment at ages 17–25 was considered in a preliminary estimation of model 2, but it had insignificant effects and the sample size was considerably reduced because many of the men had not yet married. The prior and concurrent measures of marital attachment were also quite highly correlated, suggesting substantial stability in marital cohesiveness among the married men. Therefore, we used attachment to spouse at ages 25–32 as the main indicator to increase sample size and reduce multicollinearity.

20. To assess the validity and robustness of these results, we also re-estimated all the models substituting prior adult crime in lieu of the hazard exclusion variables. Because of the strong overlap among these variables, the results were quite consistent with those presented earlier (see Sampson and Laub, 1990). In particular, the rate of arrest at ages 17–25 is correlated at .66 and .71 (both $p < .05$) with the hazard risk of exclusion at ages 17–25 and 25–32, respectively. It is not surprising then that the results converge regardless of whether we control for prior adult crime or whether we model sample selection bias (see also Table 7.7). Despite the similarity of results, our preference is for the sample selection models (and hence the majority of tables in this chapter are based on such models) because we know on a priori grounds that the excluded men are systematically different from the men for whom data are complete.

21. Age of onset of excessive drinking was measured in the social interview schedule. More detailed discussion and analysis of this variable—including validation information—are presented in Chapter 8.

22. The results in Table 7.9 maintain even when crime at ages 17–25 is simultaneously controlled. Specifically, the standardized effect of juvenile incarceration on job stability at ages 17–25, controlling for the frequency of crime at ages 17–25, is –.19 ($p < .05$). As reported in Chapter 8, the findings also remain when persistent unobserved heterogeneity among individuals in propensity to job stability is controlled.

23. In general, controlling for drinking in the prediction of later crime does not materially alter the substantive results presented earlier for job stability. Models reflecting this specification are shown in Chapter 8.

24. This model also allows us to control for exclusion risk at the age 32 interview. Given the nature of our selection equations, exclusion risk is highly correlated with incarceration at ages 17–25 and crime frequency at ages 17–25, yielding inefficient estimates when all variables are included in the same model (cf. Table 7.10, Panel A). By combining the total days incarcerated in adolescence and young adulthood, we reduce the overlap with exclusion risk and are able to assess the long-term impact on job stability.

25. For example, in models where job stability was not controlled, incarceration at ages 17–25 had a significant positive effect on crime at ages 25–32 (t-ratio = 2.07). These results support the idea that job stability helps explain the impact of incarceration, and that the collinearity between incarceration and exclusion risk does not account for the former's insignificance in Table 7.8.

26. The goodness of fit of the maximum-likelihood LISREL model estimating the simultaneous effects of job stability and crime in the full sample was excellent (chi-square of .59 with one degree of freedom; goodness of fit index = .99). The combined measurement and structural equation model of job stability and marital attachment in Figure 7.1 provided a poorer fit (chi-square of 45.8 with 11 degrees of freedom; goodness of fit index = .94). This modest fit appears to stem from violations of normality assumptions, especially regarding the dichotomous indicator of marital attachment. By freeing selected error covariances among observable indicators we were able to improve the goodness of fit slightly, but the structural parameter estimates remained the same (for example, allowing an error covariance between marital attachment and crime participation changed the latent reciprocal effect of social bonds on crime only to −.61 from −.62). Given this invariance of structural parameter estimates in conjunction with both the lack of theoretical guidance on error covariances and the risk of capitalizing on chance variation in the sample (see Alwin, 1988: 116), the model represented in Figure 7.1 is preferred.

27. To be safe, however, we checked the data against the assumption of proportionality using graphical procedures outlined by Allison (1984: 39). The data were first grouped into strata defined by our key full-sample independent variables split at the mean (that is, low job stability versus high job stability; low juvenile delinquency versus high juvenile delinquency). Then the logged-hazard rates and survival functions were plotted against logged-time for each stratum. If the requirement of proportional hazards is met, we would expect the plots to be roughly parallel for each stratum. That is exactly what we found, not only for total arrests (that is, any crime) but

for property crime, violent crime, and drunkenness arrests as well. The initial results and plots also indicated that our exogenous strata were related to the survival function in the manner predicted by theory. For example, the survival rates for men with high job stability at age 25 were .80 in the age period 25-26, .70 for ages 26-27, .66 for ages 27-28, .58 for ages 28-29, and .52 for ages 29-30. The corresponding survival rates for men with low job stability were .58, .44, .36, .28, and .24, respectively. In short, the graphical analysis supported the assumption of proportional hazards and indicated that time until failure was related to our strata in the expected manner.

8. Comparative Models of Crime and Deviance

1. Although by design the control-group subjects had no arrests before the study began, 10 percent were in fact arrested between the time of examination (mean age 14) and age 17 (see Chapter 3). For the control group we thus examine the frequency of post-interview arrests as juveniles. We do not adjust for juvenile incarceration time among control-group members because it was such a rare event and hence was not coded.

2. Given that the control group generated little if any incarceration time as adults, length of control-group incarceration was neither coded nor used as an exogenous variable in predicting models of exclusion risk. Despite this difference in model specification, the control-group sample-selection models corresponded to substantive expectations (for instance, the primary predictor of exclusion at ages 17-25 was length of military service, and younger control-group members were more likely to be excluded than older members).

3. Nevertheless, we re-estimated all OLS models with Poisson and negative binomial regression. Probably because of limited skewness, the results were substantively identical. For simplicity we thus present the OLS results for the breadth of crime and deviance scale.

4. In Table 8.4 and the remaining tables in this chapter, juvenile arrest frequency for the delinquent group measures the annualized number of arrests per day free under age 17. The corresponding measure for the control group is the number of arrests between the interview date (average age 14) and the subject's seventeenth birthday.

5. Although the model specification was slightly different, the results in Table 8.4 are replicated when the breadth of crime and deviance scale is expanded to ages 17-32. For example, the standardized effects of age 17-25 job stability and marital attachment on crime/deviance at ages 17-32 are −.27 and −.40, respectively, for the delinquent group ($p < .05$). The corresponding coefficients for the control group are −.28 and −.40 ($p < .05$).

6. Because we have no unofficial reports of deviance available at ages 32-45 as we do for earlier ages, we must rely on official record data. As noted

earlier, the skewed distribution of arrests among the controls at ages 32–45 resembles a simple dichotomy, and hence we estimate a ML logistic model of crime participation. Nevertheless, negative binomial results for crime frequency were quite similar.

7. Information for this measure was derived from the social investigation interview with the subject and other knowledgeable informants, supplemented by extensive record checks (see Glueck and Glueck, 1968: 83–84). For example, not only were criminal records checked, but assessments of deviance were obtained from social welfare, mental health, school, and employment records as well.

8. The interaction of attachment and spouse's deviance correlated highly with constituent variables and did not add substantively to the model. Also, the results in Table 8.6 are fully replicated when we consider the frequency of arrests among delinquents and controls. For example, marital attachment has a standardized effect of −.31 (t-ratio = −3.48) on arrests per year free among the delinquents, controlling for deviance of spouse.

9. As in the analyses for deviance of spouse, we estimate "trimmed" models that drop insignificant predictors in Tables 8.4 and 8.5.

10. We also estimated even stricter models that controlled for unofficial drinking *and* the frequency of drunkenness arrests at ages 17–25 in predicting crime at ages 25–32. These models are somewhat ambiguous theoretically because drinking at ages 17–25 may mediate some of the instantaneous effects of job stability at ages 17–25, or vice versa. Still, the basic message remained intact, especially for job stability. For example, the t-ratios reflecting the effect of job stability at ages 17–25 on crime/deviance and crime frequency at ages 25–32—controlling for concurrent drinking (official and unofficial)—were −4.45 and −4.37, respectively, for the control group. The corresponding delinquent-group t-ratios were −5.41 and −5.87. The validation results were consistent for marital attachment except for age 25–32 crime among the control-group subjects. Here the effects of marital attachment at ages 17–25 were insignificant when age 17–25 drinking was controlled. When we controlled for drinking *prior* to age 20 in Table 8.7, though, the effect of marital attachment remained intact for the control subjects. This finding suggests that later drinking may mediate the prior effects of marital attachment on age 25–32 crime among the controls. For the other models, however, the effects of marital attachment were quite similar despite accounting for concurrent drinking.

Finally, we extended the analysis to a consideration of the effects of social bonds at ages 25–32 on age 32–45 crime, again controlling for prior drinking. Within both groups job stability had consistent negative effects on crime, a finding that maintained using OLS models of logged frequencies and negative binomial models of raw arrest counts.

11. Recall that race and gender do not vary by the nature of the research

design. In the follow-ups, age is also controlled since the independent and dependent variables refer to the same age period (that is, ages 17–25 and ages 25–32). For example, even though a boy may have entered the study at age 12 and another at age 16 (the range was 10–17), the follow-ups were conducted on or near the 25th and 32nd birthdays of both individuals and have the same reference period. The exception was in the event history models for the delinquent group in Chapter 7, where age at release was controlled.

12. We even re-estimated all comparative models controlling for final educational attainment, residential mobility, neighborhood poverty, and religiosity in adulthood. The significant negative effects of job stability and marital attachment held up, and the additional controls were inconsistent.

13. The expected value of u_i is zero, and the covariance of $[e_{it}, u_i]$ is also assumed to be zero (that is, the individual-specific term and random errors are assumed to be uncorrelated across individuals). However, the combined disturbances—$e_{it} + u_i$—may be correlated over time. For example, in a two-wave model the correlation would be of the form: $[e_{i1} + u_i, e_{i2} + u_i]$, estimated by dividing the variance of u_i by the sum of variances of u_i and the random error components (for details see Greene, 1989: 162).

14. The primary purpose of Nagin and Paternoster's (1991) analyses was to distinguish between state dependence and population heterogeneity interpretations of the link between past and future criminality (see also Chapters 6 and 7). Our emphasis is somewhat different—we seek to establish the robustness of our findings to random-effects models that incorporate persistent unobserved heterogeneity in the error terms.

15. We use arrest frequencies as dependent variables since they are measured in the same manner at ages 25–32 and 32–45 (recall that there are no unofficial measures at ages 32–45). This specification is supported by the general convergence of earlier results using OLS, logistic, and negative binomial estimation procedures. The LIMDEP program for panel data (see Greene, 1989) was employed to estimate the model.

16. Replication of our job stability analyses in Chapter 7 with a "random-effects" model also produced substantively identical results. The GLS t-ratio reflecting the overall effect of incarceration in adolescence and young adulthood on job stability at ages 17–25 and 25–32, controlling for prior crime, sample exclusion risk, and drinking, was −2.47 ($p < .05$). Approximately 40 percent of the error covariance over time in predicting job stability was due to individual-specific heterogeneity. The negative effect of incarceration on later job stability (cf. Tables 7.9 and 7.10) thus maintains despite controlling for a nontrivial level of persistent unobserved heterogeneity.

17. Although raw change scores have been criticized, recent work suggests that they are an appropriate way to study change (Allison, 1990). We thus

use change scores to provide an alternative to models in which both prior and concurrent levels of independent variables are simultaneously considered.

18. This general conclusion holds not only for persistent unobserved heterogeneity models, but for LISREL models where social bonding was specified as a latent construct tapped by the fallible indicators of job stability and marital attachment. For this measurement model we were restricted to the subsample of married men. Adult crime was specified as a latent construct underlying the covariance between the frequency of arrests and the summary measure of the breadth of crime participation. Controlling for prior adult crime, delinquency, and exclusion risk, the standardized latent effect of social bonds at ages 17–25 on crime at ages 25–32 was −.42 (t-ratio = −4.47) and −.35 (t-ratio = −2.75) for the delinquents and controls, respectively. Moreover, by estimating the contemporaneous influence of social bonding at ages 25–32 on crime and setting lagged effects to zero, we also estimated a simultaneous equation model. (In this model the effects of juvenile delinquency were assumed to influence adult social bonds only through adult crime.) The results indicated that while crime at ages 25–32 did influence social bonding, the reciprocal effect of social bonding on crime was significant and strong for both the control and delinquent groups (t-ratios = −3.49 and −5.07, respectively). Although these results must be viewed with caution because of the varying assumptions required to estimate the models, both the reciprocal and lagged model specifications suggest that even when measurement error is modeled, the basic theoretical picture is maintained.

9. Exploring Life Histories

1. Kidder and Fine (1987) distinguish two types of qualitative data. The first, referred to as "big Q," includes field work, participant observation, or ethnography. The chief characteristic of big Q is that "it consists of a continually changing set of questions without a structured design" (1987: 59). The second type of qualitative data is "small q," which "consists of open-ended questions embedded in a survey or experiment that has a structure or design" (1987: 59). The Gluecks' qualitative data are of the second variety.

2. Because of resource limitations plus the fact that case records for the control group are not yet part of the Glueck data archive held at the Murray Research Center, we decided to restrict the qualitative analysis to the delinquent subjects in the *UJD* study. Furthermore, we felt that by focusing on this group we were able to address perhaps the most important question of this research: what accounts for persistence (or desistance) in criminal behavior in adulthood among a sample of adolescent offenders?

3. In a somewhat similar approach, Giordano (1989) analyzes two sets of

negative cases with respect to control theory—youths with low levels of attachment to parents who are not delinquent and youths with high levels of attachment who are delinquent. Her interesting study points out the theoretical potential of analyzing negative cases rather than ignoring them.

4. Interestingly, we found that some spouses knew of their husband's delinquent past whereas other spouses were totally unaware. For instance, the wife of Case #040 stated, "I do not believe in holding this in for him since we all make mistakes when we are young." In contrast, Case #813 stated that he would be "apprehensive of the consequences if his wife knew of his record."

5. Supporting our earlier quantitative results, several of the life histories we examined revealed behavioral difficulties during military service. For example, Case #390 was found guilty of being AWOL, breaking and entering, stealing, and not getting up for reveille. Eventually, this subject received an "Undesirable Discharge" from the Navy. This pattern of continuity in antisocial behavior was found for many of the men in the delinquent sample.

6. It should be noted that the delinquent subjects were sometimes rejected for military service by the Selective Service Board because of their criminal records. According to the Gluecks' interviewer, the label "psychopathic personality" was a general category used by the Selective Service to classify boys with records.

7. Clausen (1991) found that those less competent in adolescence did not have fewer turning points than competent adolescents. However, less competent adolescents had more difficult turning points.

10. Summing Up and Looking Ahead

1. Data limitations precluded the estimation of all substantive relationships implied in Figure 10.1 (for example, reciprocal paths of adult social bonds and crime). There are also numerous other measures and concepts related to informal social control, social capital, and structural context that are germane to the study of crime. In addition, the integration of our social control model with other perspectives such as social learning theory (see especially Akers, 1989) is beyond the scope of this book. Figure 10.1 is simply meant to represent the best fit between our theoretical conceptualization and the nature of the Gluecks' data on crime and deviance over the life course.

2. It should be reiterated that the Gluecks' measures of peer group influence may be confounded by the sampling design of the study. In addition, the Gluecks' ideological stance led them to dismiss peers as an important causal variable (see Laub and Sampson, 1991). Clearly, better measures of the nature of friendship groupings between delinquent and nondelinquent

companions are needed, as are improved techniques to sort out the causal ordering problems (see Giordano et al., 1986 and Gauvreau, 1991).

3. The difficulty in estimating simultaneous equation models—even with longitudinal data—is not unique to the Glueck data (see especially Thornberry et al., 1991).

REFERENCES

Abbott, Andrew, and Andrea Hrycak. 1990. Measuring Resemblance in Sequence Data: An Optimal Matching Analysis of Musicians' Careers. *American Journal of Sociology* 96: 144–185.

Abramson, Jill, and Barbara Franklin. 1986. *Where They Are Now: The Story of the Women of Harvard Law 1974*. New York: Doubleday.

Agnew, Robert. 1991. The Interactive Effects of Peer Variables on Delinquency. *Criminology* 29: 47–72.

Akers, Ronald. 1985. *Deviant Behavior: A Social Learning Approach*. Belmont, Calif.: Wadsworth.

——— 1989. A Social Behaviorist's Perspective on Integration of Theories of Crime and Deviance. Pp. 23–36 in *Theoretical Integration in the Study of Deviance and Crime: Problems and Prospects*, ed. Steven Messner, Marvin Krohn, and Allen Liska. Albany: State University of New York Press.

Aldrich, John, and Forrest Nelson. 1984. *Linear Probability, Logit, and Probit Models*. Beverly Hills, Calif.: Sage.

Allison, Paul. 1984. *Event History Analysis*. Beverly Hills, Calif.: Sage.

——— 1990. Change Scores as Dependent Variables in Regression Analysis. Pp. 93–114 in *Sociological Methodology, 1989–90*, ed. Clifford Clogg. Oxford: Basil Blackwell.

Alwin, Duane. 1988. Structural Equation Models in Research on Human Development and Aging. Pp. 71–170 in *Methodological Issues in Aging Research*, ed. K. W. Schaie, R. T. Campbell, W. Meredith, and S. C. Rawlings. New York: Springer.

Alwin, Duane, and Robert Hauser. 1981. The Decomposition of Effects in Path Analysis. Pp. 123–140 in *Linear Models in Social Research*, ed. Peter Marsden. Beverly Hills, Calif.: Sage.

Anderson, Kathleen E., Hugh Lytton, and David M. Romney. 1986. Mothers' Interactions with Normal and Conduct-Disordered Boys: Who Affects Whom? *Developmental Psychology* 22: 604–609.

Baltes, Paul, and John Nesselroade. 1984. Paradigm Lost and Paradigm Regained: Critique of Dannefer's Portrayal of Life-Span Developmental Psychology. *American Sociological Review* 49: 841–847.

Becker, Howard. 1963. *Outsiders: Studies in the Sociology of Deviance.* New York: Free Press.

Bennett, James. 1981. *Oral History and Delinquency: The Rhetoric of Criminology.* Chicago: University of Chicago Press.

Berk, Richard A. 1983. An Introduction to Sample Selection Bias in Sociological Data. *American Sociological Review* 48: 386–398.

Berk, Richard A., and Subhash Ray. 1982. Selection Biases in Sociological Data. *Social Science Research* 11: 352–398.

Blake, Judith. 1989. *Family Size and Achievement.* Berkeley: University of California Press.

Blumstein, Alfred, Jacqueline Cohen, and David P. Farrington. 1988a. Criminal Career Research: Its Value for Criminology. *Criminology* 26:1–35.

———— 1988b. Longitudinal and Criminal Career Research: Further Clarifications. *Criminology* 26: 57–74.

Blumstein, Alfred, Jacqueline Cohen, Jeffrey A. Roth, and Christy A. Visher, eds. 1986. *Criminal Careers and Career Criminals.* Washington, D.C.: National Academy Press.

Blumstein, Alfred, David P. Farrington, and Soumyo Moitra. 1985. Delinquency Careers: Innocents, Desisters, and Persisters. Pp. 187–220 in *Crime and Justice,* Volume 6, ed. Michael Tonry and Norval Morris. Chicago: University of Chicago Press.

Bondeson, Ulla V. 1989. *Prisoners in Prison Societies.* New Brunswick, N.J.: Transaction Books.

Bordua, David. 1962. Some Comments on Theories of Group Delinquency. *Sociological Inquiry* 32: 245–260.

Brace, Charles Loring. 1872. *The Dangerous Classes of New York, and Twenty Years' Work among Them.* New York: Wynkoop.

Braithwaite, John. 1989. *Crime, Shame, and Reintegration.* Cambridge: Cambridge University Press.

Brim, Orville G., Jr., and Jerome Kagan. 1980. Constancy and Change: A View of the Issues. Pp. 1–25 in *Constancy and Change in Human Development,* ed. Orville G. Brim, Jr., and Jerome Kagan. Cambridge, Mass.: Harvard University Press.

Bryk, Anthony, and Stephen Raudenbush. 1987. Application of Hierarchical Linear Models to Assessing Change. *Psychological Bulletin* 101: 147–158.

Burton, Velmer, Francis Cullen, and Lawrence Travis. 1987. The Collateral Consequences of a Felony Conviction: A National Study of State Statutes. *Federal Probation* 51: 52–60.

Cabot, Richard C. 1926. *Facts on the Heart.* Philadelphia: Saunders.

Cairns, Robert B. 1986. Phenomena Lost: Issues in the Study of Development. Pp. 97–111 in *The Individual Subject and Scientific Psychology,* ed. J. Valsiner. New York: Plenum.

Callwood, June. 1954. Will Your Youngster Turn to Crime? *McLean's Magazine,* September 15.

Cameron, A. Colin, and Pravin Trivedi. 1986. Econometric Models Based on Count Data: Comparisons and Applications of Some Estimators and Tests. *Journal of Applied Econometrics* 1: 29–53.

Camic, Charles. 1987. The Making of a Method: A Historical Reinterpretation of the Early Parsons. *American Sociological Review* 52: 421–439.

Campbell, Anne. 1980. Friendship as a Factor in Male and Female Delinquency. Pp. 365–389 in *Friendship and Social Relations in Children,* ed. H. Foot, A. Chapman, and J. Smith. New York: Wiley.

Campbell, Donald, and Julian Stanley. 1963. *Experimental and Quasi-Experimental Designs for Research.* Chicago: Rand-McNally.

Caspi, Avshalom. 1987. Personality in the Life Course. *Journal of Personality and Social Psychology* 53: 1203–1213.

Caspi, Avshalom, and Daryl Bem. 1990. Personality Continuity and Change across the Life Course. Pp. 549–575 in *Handbook of Personality: Theory and Research,* ed. L. A. Pervin. New York: Guilford.

Caspi, Avshalom, Daryl J. Bem, and Glen H. Elder, Jr. 1989. Continuities and Consequences of Interactional Styles across the Life Course. *Journal of Personality* 57: 375–406.

Caspi, Avshalom, Glen H. Elder, Jr., and Daryl J. Bem. 1987. Moving against the World: Life-Course Patterns of Explosive Children. *Developmental Psychology* 23: 308–313.

———— 1988. Moving Away from the World: Life-Course Patterns of Shy Children. *Developmental Psychology* 24: 824–831.

Caspi, Avshalom, Glen H. Elder, Jr., and Ellen S. Herbener. 1990. Childhood Personality and the Prediction of Life-Course Patterns. Pp. 13–35 in *Straight and Devious Pathways from Childhood to Adulthood,* ed. Lee Robins and Michael Rutter. Cambridge: Cambridge University Press.

Caspi, Avshalom, and Ellen Herbener. 1990. Continuity and Change: Assortative Marriage and the Consistency of Personality in Adulthood. *Journal of Personality and Social Psychology* 58: 250–258.

Caspi, Avshalom, and Terrie E. Moffitt. 1992. The Continuity of Maladaptive Behavior: From Description to Understanding in the Study of Antisocial Behavior. In *Manual of Developmental Psychopathology,* ed. Dante Cicchetti and Donald Cohen. New York: Wiley.

Cernkovich, Stephen A., and Peggy C. Giordano. 1987. Family Relationships and Delinquency. *Criminology* 25: 295–321.

Cernkovich, Stephen A., Peggy C. Giordano, and M. D. Pugh. 1985. Chronic Offenders: The Missing Cases in Self-Report Delinquency Research. *Journal of Criminal Law and Criminology* 76: 705–732.

Chung, Ching-Fan, Peter Schmidt, and Ann D. Witte. 1991. Survival Analysis: A Survey. *Journal of Quantitative Criminology* 7: 59–98.

Clausen, John. 1990. Turning Point as a Life Course Concept: Meaning and Measurement. Paper presented at the annual meeting of the American Sociological Association, Washington, D.C.

——— 1991. Adolescent Competence and the Shaping of the Life Course. *American Journal of Sociology* 96: 805–842.

Cline, Hugh F. 1980. Criminal Behavior over the Life Span. Pp. 641–674 in *Constancy and Change in Human Development,* ed. Orville G. Brim, Jr., and Jerome Kagan. Cambridge, Mass.: Harvard University Press.

Cohen, Albert K. 1959. The Study of Social Disorganization and Deviant Behavior. Pp. 461–484 in *Sociology Today: Problems and Prospects,* ed. Robert K. Merton, Leonard Broom, and Leonard S. Cottrell, Jr. New York: Basic Books.

Cohen, Albert K., Alfred Lindesmith, and Karl Schuessler, eds. 1956. *The Sutherland Papers.* Bloomington: Indiana University Press.

Cohen, Lawrence E. 1987. Throwing Down the Gauntlet: A Challenge to the Relevance of Sociology for the Etiology of Criminal Behavior. *Contemporary Sociology* 16: 202–205.

Coleman, James S. 1988. Social Capital in the Creation of Human Capital. *American Journal of Sociology* 94: S95–120.

——— 1990. *Foundations of Social Theory.* Cambridge, Mass.: Harvard University Press.

Cook, Philip J. 1975. The Correctional Carrot: Better Jobs for Parolees. *Policy Analysis* 1: 11–54.

Cook, Thomas D. 1985. Postpositivist Critical Multiplism. Pp. 21–62 in *Social Science and Social Policy,* ed. R. Lance Shotland and Melvin M. Mark. Beverly Hills, Calif.: Sage.

Cook, Thomas D., and Donald T. Campbell. 1979. *Quasi-Experimentation: Design and Analysis Issues for Field Settings.* Chicago: Rand McNally.

Cox, D. R. 1972. Regression Models and Life Tables. *Journal of the Royal Statistical Society,* Series B 34: 187–202.

Crutchfield, Robert D. 1989. Labor Stratification and Violent Crime. *Social Forces* 68: 489–512.

Current Biography Yearbook. 1957. Glueck, Sheldon, and Eleanor Touroff. 18: 10–12.

Cusson, Maurice, and Pierre Pinsonneault. 1986. The Decision to Give up Crime. Pp. 72–82 in *The Reasoning Criminal: Rational Choice Perspectives of Offending,* ed. D. B. Cornish and Ronald V. Clarke. New York: Springer-Verlag.

Dannefer, Dale. 1984. Adult Development and Social Theory: A Paradigmatic Reappraisal. *American Sociological Review* 49: 100–116.

Davis, Kenna F. 1992. Patterns of Specialization and Escalation in Crime: A

Longitudinal Analysis of Juvenile and Adult Arrest Transitions in the Glueck Data. Ph.D. dissertation, University of Illinois, Urbana-Champaign.

Dressler, David. 1955. You The Newly Married: The Young Parent Can Prevent Delinquency. *Everywoman's Magazine* (September).

Dunn, Judy. 1988. Normative Life Events as Risk Factors in Childhood. Pp. 227–244 in *Studies of Psychosocial Risk: The Power of Longitudinal Data*, ed. Michael Rutter. Cambridge: Cambridge University Press.

Durkheim, Emile. [1897] 1951. *Suicide*. Trans. J. Spaulding and G. Simpson. New York: Free Press.

Earls, Felton, and Kenneth C. Jung. 1987. Temperament and Home Environment Characteristics as Causal Factors in the Early Development of Childhood Psychopathology. *Journal of the American Academy of Child and Adolescent Psychiatry* 26: 491–498.

Elder, Glen H., Jr. 1974. *Children of the Great Depression*. Chicago: University of Chicago Press.

——— 1975. Age Differentiation and the Life Course. Pp. 165–190 in *Annual Review of Sociology*, Volume 1, ed. Alex Inkeles. Palo Alto, Calif.: Annual Reviews.

——— 1980. Adolescence in Historical Perspective. Pp. 3–46 in *Handbook of Adolescent Psychology*, ed. Joseph Adelson. New York: John Wiley and Sons.

——— 1985. Perspectives on the Life Course. Pp. 23–49 in *Life Course Dynamics*, ed. Glen H. Elder, Jr. Ithaca: Cornell University Press.

——— 1986. Military Times and Turning Points in Men's Lives. *Developmental Psychology* 22: 233–245.

——— 1992. The Life Course. Pp. 1120–1130 in *The Encyclopedia of Sociology*, Volume 3, ed. Edgar F. Borgatta and Marie L. Borgatta. New York: Macmillan.

Elder, Glen H., Jr., and Avshalom Caspi. 1990. Studying Lives in a Changing Society: Sociological and Personological Explorations. Pp. 201–247 in *Studying Persons and Lives*, ed. A. I. Rabin, Robert Zucker, and Susan Frank. New York: Springer.

Elder, Glen H., Jr., Avshalom Caspi, and Linda Burton. 1988. Adolescent Transitions in Developmental Perspective: Sociological and Historical Insights. Pp. 151–179 in *Minnesota Symposium on Child Psychology*, Volume 1, ed. M. Gunnar. Hillsdale, N.J.: Erlbaum.

Elliott, Delbert, David Huizinga, and Suzanne Ageton. 1985. *Explaining Delinquency and Drug Use*. Beverly Hills, Calif.: Sage.

Elliott, Delbert, David Huizinga, and Scott Menard. 1989. *Multiple Problem Youth: Delinquency, Substance Use, and Mental Health Problems*. New York: Springer-Verlag.

Faculty Committee Report. 1954. The Behavioral Sciences at Harvard. Sheldon and Eleanor T. Glueck Papers. Cambridge, Mass.: Harvard Law School Library.

Farrington, David P. 1979. Longitudinal Research on Crime and Delinquency. Pp. 289–348 in *Crime and Justice,* Volume 1, ed. Norval Morris and Michael Tonry. Chicago: University of Chicago Press.

———— 1986a. Age and Crime. Pp. 189–250 in *Crime and Justice,* Volume 7, ed. Michael Tonry and Norval Morris. Chicago: University of Chicago Press.

———— 1986b. Stepping Stones to Adult Criminal Careers. Pp. 359–384 in *Development of Antisocial and Prosocial Behavior,* ed. Dan Olweus, Jack Block, and Marian Radke-Yarrow. New York: Academic Press.

———— 1987. Early Precursors of Frequent Offending. In *From Children to Citizens,* Volume III: *Families, Schools, and Delinquency Prevention,* ed. James Q. Wilson and Glenn C. Loury. New York: Springer-Verlag.

———— 1988. Studying Changes within Individuals: The Causes of Offending. Pp. 158–183 in *Studies of Psychosocial Risk: The Power of Longitudinal Data,* ed. Michael Rutter. Cambridge: Cambridge University Press.

———— 1989. Later Adult Life Outcomes of Offenders and Nonoffenders. Pp. 220–244 in *Children at Risk: Assessment, Longitudinal Research, and Intervention,* ed. M. Brambring, F. Losel, and H. Skowronek. New York: Walter de Gruyter.

———— 1990. Age, Period, Cohort, and Offending. Pp. 51–75 in *Policy and Theory in Criminal Justice: Contributions in Honour of Leslie T. Wilkins,* ed. Don M. Gottfredson and Ronald V. Clark. Aldershot: Avebury.

Farrington, David P., Bernard Gallagher, Lynda Morley, Raymond J. St. Ledger, and Donald J. West. 1986. Unemployment, School Leaving, and Crime. *British Journal of Criminology* 26: 335–356.

Farrington, David P., G. Gundry, and Donald J. West. 1975. The Familial Transmission of Criminality. *Medicine, Science, and Law* 15: 177–186.

Farrington, David P., and Rolf Loeber. 1989. Relative Improvement over Chance (RIOC) and Phi as Measures of Predictive Efficiency and Strength of Association in 2 × 2 Tables. *Journal of Quantitative Criminology* 5: 201–213.

Farrington, David P., Lloyd Ohlin, and James Q. Wilson. 1986. *Understanding and Controlling Crime: Toward a New Research Strategy.* New York: Springer-Verlag.

Farrington, David P., and Roger Tarling, eds. 1985. *Prediction in Criminology.* Albany: State University of New York Press.

Featherman, David, Dennis Hogan, and Aage Sorenson. 1984. Entry in Adulthood: Profiles of Young Men in the 1950s. Pp. 160–203 in *Life-Span Development and Behavior,* ed. Paul Baltes and Orville Brim. Orlando: Academic.

Featherman, David, and Richard Lerner. 1985. Ontogenesis and Sociogenesis: Problematics for Theory and Research about Development and Socialization across the Lifespan. *American Sociological Review* 50: 659–676.

Federal Bureau of Investigation. 1990. *Age-Specific Arrest Rates and Race-Specific Arrest Rates for Selected Offenses.* Washington, D.C.: U.S. Department of Justice.

Federal Probation. 1951. *Unraveling Juvenile Delinquency:* A Symposium of Reviews. 15: 52–58.

Fisher, Joseph, and Robert Mason. 1981. The Analysis of Multicollinear Data in Criminology. Pp. 99–125 in *Methods in Quantitative Criminology,* ed. James A. Fox. New York: Academic.

Flanagan, Timothy, and Katherine Maguire, eds. 1990. *Sourcebook of Criminal Justice Statistics: 1989.* Washington, D.C.: Government Printing Office.

Frankfurter, Felix. 1934. Introduction to *One Thousand Juvenile Delinquents,* by Sheldon Glueck and Eleanor Glueck. Cambridge, Mass.: Harvard University Press.

Freeman, Richard. 1987. The Relation of Criminal Activity to Black Youth Employment. *Review of Black Political Economy* (Summer-Fall): 99–107.

—— 1992. Crime and the Employment of Disadvantaged Youth. Paper presented at the Urban Poverty Workshop, University of Chicago, February 14.

Garofalo, James, and John H. Laub. 1978. The Fear of Crime: Broadening Our Perspective. *Victimology* 3: 242–253.

Gartner, Rosemary, and Irving Piliavin. 1988. The Aging Offender and the Aged Offender. Pp. 287–315 in *Life-Span Development and Behavior,* Volume 9, ed. Paul B. Baltes, David L. Featherman, and Richard M. Lerner. Hillside, N.J.: Lawrence Erlbaum Associates.

Gauvreau, Sandra. 1991. Social Selection or Social Causation? Untangling the Peer-Delinquency Relationship. Unpublished manuscript, University of Chicago.

Geis, Gilbert. 1966. Review of *Ventures in Criminology. Journal of Criminal Law, Criminology, and Police Science* 57:187–188.

—— 1970. Review of *Delinquents and Nondelinquents in Perspective. Crime and Delinquency* 16:118–120.

Gibbens, T. C. N. 1984. Borstal Boys after 25 Years. *British Journal of Criminology* 24: 49–62.

Gilboy, Elizabeth Waterman. 1936. Interview with Eleanor Touroff Glueck. *Barnard College Alumnae Monthly* 11–12.

Giordano, Peggy. 1989. Confronting Control Theory's Negative Cases. Pp. 261–278 in *Theoretical Integration in the Study of Deviance and Crime,* ed. Steven Messner, Marvin Krohn, and Allen Liska. Albany: State University of New York Press.

Giordano, Peggy C., Stephen A. Cernkovich, and M. D. Pugh. 1986. Friendships and Delinquency. *American Journal of Sociology* 91: 1170–1202.

Gittelman, Rachel. 1980. The Role of Psychological Tests for Differential Diagnosis in Child Psychiatry. *Journal of the American Academy of Child Psychiatry* 19: 413–438.

Glaser, Daniel. 1969. *The Effectiveness of a Prison and Parole System,* abridged ed. Indianapolis: Bobbs-Merrill.

Glenn, Norval D. 1981. Age, Birth Cohorts, and Drinking: An Illustration of the Hazards of Inferring Effects from Cohort Data. *Journal of Gerontology* 36: 567–582.

Glueck, Bernard. 1916. *Studies in Forensic Psychiatry.* Boston: Little, Brown.

—— 1918. A Study of Six Hundred and Eight Admissions to Sing Sing Prison. *Mental Hygiene* 2: 85–151.

Glueck, Eleanor T. 1927. *Community Use of Schools.* Baltimore: Williams and Wilkins.

—— 1936. *Evaluative Research in Social Work.* New York: Columbia University Press.

—— 1966. Identification of Potential Delinquents at 2–3 Years of Age. *International Journal of Psychiatry* 12: 5–16.

Glueck, Sheldon. 1925. *Mental Disorder and the Criminal Law.* Boston: Little, Brown.

—— 1956. Theory and Fact in Criminology. *British Journal of Delinquency* 7: 92–109.

—— 1960. Ten Years of *Unraveling Juvenile Delinquency:* An Examination of Criticisms. *Journal of Criminal Law, Criminology, and Police Science* 51: 283–308.

—— 1962. *Law and Psychiatry: Cold War or Entente Cordiale?* Baltimore: The Johns Hopkins Press.

—— 1964. Remarks in Honor of William Healy, M.D. *Mental Hygiene* 48: 318–322.

Glueck, Sheldon, and Eleanor Glueck. 1930. *500 Criminal Careers.* New York: A. A. Knopf.

—— 1934a. *Five Hundred Delinquent Women.* New York: A. A. Knopf.

—— 1934b. *One Thousand Juvenile Delinquents.* Cambridge, Mass.: Harvard University Press.

—— 1937. *Later Criminal Careers.* New York: The Commonwealth Fund.

—— 1938. Letter to Dr. Elizabeth Hincks, 2/14/38. Sheldon and Eleanor T. Glueck Papers. Cambridge, Mass.: Harvard Law School Library.

—— 1939. Social Case Histories—Policy Memo. Sheldon and Eleanor T. Glueck Papers. Cambridge, Mass.: Harvard Law School Library.

—— 1940. *Juvenile Delinquents Grown Up.* New York: The Commonwealth Fund.

—— 1943. *Criminal Careers in Retrospect.* New York: The Commonwealth Fund.

—— 1945. *After-Conduct of Discharged Offenders.* London: Macmillan.

—— 1950. *Unraveling Juvenile Delinquency.* New York: The Commonwealth Fund.

—— 1951. Note of Plans for Further "Unraveling" Juvenile Delinquency. *Journal of Criminal Law, Criminology, and Police Science* 41:759–762.

———— 1952. *Delinquents in the Making.* New York: Harper and Row.

———— 1956. *Physique and Delinquency.* New York: Harper and Row.

———— 1959. *Predicting Delinquency and Crime.* Cambridge, Mass.: Harvard University Press.

———— 1962. *Family Environment and Delinquency.* London: Routledge and Kegan Paul.

———— 1964. *Ventures in Criminology.* Cambridge, Mass.: Harvard University Press.

———— 1968. *Delinquents and Nondelinquents in Perspective.* Cambridge, Mass.: Harvard University Press.

———— 1970. *Toward a Typology of Juvenile Delinquency.* New York: Grune and Stratton.

———— 1974. *Of Delinquency and Crime: A Panorama of Years of Search and Research.* Springfield, Ill.: Charles C. Thomas.

Goring, Charles. [1913] 1972. *The English Convict.* Montclair, N.J.: Patterson Smith.

Gottfredson, Michael, and Travis Hirschi. 1986. The True Value of Lambda Would Appear to be Zero: An Essay on Career Criminals, Criminal Careers, Selective Incapacitation, Cohort Studies, and Related Topics. *Criminology* 24: 213–234.

———— 1987. The Methodological Adequacy of Longitudinal Research on Crime. *Criminology* 25: 581–614.

———— 1988. Science, Public Policy, and the Career Paradigm. *Criminology* 26: 37–55.

———— 1990. *A General Theory of Crime.* Stanford: Stanford University Press.

Gove, Walter R. 1985. The Effect of Age and Gender on Deviant Behavior: A Biopsychosocial Perspective. Pp. 115–144 in *Gender and the Life Course,* ed. Alice S. Rossi. New York: Aldine.

Gove, Walter R., and Robert D. Crutchfield. 1982. The Family and Juvenile Delinquency. *Sociological Quarterly* 23: 301–319.

Greene, William. 1989. *LIMDEP.* New York: Econometric Software.

Hagan, John. 1989. *Structural Criminology.* New Brunswick, N.J.: Rutgers University Press.

———— 1991. Destiny and Drift: Subcultural Preferences, Status Attainments, and the Risks and Rewards of Youth. *American Sociological Review* 56: 567–582.

Hagan, John, and Alberto Palloni. 1988. Crimes as Social Events in the Life Course: Reconceiving a Criminological Controversy. *Criminology* 26: 87–100.

———— 1990. The Social Reproduction of a Criminal Class in Working-Class London, circa 1950–1980. *American Journal of Sociology* 96: 265–299.

Harvard Law Review. 1951. A Symposium on *Unraveling Juvenile Delinquency.* 64: 1022–1041.

Healy, William. 1915. *The Individual Delinquent*. Boston: Little, Brown.

Healy, William, and Augusta F. Bronner. 1926. *Delinquents and Criminals: Their Making and Unmaking*. New York: Macmillan.

Heckman, James J. 1979. Sample Selection Bias as a Specification Error. *Econometrica* 47: 153–161.

Hindelang, Michael J. 1981. Variations in Sex-Race-Age-Specific Incidence Rates of Offending. *American Sociological Review* 46: 461–474.

Hindelang, Michael J., Travis Hirschi, and Joseph G. Weis. 1981. *Measuring Delinquency*. Beverly Hills, Calif.: Sage.

Hinds, M. 1990. Number of Killings Soars in Big Cities Across U.S. *New York Times*, July 18, p. 1.

Hirschi, Travis. 1969. *Causes of Delinquency*. Berkeley: University of California Press.

―――― 1983. Crime and the Family. Pp. 53–68 in *Crime and Public Policy*, ed. James Q. Wilson. San Francisco: Institute for Contemporary Studies.

―――― 1991. Family Structure and Crime. Pp. 43–66 in *When Families Fail: The Social Costs*, ed. Bryce J. Christensen. Lanham, Md.: University Press.

Hirschi, Travis, and Michael Gottfredson. 1983. Age and the Explanation of Crime. *American Journal of Sociology* 89: 552–584.

Hirschi, Travis, and Hanan C. Selvin. 1967. *Delinquency Research: An Appraisal of Analytic Methods*. New York: The Free Press.

Hoffman, Lois Wladis. 1974. Effects of Maternal Employment on the Child: A Review of the Research. *Developmental Psychology* 10: 204–228.

Hogan, Dennis P. 1978. The Variable Order of Events in the Life Course. *American Sociological Review* 43: 573–586.

―――― 1980. The Transition to Adulthood as a Career Contingency. *American Sociological Review* 45: 261–276.

Horwitz, Allan V. 1990. *The Logic of Social Control*. New York: Plenum Press.

Huesmann, L. Rowell, Leonard D. Eron, Monroe M. Lefkowitz, and Leopold O. Walder. 1984. Stability of Aggression over Time and Generations. *Developmental Psychology* 20: 1120–1134.

Huizinga, David, Finn-Aage Esbensen, and Anne Wylie Weiher. 1991. Are There Multiple Paths to Delinquency? *Journal of Criminal Law and Criminology* 82: 83–118.

James, G. 1991. New York Killings Set Record in 1990. *New York Times*, April 23, p. A14.

Janowitz, Morris. 1975. Sociological Theory and Social Control. *American Journal of Sociology* 81: 82–108.

Jencks, Christopher. 1992. *Rethinking Social Policy: Race, Poverty, and the Underclass*. Cambridge, Mass.: Harvard University Press.

Jensen, Gary F. 1976. Race, Achievement, and Delinquency: A Further Look at *Delinquency in a Birth Cohort*. *American Journal of Sociology* 82: 379–387.

Jessor, Richard. 1983. The Stability of Change: Psychosocial Development from Adolescence to Young Adulthood. Pp. 321–341 in *Human Development: An Interactional Perspective*, ed. David Magnusson and Vernon Allen. New York: Academic.

Jessor, Richard, John E. Donovan, and Frances M. Costa. 1991. *Beyond Adolescence: Problem Behavior and Young Adult Development*. Cambridge: Cambridge University Press.

Jessor, Richard, and Shirley Jessor. 1977. *Problem Behavior and Psychosocial Development: A Longitudinal Study of Youth*. New York: Academic.

Jick, Todd. 1979. Mixing Qualitative and Quantitative Methods: Triangulation in Action. *Administrative Science Quarterly* 24: 602–611.

Johnson, Richard E. 1979. *Juvenile Delinquency and Its Origins: An Integrated Theoretical Approach*. Cambridge: Cambridge University Press.

——— 1986. Family Structure and Delinquency: General Patterns and Gender Differences. *Criminology* 24: 65–84.

Joreskog, Karl, and Dag Sorbom. 1984. *LISREL VI: Analysis of Linear Structural Relationships by the Method of Maximum Likelihood, Instrumental Variables, and Least Squares Methods*. Mooresville, Indiana: Scientific Software.

Journal of Criminal Law, Criminology, and Police Science. 1951. Unraveling Juvenile Delinquency: A Symposium of Reviews. 41: 732–759.

Kamim, Leon J. 1986. Is Crime in the Genes? The Answer May Depend on Who Chooses What Evidence. *Scientific American* 254: 22–27.

Katz, Jack. 1988. *Seductions of Crime*. New York: Basic Books.

Kercher, Kyle. 1988. Criminology. Pp. 294–316 in *The Future of Sociology*, ed. Edgar F. Borgatta and Karen S. Cook. Beverly Hills, Calif.: Sage.

Kerlinger, Fred. 1973. *Foundations of Behavioral Research*, 2nd ed. New York: Holt, Rinehart and Winston.

Kessler, Ronald, and David Greenberg. 1981. *Linear Panel Analysis: Models of Quantitative Change*. New York: Academic.

Kidder, Louise H., and Michelle Fine. 1987. Qualitative and Quantitative Methods: When Stories Converge. Pp. 57–75 in *Multiple Methods in Program Evaluation*, ed. M. Mark and R. Shotland. San Francisco: Jossey-Bass.

Kiecolt, K. J., and L. Nathan. 1985. *Secondary Analysis of Survey Data*. Beverly Hills, Calif.: Sage.

King, Gary. 1988. Statistical Models for Political Science Event Counts: Bias in Conventional Procedures and Evidence for the Exponential Poisson Regression Model. *American Journal of Political Science* 32: 838–863.

Knight, B. J., S. G. Osborn, and D. West. 1977. Early Marriage and Criminal Tendency in Males. *British Journal of Criminology* 17: 348–360.

Koop, C. Everett, and George D. Lundberg. 1992. Violence in America: A Public Health Emergency. *Journal of the American Medical Association* 267: 3075–3076.

Kornhauser, Ruth. 1978. *Social Sources of Delinquency*. Chicago: University of Chicago Press.

Kotlowitz, Alex. 1991. *There Are No Children Here: The Story of Two Boys Growing Up in the Other America*. New York: Doubleday.

LaBrie, Richard. 1970a. Verification of the Glueck Prediction Table by Mathematical Statistics Following a Computerized Procedure of Discriminant Function Analysis. *Journal of Criminal Law and Criminology* 61: 229–234.

———— 1970b. Appendix B: Multivariate Discriminant Function Analyses on Glueck Data. Pp. 113–155 in Sheldon Glueck and Eleanor Glueck, *Toward a Typology of Juvenile Offenders*. New York: Grune and Stratton.

Larzelere, Robert E., and Gerald R. Patterson. 1990. Parental Management: Mediator of the Effect of Socioeconomic Status on Early Delinquency. *Criminology* 28: 301–323.

Laub, John H. 1983a. Urbanism, Race, and Crime. *Journal of Research in Crime and Delinquency* 20:183–198.

———— 1983b. *Criminology in the Making: An Oral History*. Boston: Northeastern University Press.

Laub, John H., and Robert J. Sampson. 1988. Unraveling Families and Delinquency: A Reanalysis of the Gluecks' Data. *Criminology* 26:355–380.

———— 1991. The Sutherland-Glueck Debate: On the Sociology of Criminological Knowledge. *American Journal of Sociology* 96: 1402–1440.

Laub, John H., Robert J. Sampson, and Kenna Kiger. 1990. Assessing the Potential of Secondary Data Analysis: A New Look at the Gluecks' *Unraveling Juvenile Delinquency* Data. Pp. 241–257 in *Measurement Issues in Criminology*, ed. Kimberly Kempf. New York: Springer-Verlag.

Lazarsfeld, Paul F. 1955. Interpretation of Statistical Relations as a Research Operation. Pp. 115–125 in *The Language of Social Research*, ed. Paul F. Lazarsfeld and Morris Rosenberg. Glencoe, Ill.: Free Press.

Lemann, Nicholas. 1991. The Other Underclass. *The Atlantic* 268:96–110.

Lemert, Edwin. 1951. *Social Pathology*. New York: McGraw-Hill.

Liska, Allen, and Mark Reed. 1985. Ties to Conventional Institutions and Delinquency: Estimating Reciprocal Effects. *American Sociological Review* 50: 547–560.

Loeber, Rolf. 1982. The Stability of Antisocial Child Behavior: A Review. *Child Development* 53: 1431–1446.

Loeber, Rolf, and Thomas Dishion. 1983. Early Predictors of Male Delinquency: A Review. *Psychological Bulletin* 94: 68–99.

Loeber, Rolf, and Marc LeBlanc. 1990. Toward a Developmental Criminology. Pp. 375–437 in *Crime and Justice*, Volume 12 , ed. Michael Tonry and Norval Morris. Chicago: University of Chicago Press.

Loeber, Rolf, and Magda Stouthamer-Loeber. 1986. Family Factors as Correlates and Predictors of Juvenile Conduct Problems and Delinquency. In *Crime and Justice*, Volume 7, ed. Michael Tonry and Norval Morris. Chicago: University of Chicago Press.

———— 1987. Prediction. Pp. 325–382 in *Handbook of Juvenile Delinquency*, ed. Herbert C. Quay. New York: Wiley.

Loeber, Rolf, Magda Stouthamer-Loeber, Welmoet Van Kammen, and David P. Farrington. 1991. Initiation, Escalation and Desistance in Juvenile Offending and Their Correlates. *Journal of Criminal Law and Criminology* 82: 36–82.

Loftin, Colin, and David McDowall. 1988. The Analysis of Case-Control Studies in Criminology. *Journal of Quantitative Criminology* 4: 85–98.

Long, Jancis V. F., and George E. Vaillant. 1984. Natural History of Male Psychological Health, XI: Escape from the Underclass. *American Journal of Psychiatry* 141: 341–346.

Loury, Glenn C. 1987. The Family as Context for Delinquency Prevention: Demographic Trends and Political Realities. Pp. 3–26 in *From Children to Citizens*, Volume III: *Families, Schools, and Delinquency Prevention*, ed. James Q. Wilson and Glenn C. Loury. New York: Springer-Verlag.

Lytton, Hugh. 1990. Child and Parent Effects in Boys' Conduct Disorder: A Reinterpretation. *Developmental Psychology* 26: 683–697.

Maccoby, Eleanor E. 1958. Children and Working Mothers. *Children* 5: 83–89.

Magnusson, David, and Lars R. Bergman. 1988. Individual and Variable-Based Approaches to Longitudinal Research on Early Risk Factors. Pp. 45–61 in *Studies of Psychosocial Risk: The Power of Longitudinal Data*, ed. Michael Rutter. Cambridge: Cambridge University Press.

———— 1990. A Pattern Approach to the Study of Pathways from Childhood to Adulthood. Pp. 101–115 in *Straight and Devious Pathways from Childhood to Adulthood*, ed. Lee Robins and Michael Rutter. Cambridge: Cambridge University Press.

Markus, Gregory. 1979. *Analyzing Panel Data*. Beverly Hills, Calif.: Sage.

Matsueda, Ross L. 1982. Testing Control Theory and Differential Association: A Causal Modeling Approach. *American Sociological Review* 47: 489–504.

———— 1989. The Dynamics of Moral Beliefs and Minor Deviance. *Social Forces* 68: 428–457.

Mauer, Mark. 1990. Young Black Men and the Criminal Justice System: A Growing National Problem. Washington, D.C.: The Sentencing Project.

McCord, Joan. 1979. Some Child-Rearing Antecedents of Criminal Behavior in Adult Men. *Journal of Personality and Social Psychology* 37: 1477–1486.

———— 1980. Patterns of Deviance. Pp. 157–165 in *Human Functioning in Longitudinal Perspective*, ed. S. B. Sells, Rick Crandall, Merrill Roff, John S. Strauss, and William Pollin. Baltimore: Williams and Wilkins.

———— 1990. Crime in Moral and Social Contexts. *Criminology* 28: 1–26.

McCord, William, and Joan McCord. 1959. *Origins of Crime.* New York: Columbia University Press.

———— 1960. *Origins of Alcoholism.* Stanford: Stanford University Press.

Modell, John. 1989. *Into One's Own: From Youth to Adulthood in the United States, 1920–1975.* Berkeley: University of California Press.

Moffitt, Terrie E. 1991. Life-course Persistent and Adolescence Limited Antisocial Behavior: A Developmental Taxonomy. Unpublished paper, University of Wisconsin–Madison.

Morgan, Thomas B. 1960. Now We Can Spot Delinquents Early. *Think Magazine* (March).

Nagin, Daniel. 1991. The Stability of the Link between Individual Differences at Childhood and Adult Criminality. Unpublished paper, Carnegie Mellon University.

Nagin, Daniel, and Raymond Paternoster. 1991. On the Relationship of Past and Future Participation in Delinquency. *Criminology* 29: 163–190.

Offord, D. R. 1982. Family Backgrounds of Male and Female Delinquents. In *Abnormal Offenders: Delinquency and the Criminal Justice System,* ed. J. Gunn and David P. Farrington. Chichester: Wiley.

Olweus, Dan. 1979. Stability of Aggressive Reaction Patterns in Males: A Review. *Psychological Bulletin* 86: 852–875.

———— 1980. Familial and Temperamental Determinants of Aggressive Behavior in Adolescent Boys: A Causal Analysis. *Developmental Psychology* 16: 644–660.

———— 1983. Low School Achievement and Aggressive Behavior in Adolescent Boys. Pp. 353–365 in *Human Development: An Interactional Perspective,* ed. David Magnusson and Vernon L. Allen. New York: Academic.

Osborn, S. G. 1980. Moving Home, Leaving London, and Delinquent Trends. *British Journal of Criminology* 20: 54–61.

Osborn, S. G., and Donald J. West. 1979. Marriage and Delinquency: A Postscript. *British Journal of Criminology* 19: 254–256.

Osgood, D. Wayne. 1990. Covariation among Adolescent Problem Behaviors. Unpublished paper, University of Nebraska.

Osgood, D. Wayne, Lloyd D. Johnston, Patrick M. O'Malley, and Jerald G. Bachman. 1988. The Generality of Deviance in Late Adolescence and Early Adulthood. *American Sociological Review* 53: 81–93.

Patterson, Gerald R. 1980. Children Who Steal. Pp. 73–90 in *Understanding Crime: Current Theory and Research,* ed. Travis Hirschi and Michael Gottfredson. Beverly Hills, Calif.: Sage.

———— 1982. *Coercive Family Process.* Eugene, Oreg.: Castalia.

———— 1984. Siblings: Fellow Travelers in Coercive Family Processes. Pp.

173–215 in *Advances in the Study of Aggression,* Volume 1, ed. Robert J. Blanchard and D. Caroline Blanchard. New York: Academic.

———— 1986. The Contribution of Siblings to Training for Fighting: A Microsocial Analysis. Pp. 235–261 in *Development of Antisocial and Prosocial Behavior: Research, Theories, and Issues,* ed. Dan Olweus, Jack Block, and Marian Radke-Jarrow. New York: Academic.

Patterson, Gerald R., Barbara D. DeBaryshe, and Elizabeth Ramsey. 1989. A Developmental Perspective on Antisocial Behavior. *American Psychologist* 44: 329–335.

Patterson, Gerald R., and Thomas J. Dishion. 1985. Contributions of Families and Peers to Delinquency. *Criminology* 23: 63–79.

Petersen, Trond. 1985. A Comment on Presenting Results from Logit and Probit Models. *American Sociological Review* 50: 130–131.

Plewis, Ian. 1985. *Analysing Change: Measurement and Explanation Using Longitudinal Data.* New York: Wiley.

Porterfield, A. 1946. *Youth in Trouble.* Fort Worth, Tex.: Leo Potisham Foundation.

Potts, David P. 1965. Social Ethics at Harvard, 1881–1931: A Study in Academic Activism. Pp. 91–128 in *Social Sciences at Harvard, 1860–1920,* ed. Paul Buck. Cambridge, Mass.: Harvard University Press.

Rand, Alicia. 1987. Transitional Life Events and Desistance from Delinquency and Crime. Pp. 134–162 in *From Boy to Man: From Delinquency to Crime,* ed. Marvin Wolfgang, Terence P. Thornberry, and Robert M. Figlio. Chicago: University of Chicago Press.

Reiss, Albert J., Jr. 1951a. Delinquency as the Failure of Personal and Social Control. *American Sociological Review* 16: 196–207.

———— 1951b. *Unraveling Juvenile Delinquency.* II. An Appraisal of the Research Methods. *American Journal of Sociology* 57:115–120.

Rindfuss, Ronald, C. Gray Swicegood, and Rachel Rosenfeld. 1987. Disorder in the Life Course: How Common and Does It Matter? *American Sociological Review* 52: 785–801.

Robins, Lee N. 1966. *Deviant Children Grown Up.* Baltimore: Williams and Wilkins.

———— 1978. Sturdy Childhood Predictors of Adult Antisocial Behavior: Replications from Longitudinal Studies. *Psychological Medicine* 8: 611–622.

Robins, Lee N., and Shirley Y. Hill. 1966. Assessing the Contribution of Family Structure, Class and Peer Groups to Juvenile Delinquency. *Journal of Criminal Law, Criminology, and Police Science* 57: 325–334.

Robins, Lee N., and Kathryn Strother Ratcliff. 1980. Childhood Conduct Disorders and Later Arrest. Pp. 248–263 in *The Social Consequences of Psychiatric Illness,* ed. Lee N. Robins, Paula J. Clayton, and John K. Wing. New York: Brunner/Mazel.

Robins, Lee N., Patricia A. West, and Barbara L. Herjanic. 1975. Arrests and Delinquency in Two Generations: A Study of Black Urban Families and Their Children. *Journal of Child Psychology and Psychiatry* 16: 125–140.

Rogosa, David. 1988. Myths about Longitudinal Research. Pp. 171–209 in *Methodological Issues in Aging Research,* ed. K. W. Schaie, R. T. Campbell, W. Meredith, and S. C. Rawlings. New York: Springer.

Rogosa, David, D. Brandt, and M. Zimowski. 1982. A Growth Curve Approach to the Measurement of Change. *Psychological Bulletin* 92: 726–748.

Rowe, Alan, and Charles Tittle. 1977. Life Cycle Changes and Criminal Propensity. *Sociological Quarterly* 18: 223–236.

Rowe, David. 1985. Sibling Interaction and Self-Reported Delinquent Behavior: A Study of 265 Twin Pairs. *Criminology* 23: 223–240.

Rowe, David, and D. Wayne Osgood. 1984. Heredity and Sociological Theories of Delinquency: A Reconsideration. *American Sociological Review* 49:526–540.

Rutter, Michael. 1988. Longitudinal Data in the Study of Causal Processes: Some Uses and Some Pitfalls. Pp. 1–28 in *Studies of Psychosocial Risk: The Power of Longitudinal Data,* ed. Michael Rutter. Cambridge: Cambridge University Press.

—— 1989. Age as an Ambiguous Variable in Developmental Research: Some Epidemiological Considerations from Developmental Psychopathology. *International Journal of Behavioral Development* 12: 1–34.

Rutter, Michael, and Henri Giller. 1983. *Juvenile Delinquency: Trends and Perspectives.* New York: Guilford Press.

Rutter, Michael, D. Quinton, and J. Hill. 1990. Adult Outcomes of Institution-reared Children: Males and Females Compared. Pp. 135–157 in *Straight and Devious Pathways from Childhood to Adulthood,* ed. Lee N. Robins and Michael Rutter. Cambridge: Cambridge University Press.

Sampson, Robert J. 1986. Effects of Socioeconomic Context on Official Reaction to Juvenile Delinquency. *American Sociological Review* 51: 876–885.

—— 1987. Urban Black Violence: The Effect of Male Joblessness and Family Disruption. *American Journal of Sociology* 93: 348–382.

—— 1988. Local Friendship Ties and Community Attachment in Mass Society: A Multi-Level Systemic Model. *American Sociological Review* 53: 766–779.

Sampson, Robert J., and John H. Laub. 1990. Crime and Deviance over the Life Course: The Salience of Adult Social Bonds. *American Sociological Review* 55: 609–627.

Schmidt, Peter, and Ann Dryden Witte. 1988. *Predicting Recidivism Using Survival Models.* New York: Springer-Verlag.

Schneider, Alexander J. N., Cyrus W. LaGrone, Jr., Eleanor T. Glueck, and Sheldon Glueck. 1944. Prediction of Behavior of Civilian Delinquents in the Armed Forces. *Mental Hygiene* 28:456–475.

Shannon, Lyle. 1988. *Criminal Career Continuity: Its Social Context*. New York: Human Sciences Press.

Shaw, Clifford R. 1930. *The Jack-Roller: A Delinquent Boy's Own Story*. Chicago: University of Chicago Press.

Shaw, Clifford R., and Henry McKay. 1942. *Juvenile Delinquency and Urban Areas*. Chicago: University of Chicago Press.

Short, James F., Jr. 1969. Book Review of *Delinquents and Nondelinquents in Perspective*. *American Sociological Review* 34: 981–983.

Short, James F., Jr., and Ivan Nye. 1957. Reported Behavior as a Criterion of Deviant Behavior. *Social Problems* 5: 207–213.

—— 1958. Extent of Unrecorded Juvenile Delinquency: Tentative Conclusions. *Journal of Criminal Law and Criminology* 49: 296–302.

Shover, Neal. 1985. *Aging Criminals*. Beverly Hills, Calif.: Sage.

Shover, Neal, and Carol Y. Thompson. 1992. Age, Differential Expectations, and Crime Desistance. *Criminology* 30: 89–104.

Siegel, Larry. 1989. *Criminology*, 3rd ed. St. Paul: West Publishing.

Smith, Douglas, and Raymond Paternoster. 1990. Formal Processing and Future Delinquency: Deviance Amplification as Selection Artifact. *Law and Society Review* 24: 1109–1131.

Snodgrass, Jon. 1972. *The American Criminological Tradition: Portraits of the Men and Ideology in a Discipline*. Ann Arbor, Mich.: University Microfilms.

Stolzenberg, Ross, and Daniel Relles. 1990. Theory Testing in a World of Constrained Research Design: The Significance of Heckman's Censored Sampling Bias Correction for Nonexperimental Research. *Sociological Methods and Research* 18: 395–415.

Sutherland, Edwin H., and Chic Conwell. 1937. *The Professional Thief*. Chicago: University of Chicago Press.

Sutherland, Edwin H., and Donald R. Cressey. 1978. *Principles of Criminology*. Philadelphia: J. B. Lippincott.

Thernstrom, Stephan. 1973. *The Other Bostonians: Poverty and Progress in the American Metropolis, 1880–1970*. Cambridge, Mass.: Harvard University Press.

Thornberry, Terence P. 1987. Toward an Interactional Theory of Delinquency. *Criminology* 25: 863–891.

Thornberry, Terence P., Alan J. Lizotte, Marvin D. Krohn, Margaret Farnworth, and Sung Joon Jang. 1991. Testing Interactional Theory: An Examination of Reciprocal Causal Relationships among Family, School, and Delinquency. *Journal of Criminal Law and Criminology* 82: 3–35.

Tonry, Michael, Lloyd E. Ohlin, and David P. Farrington. 1991. *Human Development and Criminal Behavior: New Ways of Advancing Knowledge*. New York: Springer-Verlag.

Tracy, Paul E., Marvin Wolfgang, and Robert M. Figlio. 1990. *Delinquency Careers in Two Birth Cohorts*. New York: Plenum.

Vaillant, George E. 1977. *Adaptation to Life*. Boston: Little, Brown.

—— 1983. *The Natural History of Alcoholism*. Cambridge, Mass.: Harvard University Press.

Vold, George, and Thomas Bernard. 1986. *Theoretical Criminology*, 3rd ed. New York: Oxford.

Wallerstein, James, and Clement J. Wyle. 1947. Our Law-Abiding Law-Breakers. *Probation* 25: 107–112.

Weis, Joseph G. 1986. Issues in the Measurement of Criminal Careers. Pp. 1–51 in *Criminal Careers and Career Criminals*, ed. Alfred Blumstein, Jacqueline Cohen, Jeffrey A. Roth, and Christy A. Visher. Washington, D.C.: National Academy Press.

Werner, Emily E., and Ruth S. Smith. 1982. *Vulnerable but Invincible*. New York: McGraw-Hill.

West, Donald J. 1982. *Delinquency: Its Roots, Careers, and Prospects*. London: Heinemann.

West, Donald J., and David P. Farrington. 1973. *Who Becomes Delinquent?* London: Heinemann.

—— 1977. *The Delinquent Way of Life*. London: Heinemann.

White, Jennifer L., Terrie E. Moffitt, Felton Earls, Lee N. Robins, and Phil A. Silva. 1990. How Early Can We Tell? Predictors of Childhood Conduct Disorder and Adolescent Delinquency. *Criminology* 28: 507–533.

Wiatrowski, Michael D., David B. Griswold, and Mary K. Roberts. 1981. Social Control Theory and Delinquency. *American Sociological Review* 46: 525–541.

Wilkins, Leslie T. 1969. Data and Delinquency. *Yale Law Journal* 78: 731–737.

Wilkinson, Karen. 1974. The Broken Family and Juvenile Delinquency: Scientific Explanation or Ideology? *Social Problems* 21: 726–739.

Wilson, Harriet. 1980. Parental Supervision: A Neglected Aspect of Delinquency. *British Journal of Criminology* 20: 203–235.

Wilson, James Q. 1983. Raising Kids. *The Atlantic*, October, pp. 45–56.

Wilson, James Q., and Richard Herrnstein. 1985. *Crime and Human Nature*. New York: Simon and Schuster.

Wilson, William Julius. 1987. *The Truly Disadvantaged: The Inner City, the Underclass, and Public Policy*. Chicago: University of Chicago Press.

Wolfgang, Marvin, Robert Figlio, and Thorsten Sellin. 1972. *Delinquency in a Birth Cohort*. Chicago: University of Chicago Press.

Wolfgang, Marvin E., Robert Figlio, and Terence P. Thornberry. 1978. *Evaluating Criminology*. New York: Elsevier.

Wolfgang, Marvin E., Terence P. Thornberry, and Robert Figlio. 1987. *From Boy to Man: From Delinquency to Crime*. Chicago: University of Chicago Press.

Worcester, Jane. 1956. Appendix A: Explanation of Statistical Method. Pp. 276–283 in Sheldon Glueck and Eleanor Glueck, *Physique and Delinquency*. New York: Harper and Row.

INDEX